A SANSKRIT GRAMMAR

FOR STUDENTS

Note from the Publishers

This edition has been thoroughly recomposed with the main objective to provide a better printed text to the students/scholars. Though we have been conscious enough to avoid misprints, still a few errors might have gone unnoticed. We would be grateful to the users for calling our attention to such misprints/errors to help us rectify these in the future editions.

D.K. PRINTWORLD (P) LTD.

A SANSKRIT GRAMMAR FOR STUDENTS

ARTHUR A. MACDONELL

PRINTWORLD

Publishers of Indian Traditions

Cataloging in Publication Data — DK

Macdonell, Arthur Anthony, 1854-1930.

A Sanskrit grammar for students.
Includes indexes.

1. Sanskrit language — Grammar. I. Title.

ISBN: 978-81-246-0094-8 (Hardbound)
ISBN: 978-81-246-0095-5 (Paperback)

Third Edition : Oxford, 1926
Reprinted in this form in 1997
Reissued in 2001, 2004, 2008, 2015

Published and printed by:
D.K. Printworld (P) Ltd.
Regd. Office : *Vedaśrī*, F-395, Sudarshan Park
(Metro Station: Ramesh Nagar)
New Delhi - 110 015
Phones : (011) 2545 3975; 2546 6019
Fax : (011) 2546 5926
e-mail : indology@dkprintworld.com
Web : www.dkprintworld.com

PREFACE TO THIRD EDITION

In preparing a new edition of this grammar I have found misprints requiring correction to be few and insignificant. The alterations that seemed necessary are nearly all concerned with facilitating the use of the book for students. One of these is the indication of the relevant number of chapter and paragraph on the inside top corner of each page. Since the grammar is intended to supply a complete account of Classical Sanskrit, many paragraphs may be omitted till a later stage of study. I therefore here append a list of those which are essential for absolute beginners and thus constitute a virtual primer of Classical Sanskrit.

I : 1-7, 8-12, 13. II : 16-22, 27, 30-34, 36 A.B., 37, 38, 40, 42-44, 45, 1.2, 52-55, 65, 67. III : 70, 71, 73, 74, 77, 85, 87, 90, 1, 97, 100, 101 D (p. 63), 103, 1, 2, 109-111, 120. IV : 121-128, 131, 132 (only Pres. Par., pp. 92, 98), 135, 136, 138, 1 (only √ *tud.*, Par.), 141a (only Par.), 143, 1 (only Par.), 147 (only Par.), 148 (only *adām*), 151 (only Par.), 154 (only Pres.), 156, 160, 1, 2, 162, 163, 167, 168, 169, 172, 175.

When the student has gone through these paragraphs he will be quite prepared to begin reading. Any new grammatical forms he now meets with he will be able to find explained in the paragraphs that have been passed over. In this way he will understand, with the aid of a vocabulary, every word in the first canto of the *Story of Nala* within the course of a month, and know all the grammar necessary for reading easy Sanskrit texts.

Since the appearance of the second edition of this work (1911) my *Vedic Grammar for Students* was published (1916). Though this new book seemed at first sight to make Appendix III superfluous in the present work (pp. 236-44), I decided to retain it as presenting Vedic grammar in an abridged form and rendering it easier for absolute beginners to master.

A.A.M.

20 BARDWELL ROAD
OXFORD.
November, 1926.

PREFACE TO SECOND EDITION

THE original form of the present work was my abridgement (1886) of Max Müller's Sanskrit Grammar (2nd ed., 1870). That abridgement was the outcome of what I had found by experience, both as a learner and a teacher, to be unessential in an elementary grammar. It was also partly due to my conviction that the existing Sanskrit grammars, being too much dominated by the system of Pāṇini, rendered Sanskrit unnecessarily hard to learn. The introductory sketch of the history of Sanskrit grammar prefixed to the present volume will, I think, sufficiently show that the native Indian system is incompatible with the practical methods of teaching and learning in the West.

In the first edition of this grammar, published in 1901, the earlier book was transformed into an entirely new work. Though, on the whole, considerably enlarged it showed many omissions. For I made it my guiding principle to leave out all matter that is found exclusively in Vedic literature or in the Hindu grammarians, the aim I had in view being to describe only such grammatical forms as are to be met with in the actual literature of post-Vedic Sanskrit. The student of Sanskrit grammar would thus not be burdened with matter which could never be of any practical use to him. Hence I refrained from employing, even in a paradigm, any word not to be found in the literature; though for the sake of completeness I here often gave inflected forms represented only by other words of the same type. The purpose of the book, then, was not to supply a mass of forms and rules mainly useful for answering examination questions more or

less mechanically, but to provide the student with the full grammatical equipment necessary for reading any Sanskrit text with ease and exactness.

The present edition has undergone a thorough revision aided by the experience of ten more years' teaching and by the suggestions of pupils and others who have used the first edition. The improvements chiefly consist of additions, which have increased the size of the book by twenty-four pages.

An entirely new portion of the grammar are the three sections comprised in pages 159-168. The first (182) deals with nominal stem formation, giving an account of the primary and secondary suffixes, and thus furnishing the student with a more complete insight into the structure of Sanskrit words than the first edition supplied. In connexion with these suffixes a survey (183) of the rules of gender is added. The third new section (184) describes the formation of verbal compounds. The most noticeable case of expansion is otherwise to be found in the rules about the treatment of final dental *n* in Sandhi: these now give a complete account (36, 40) of the changes undergone by that letter. In the accidence a few new paradigms have been introduced, such as *grāvan* (90, 4), and additional forms have been given, as in the difficult s-aorist of *dah*, where (144, 5) even middle forms, though not occurring in that verb, are supplied as a model for other verbs presenting similar difficulties of euphonic combination. Other improvements are intended to facilitate the use of the grammar. Thus in the list of verbs (Appendix I) abbreviations have been added to indicate the various forms which beginners have otherwise often found difficulty in identifying. Again, the Sanskrit Index has been made both fuller and more explanatory (see e.g. *prākṛta*). A decidedly practical improvement is the substitution of a brief synopsis of the subject-matter for an elaborate table of contents at the beginning, and the addition of a General Index

at the end. All these extensions and changes will, I feel sure, be found to have considerably increased the practical value of the grammar both in matter and form.

As in the first edition, the book is transliterated throughout, excepting the list of verbs (Appendix I) and the syntactical examples at the end (180; 190-218). The system of transliteration remains the same, being that which is now most generally adopted in the West. This system includes the use of *ṛ* (to be pronounced with a syllabic value, as the *r* in French *chambre*) to represent the weak grade of the syllables *ar* and *ra*.

The improvements appearing in this edition are largely due to the suggestions of former pupils or of friends. The gentlemen to whom I owe thanks for their advice are — Prof. E.J. Rapson; Dr. James Morison; Mr. M.L. Puri, B.A., of Exeter College; Mr. Horace Hart, M.A., Controller of the University Press; and especially Mr. T.E. Moir, I.C.S., of Wadham College, as well as Dr. F.W. Thomas, Librarian of the India Office. Mr. J.C. Pembrey, Hon. M.A., Oriental Reader of the University Press, has read with his usual care the proofs of this edition, which is separated by no less an interval than sixty-four years from the first Sanskrit Grammar which he (together with his father) corrected for the press, that of Prof. H.H. Wilson, in 1847. To Dr. A.B. Keith I am indebted for reading the proofs of this as well as of all the other books I have published since 1900. I must take this opportunity of thanking him not only for having read the proofs of the whole of my *Vedic Grammar*, but also for having passed several sheets of that work through the press for me during my absence in India between September, 1907, and April, 1908.

A.A. MACDONELL.

107 BANBURY ROAD, OXFORD.
July, 1911.

INTRODUCTION

BRIEF HISTORY OF SANSKRIT GRAMMAR

THE first impulse to the study of grammar in India was given by the religious motive of preserving intact the sacred Vedic texts, the efficacy of which was believed to require attention to every letter. Thus, aided by the great transparency of the Sanskrit language, the ancient Indian grammarians had by the fifth century BC arrived at scientific results unequalled by any other nation of antiquity. It is, for instance, their distinctive achievement to have recognized that words for the most part consist on the one hand of roots, and on the other of affixes, which, when compounded with the former, modify the radical sense in various ways.

The oldest grammar that has been preserved is Pāṇini's. It already represents a fully developed system, its author standing at the end of a long line of predecessors, of whom no fewer than sixty-four are mentioned, and the purely grammatical works of all of whom, owing to the excellence and comprehensiveness of his work, have entirely perished.

Pāṇini is considerably later than Yāska (probably about 500 BC), whom he mentions, and between whom and himself a good number of important grammarians intervene. On the other hand, Pāṇini is much older than his interpreter Patañjali, who probably dates from the latter half of the second century BC, the two being separated by another eminent grammarian, Kātyāyana. Pāṇini himself uses the word *yavanānī*, which Kātyāyana explains as 'writing of the Yavanas' (i.e. Iāones or Greeks). Now it is not at all likely that the Indians should have become acquainted with Greek writing before the invasion of Alexander in 327 BC. But the natives of the extreme north-west, of whom Pāṇini in all probability was one, would naturally have become acquainted with it soon after that date. They must, however, have grown familiar with it before a grammarian would make a rule as to how to form from Yavana, 'Greek,'

a derivative form meaning 'Greek writing'. It seems therefore hardly possible to place Pāṇini earlier than about 300 BC.

Pāṇini's grammar consists of nearly 4,000 rules divided into eight chapters. Being composed with the utmost imaginable brevity, each Sūtra or aphorism usually consists of only two or three words, and the whole work, if printed continuously in medium-sized Devanāgarī type, would not occupy more than about thirty-five pages of the present volume. And yet this grammar describes the entire Sanskrit language in all the details of its structure, with a completeness which has never been equalled elsewhere. It is at once the shortest and fullest grammar in the world.

In his endeavour to give an exhaustive survey of the *bhāṣā* or classical Sanskrit with a view to correct usage, Pāṇini went on to include within the scope of his grammar the language of the sacred texts, which was no longer quite intelligible. He accordingly gives hundreds of rules about the Veda, but without completeness. His account of the Vedic language, taken as a whole, thus shows many gaps, important matters being often omitted, while trifles are noticed. In this part of his work Pāṇini shows a decided incapacity to master his subject-matter, attributing to the Veda the most unbounded grammatical license, especially in interchanging or dropping inflections.

The grammar of Pāṇini is a *śabdānuśāsana,* or 'Treatise on Words', the fundamental principle of which is, that all nouns are derived from verbs. Starting with the simplest elements into which words can be analysed, root, affix and termination, Pāṇini shows how nominal and verbal stems are formed from roots and complete words from stems. He at the same time indicates the functions which words acquire by the addition of formative elements and by being compounded with other words. It is a peculiarity of Pāṇini's word-formation, that he recognizes derivation by suffixes only. Thus when a verbal root like *bhid*, 'to pierce,' is used in the nominal sense of 'piercer', he has recourse to the highly artificial expedient of assuming an imaginary suffix, for which a blank is substituted!

Yāska records that the universality of Śākaṭāyana's principle of nouns being derived from verbs was contested by Gārgya, who objected to the forced etymologies resulting from a general

application of this principle. Gārgya maintained that if *aśva*, 'horse,' for instance, were derived from *aś*, 'to travel,' not only would everything that travels be called *aśva*, and everything be named after all its activities, but states of being (*bhāva*) would be antecedent to things (which are presupposed by those states).

Pāṇini makes a concession to Gārgya's objection by excluding all words the derivation of which is difficult owing to their form or meaning, as *aśva*, 'horse,' *go*, 'cow,' and *puruṣa*, 'man.' Primary nouns of this kind had been collected before Pāṇini's time in a special list, in which they were often forcibly derived from verbal roots by means of a number of special suffixes. The first of these suffixes being *u*, technically called *uṇ*, the whole list of these formations received the name of *uṇādi* ('beginning with *uṇ*'). Pāṇini refers to all such words as ready-made stems, the formation of which does not concern him.

The Uṇādi list which Pāṇini had before him survives, in a somewhat modified form, as the Uṇādi Sūtra with the commentary (dating probably from the thirteenth century AD) of Ujjvaladatta. In its extant shape this Sūtra contains some late words, such as *dīnāra* (Lat. denarius), a noun which cannot have come into use in India much before 100 AD.

The proper object of Pāṇini's grammar being derivation, he does not deal with phonetics as such, but only incidentally as affecting word-formation, or the combination of words in a sentence. He therefore does not give general rules of phonetic change, but since his analyses, unlike those of the Uṇādi Sūtra, move within the bounds of probability and are generally correct, being in many cases confirmed by comparative philology, he actually did discover several phonetic laws. The most important of these was the interchange of vowels with their strong grades *guṇa* and *vṛddhi* (cp. 17), which Grimm called *ablaut*, and which comparative grammar traces to the original Indo-European language. The other great phonetic discoveries of the Indians had already been made by Pāṇini's predecessors, the authors of the original Prātiśākhyas, the phonetic treatises of the Vedic schools.

Pāṇini also treats of the accents of words in derivation and in the sentence, but with syntax in our sense he does not deal, perhaps owing to the simplicity of the sentence in Sanskrit.

The general plan of Pāṇini's work is as follows: Book i. contains the technical terms of the grammar and its rules of interpretation; ii. deals with nouns in composition and case relations; iii. teaches how suffixes are to be attached to verbal roots; iv. and v. explain the same process with regard to nominal stems; vi. and vii. describe the accent and phonetic changes in the formation of words, while viii. treats of words in a sentence. This general plan is, however, constantly interrupted by single rules or by a series of rules, which were added by the author as a result of progressive grammatical studies, or transferred from their natural context to their present position in order to economize words.

In formulating his rules, Pāṇini makes it his aim to express them in as abstract and general a way as possible. In this he occasionally goes so far as to state a general rule for a single case; while, on the other hand, he sometimes fails to collect a number of related phenomena under a single head.

In carrying out the principle of extreme conciseness dominating his grammar, Pāṇini resorts to various devices, such as ellipse of the verb, the use of the cases in a special technical sense, and the employment of heading rules (*adhikāra*) which must be supplied with a number of subordinate rules that follow. By such means a whole rule can often be expressed by a single word. Thus the ablative *dhātoḥ*, literally 'after a root', not only means 'to a root the following suffixes are attached', but is also an *adhikāra* extending its influence (*anuvṛtti*) over some 540 subsequent aphorisms.

The principle of brevity is, moreover, notably applied in the invention of technical terms. Those of Pāṇini's terms which are real words, whether they describe the phenomenon, as *sam-āsa*, 'compound,' or express a category by an example, as *dvi-gu* ('two-cow'), 'numeral compound,' are probably all borrowed from predecessors. But most of his technical terms are arbitrary groups of letters resembling algebraic symbols. Only a few of these are abbreviations of actual words, as *it*, 'indicatory letter,' from *iti*, 'thus.' Most of them are the result of great deliberation, being chiefly composed of letters rarely occurring in the language. Thus the letter *l* was taken as a symbol of the personal endings of the verb; combined with a cerebral *ṭ* it refers to a primary tense or mood, but combined with a guttural *ṅ* it denotes a secondary tense or mood. Thus *laṭ, liṭ, luṭ, leṭ, loṭ,* mean present, perfect,

future, subjunctive, and imperative respectively; *laṅ, luṅ, liṅ*, imperfect, aorist, and potential.

Pāṇini's grammar begins with the alphabet arranged on scientific principles. To several of its letters is attached an *it* or *anubandha* (indicatory letter), by means of which can be formed convenient contractions (called *pratyāhāra*) designating different groups of letters. The vowels are arranged thus : *a i u-ṇ, ṛ ḷ-k, e o-ṅ, ai au-c.* By means of the indicatory letter at the end of the group, all the simple vowels can be expressed by *ak*, the simple vowels together with the diphthongs by *ac.* As the last letter in Sanskrit is *h*, written *ha-l*, the entire alphabet is expressed by the symbol *al* (much as if we were to express it by *az*). Indicatory letters are also attached to suffixes, roots, and words in order to point to certain rules as applicable to them, thus aiding the memory as well as promoting brevity.

Pāṇini's work has two appendixes, to which it refers. One of these is the *Dhātu-pāṭha*, or 'List of Verbal Roots', arranged according to conjugational classes, the mode of inflexion being expressed by accents and indicatory letters. A striking fact about this collection is that of its 2,000 roots (many of which are, however, merely variants of one form) only about 800 have yet been found in Sanskrit literature, while it omits about fifty Vedic verbs. The second appendix is the *Gaṇa-pāṭha*, or 'List of Word-groups'. Pāṇini gives rules applicable to the whole of a group by referring to its first word. This collection, which contains many words occurring in Vedic works only, has been less well preserved than the *Dhātu-pāṭha*. The Gaṇas were metrically arranged in the *Gaṇa-ratna-mahodadhi*, or 'Ocean of the Gems of Word-groups', a work composed by Vardhamāna in 1140 AD.

Pāṇini's work very early acquired a canonical value, and has continued, for at least 2,000 years, to be the standard of usage and the foundation of grammatical studies in Sanskrit. On account of the frequent obscurity of a work which sacrifices every consideration to brevity, attempts soon began to be made to explain it, and, with the advance of grammatical knowledge, to correct and supplement its rules. Among the earliest attempts of this kind was the formulation, by unknown authors, of rules of interpretation (*paribhāṣā*), which Pāṇini was supposed to have followed in his grammar, and which are mentioned by his suc-

cessor Kātyāyana. A collection of such rules was made in the eighteenth century by Nāgoji-bhaṭṭa in his *Paribhāṣendu-śekhara*, or 'Moon-crest of Interpretative Rules.'

Next we have the Vārttikas, or 'notes' (from *vṛtti*, 'explanation'), of Kātyāyana, on 1,245, or nearly one-third, of Pāṇini's aphorisms. That grammarian belonged to the Deccan, and probably lived in the third century BC. When Kātyāyana's criticism shows him to differ from Pāṇini, an oversight on the part of the latter is usually to be assumed; but in estimating the extent of such oversights, one should not leave out of account the fact that Kātyāyana lived both later and in a part of India far removed from that of Pāṇini. Other grammarians made similar notes on Pāṇini both before and after Kātyāyana; subsequent to the latter's time are the numerous grammatical Kārikās or comments in metrical form.

All this critical work was collected by Patañjali in his extensive *Mahābhāṣya*, or 'Great Commentary', with many supplementary notes of his own. His discussions take the form of a kind of dialogue, and deals with 1,713 rules of Pāṇini. Patañjali's work probably dates, as has been said, from the latter half of the second century BC. The *Mahābhāṣya* in its turn was commented upon in the seventh century by Bhartṛhari in his *Vākyapadīya*, or 'Treatise on the Words in a Sentence', which is concerned with the philosophy of grammar, and by Kaiyaṭa probably in the thirteenth century.

About 650 AD was composed another commentary on Pāṇini, the *Kāśikā Vṛtti*, or 'Benares Commentary', the first five books being the work of Jayāditya, the last three of Vāmana. Based on a deteriorated text of Pāṇini, it contains some errors, but has the merit of conciseness and lucidity. Though much shorter than the *Mahābhāṣya*, it is particularly valuable as the oldest commentary on Pāṇini that explains every Sūtra. The examples that it gives in illustration are, as a rule, derived from older interpreters. Such borrowing was a usual practice; even Patañjali speaks of stock examples as *mūrdhābhiṣikta*, or 'consecrated' (lit. 'sprinkled on the head').

In the fifteenth century Rāmacandra endeavoured in his *Prakriyā-kaumudī*, or 'Moonlight of Method', to make Pāṇini's grammar more intelligible by rearranging its matter in a more

practical way. The *Siddhānta-kaumudī*, or 'Moonlight of Settled Conclusions', in which Bhaṭṭoji in the seventeenth century disposed Pāṇini's Sūtras in a more natural order, had a similar aim. An abridgement of this work, entitled *Laghu-(siddhānta-)kaumudī*, or 'Short Moonlight (of Settled Conclusions)', by Varadarāja, is commonly employed as a useful introduction to the native system of grammar. A belief in the infallibility of Pāṇini, which still prevails among the Pandits, has often led the above-named interpreters, from Patañjali onward, to give forced explanations of Pāṇini's rules.

Other later grammarians, not belonging to the school of Pāṇini, are on the whole of little importance. While adducing hardly any new material, they are much less complete than Pāṇini, since they omit whole sections, such as rules about Vedic forms and the accent. Introducing no new points of view, they aim solely at inventing technical devices, or at presenting their subject in a more lucid and popular form. Among these non-Pāṇinian grammarians may be mentioned the names of Candra[1], who flourished about, 650 AD[2]; the pseudo-Śākaṭāyana, who was posterior to the *Kāśikā-Vṛtti*; and the most important of them, Hemacandra (twelfth century). The *Kātantra* by Śarva-varman (of uncertain date), whose terminology has striking affinities with older works, especially the Prātiśākhyas, seems to have been the most influential of these later grammars. It served as a model for the standard Pāli grammar of Kaccāyana, and the native grammars of the Dravidians and Tibetans. Vopadeva's *Mugdha-bodha*, or 'Enlightenment of the Ignorant', a very technical work dating from the thirteenth century, has been, down to the present day, the Sanskrit grammar chiefly used in Bengal. Lastly, we have the *Sarasvatī Sūtra*, or 'Aphorisms of the Sarasvatī Grammar', by an unknown author, a work distinguished by lucidity as well as consiseness.

There are, besides, a few works dealing with special departments of the subject, which form contributions of some importance to our knowledge of Sanskrit grammar. The *Phiṭ Sūtra* of

---

1. His Grammar, the *Cāndra-vyākaraṇa*, has been edited by Prof. Brunof Liebich (Leipzig, 1902).
2. See *Vienna Oriental Journal*, 13, 308-15; *Witnernitz, Geschichte der indischen Litteratur*, ii, p. 259.

Śāntanava, composed later than the *Mahābhāṣya*, but at a time when there was still a living knowledge of the ancient accent, gives rules for the accentuation of nouns, not according to the analytical method of Pāṇini, but with reference to the finished word. As Pāṇini does not determine the gender of individual words, though he treats of feminine suffixes and does not ignore differences of gender in general, some value attaches to works dealing with the subject as a whole, especially to Hemacandra's *Liṅgānuśāsana*, or 'Treatise on Gender'.

The first Sanskrit grammar ever written by a European was composed by the German missionary Heinrich Roth, a native of Augsburg, who died at Agra in 1668, as Superior of the Jesuit College in that city. This work was never published, but the manuscript is still preserved at Rome. There is, however, in Kircher's *China Illustrata* (Amsterdam, 1667), pp. 162-63, a contribution by Roth, which contains an account of the Sanskrit alphabet with five tables in Devanāgarī characters (undoubtedly the earliest specimens of that script to be found in any book printed in Europe).[1]

The first printed European Sanskrit grammar was that of Paulinus a Sancto Bartholomaeo, written in Latin and published at Rome in 1790. This work was based partly on the MS. material left by a German Jesuit missionary named Hanxleden, who died in 1732. The first scientific grammar aiming at completeness was that of Colebrooke, published in 1805. It was followed by that of Carey in 1806. The former work was based on Pāṇini, the latter on Vopadeva. The earliest Sanskrit grammar written on European principles, and therefore of most influence on the study of Sanskrit at the beginning of the last century, was that of Wilkins (1808). The most notable among his successors have been Bopp, Benfey, and Whitney. Bopp's grammar was important owing no less to its lucidity than to its philological method. Benfey was the first to combine with the traditional material of Pāṇini a treatment of the peculiarities of the Vedic and the Epic dialects. He also largely used the aid of comparative philology for the explanation of Sanskrit forms. The American scholar Whitney was the first to attempt an

1. See Zachariae in the *Vienna Oriental Journal*, 15, 313-20.

historical grammar of Sanskrit by treating the Vedic language more fully, and explaining from it the development of classical Sanskrit. The first grammar treating Sanskrit entirely from the comparative point of view is the excellent work of Prof. J. Wackernagel, of which, however, only the first volume, dealing with phonology (1896), and the first part of the second volume (1905) treating of compounds, have yet appeared.

The best known of the Sanskrit grammars used in this country during the latter half of the nineteenth century are those of Monier-Williams and Max Müller. Both of these contain much matter derived from the native system that is of no practical utility, but rather an impediment, to the student of literary Sanskrit. All such matter has been eliminated in the present work, not from any prejudice against the Indian grammarians, but solely with the intention of facilitating the study of the subject by supplying only such grammatical data of the actual language as have been noted by scholars down to the present time. Vedic forms have also been excluded, but in order to furnish English and Indian students with the minimum material necessary for beginning to read works written in the older language, a brief outline of Vedic Grammar is given in Appendix III. My recently published *Vedic Grammar* being too elaborate for elementary students, I hope to bring out, as a parallel to the present work, a simplified Vedic Grammar, including syntax, which will afford beginners the same help in the study of Vedic literature as this grammar does in that of Sanskrit.

Though the accent is never marked in classical Sanskrit, I have, owing to its philological importance, indicated it here in transliterated words as far as it can be ascertained from Vedic texts. A short account of the Vedic accent itself will be found in Appendix III.

CONTENTS

THE DEVANĀGARĪ LETTERS

Vowels

Initial.	Medial.	Equivalent.
अ / अ		—a
आ / आ	ा	ā
इ	ि	i
ई	ी	i
उ	ु	u
ऊ	ू	ū
ऋ	ृ	ṛ (or ṛi)
ॠ	ॄ	ṝ (or ṝi)
ऌ	ॢ	ḷ (or ḷi)
ए	े	e
ऐ	ै	ai
ओ	ो	o
औ	ौ	au

Consonants

	Equivalent			Equivalent	
क	k	Gutturals	प	p	Labials
ख	k-h	Gutturals	फ	p-h	Labials
ग	g	Gutturals	ब	b	Labials
घ	g-h	Gutturals	भ	b-h	Labials
ङ	ṅ	Gutturals	म	m	Labials
च	c	Palatals	य	y	Semivowels
छ	c-h	Palatals	र	j	Semivowels
ज	j	Palatals	ल	l	Semivowels
झ / झ or झ	j-h	Palatals	व	v	Semivowels
ञ	ñ	Palatals			
ट	ṭ	Cerebrals	श	ś (or ç)	Spirants
ठ	ṭ-h	Cerebrals	ष	ṣ	Spirants
ड	ḍ	Cerebrals	स	s	Spirants
ढ	ḍ-h	Cerebrals	ह	h	Spirants
ण	ṇ	Cerebrals			
त	t	Dentals	:	ḥ (Visarga)	
थ	t-h	Dentals	˙	ṃ or ṁ (Anusvāra)	
द	d	Dentals			
ध	d-h	Dentals			
न	n	Dentals			

CHAPTER I

THE ALPHABET

1. Sanskrit (from *saṃ-skṛta*, 'elaborated') is that later phase of the literary language of ancient India which is described in the grammar of Pāṇini. In phonology it is practically identical with the earlier **Vedic** language. In accidence it has become different from the dialect of the Vedas by a process, not of growth, but of decay; a large number of older forms, including the whole subjunctive mood and all the many infinitives save one, having entirely disappeared. The chief modifications are in the vocabulary, which, while it has lost much of its old material, has been greatly extended by the accession of new words and new meanings. The difference, on the whole, between the Vedic and the Sanskrit language may be taken to be much about the same as that between Homeric and Attic Greek.

2. From the Vedic language are descended the popular dialects called **Prākrit** ('derived from the fundament,' i.e. from Sanskrit, thence 'vulgar'). The oldest extant forms of these are preserved in King Aśoka's rock inscriptions of the third century BC, one of them, under the name of Pāli, becoming the sacred literary language of the Southern Buddhists. From the ancient Prākrits, preserved in inscriptions, in entire literary works, and in parts of Sanskrit plays, are descended most of the dialects of modern India, Panjābī, Sindhī, Gujarātī, Marāṭhī, Hindī (which, with an

admixture of Arabic and Persian, is called Urdū or Hindūstānī), Bihārī, and Bengālī. The Dravidian dialects of Southern India, Telugu, Tamil, Canarese, Malayālam, though non-Āryan, are full of Sanskrit words, and their literatures are dominated by Sanskrit models.

3. A form of Semitic writing was introduced into the north-west of India by way of Mesopotamia, probably about 700 BC. The earliest Indian adaptation of this script, known from coins and inscriptions of the third century BC, is called Brāhmī or 'writing of Brahmā.' Though written from left to right it bears clear traces of having once been written from right to left. From the Brāhmī are descended all the later Indian scripts. The most important of these is the Nāgarī ('urban writing,' or perhaps 'writing of the Nāgara Brahmins' of Gujarāt) or Devanāgarī ('city writing of the gods,' a term of late but obscure origin), which assumed its characteristic shape about the middle of the eighth century AD. Sanskrit is most commonly written in Devanāgarī in Northern India, but other modern Indian characters, such as Bengālī or Oriyā, are also employed in their respective provinces; while in the non-Āryan south the Dravidian scripts are regularly used.

4. The Devanāgarī alphabet consists of forty-eight letters, thirteen vowels and thirty-five consonants (including the pure nasal called Anusvāra, and the spirant called Visarga). These represent every sound of the Sanskrit language. The arrangement of the alphabet in the table facing p. 1 is that adopted by the ancient Indian grammarians, and being thoroughly scientific, has been followed by European scholars as the lexicographical order in their Sanskrit dictionaries[1].

---

1. As Anusvāra and Visarga cause beginners much difficulty in finding words in a glossary, the following note on their alphabetical order will

5. The vowels are written differently according as they are initial or follow a consonant. They are —

(*a*) Simple vowels :

अ (-)[1] a, इ (ि) i[2], उ (ु) u, ऋ (ृ) ṛ, ऌ (ॢ) ḷ.

आ (ा) ā, ई (ी) ī, ऊ (ू) ū, ॠ (ॄ) ṝ.

(*b*) Diphthongs :

ए (े) e[3], ऐ (ै) ai[4], ओ (ो) o[3], औ (ौ) au.[5]

---

probably be useful. The unchangeable Anusvāra (before a semi-vowel, sibilant, or ह् h: cp. 42 B 1) has precedence of every other consonant: hence संवर् saṃvara, संशय् saṃśaya precede सक sa-ka. The changeable Anusvāra (10; 42 B 2) occupies the place of the nasal into which it might be changed. Thus संग saṃ-ga would be found beside सङ्ग saṅga. Similarly the unchangeable Visarga (before a hard guttural or labial) has precedence of every other consonant. Thus अन्तःकरण antaḥkaraṇa and अन्तःपुर antaḥpura follow अन्त anta and precede अन्तक anta-ka. But the changeable Visarga (before a sibilant) occupies the place of the sibilant into which it might be changed. Thus अन्तःस्थ antaḥstha would appear where अन्तस्स्थ antasstha might be written.

1. There is no sign for medial (or final) ă, as this vowel is considered to be inherent in every consonant; — e.g. क = ka.
2. Medial or final ĭ is written before the consonant after which it is pronounced; — e.g. कि ki. Originally both ĭ and ī were written as curves to the left and the right respectively above the consonant; but for the sake of clear distinction were later prolonged with a vertical downward stroke, the one on the left, the other on the right.
3. Though based, in nearly all cases, on ăi and ău respectively, e and o are at present, and have been since at least 300 BC, pronounced like the simple long vowels ē and ō in most European languages.
4. Though etymologically representating āi and āu, ai and au are at present, and have been since at least 300 BC, pronounced as ăi and ău.
5. The medial forms of the vowels are in combination with consonants; — e.g. क् k, written as follows: क ka, का kā, की kī, कि kī, कु ku,

6. The following table contains a complete classification (known to Pāṇini) of all the sounds of the Devanāgarī alphabet according to the organs of speech employed in their articulation.

	Hard (tenues)	Hard aspirates	Soft (mediæ)	Soft aspirates	(Soft) nasals	(Soft) semi-vowels.	Hard spirants	Soft Vowels Short	Long.	Diphthongs.
Gutturals	क k	ख k-h	ग g	घ g-h	ङ ṅ	ह h[3]	: ḥ[4]	अ a	आ ā	ए e ऐ ai
Palatals[1]	च c	छ c-h	ज j	झ j-h	ञ ñ	य y	श ś	इ i	ई ī	
Cerebrals[2]	ट ṭ	ठ ṭ-h	ड ḍ	ढ ḍ-h	ण ṇ	र r	ष ṣ	ऋ ṛ	ॠ ṝ	
Dentals	त t	थ t-h	द d	ध d-h	न n	ल l	स s	ऌ ḷ		
Labials	प p	फ p-h	ब b	भ b-h	म m	व v	: ḥ[5]	उ u	ऊ ū	ओ o औ au

कू kū, कृ kṛ, कॄ kṝ, क्लृ kḷ, के ke, कै kai, को ko, कौ kau. In combination with र् r, u and ū are written at the side instead of below: रु ru, रू rū.

1. The palatals, being largely derived from original gutturals under the influence of palatal vowels, were transliterated by Max Müller with italicized gutturals.
2. This term is a translation of the old native Sanskrit word *mūrdhanya*, 'produced in the head' (*mūrdhan*), i.e. on the roof or highest point of the mouth, which is nearest the upper part of the head. This class of sounds has also often been called linguals (since Bopp). They are as a rule derived from original dentals under the influence of a neighbouring crebral ṣ or r sound.
3. ह h is not a semivowel, but the soft breathing corresponding to the guttural vowel अ a, which, unlike the other simple vowels, has no semivowel of its own. It is identical with the second half of the soft aspirates g-h, &c.
4. : ḥ (Visarga) the hard breathing, corresponding to the second half of the hard aspirates k-h, &c., is regularly used at the end of a word *in pausā* for s or r, and before hard gutturals and labials. In the latter case modifications of it called Jihvāmūlīya ('formed at the root of the tongue'), a guttural spirant (= Germ. *ch*), and Upadhmānīya ('on-breathing'), the bilabial spirant *f*, were formerly employed, but have become obsolete. They were both written ≍.
5. It is important to note that in the above table only the letters in

7. Anusvāra ('after-sound'), the unmodified nasal following a vowel and differing from the nasals given in column 5, is written with a dot above the letter which it follows; — e.g. कं kaṃ. Before ल् l it is sometimes written ँ; — e.g. कँ kam̐. Its proper place was originally before the sibilants and ह् h, whence its use extended. From Anusvāra is sometimes distinguished Anunāsika ('accompanied by a nasal'), the nasalized vowel.

8. In writing the Devanāgarī alphabet, the distinctive portion of each letter is written first, then the perpendicular, and lastly the horizontal line[1]; — e.g. ̣ς, ᥰ, त ta.

9. Consonants to be pronounced without any vowel after them, are marked below with a stroke slanting from left to right, called Virāma ('stop'). Thus ak must be written अक्.

The only marks of punctuation are the sign । at the end of a half-verse or sentence, and the sign ॥ at the end of a verse or paragraph.

The elision of अ a at the beginning of a word is marked in European editions with the sign ऽ called Avagraha ('separation'); — e.g. तेऽपि te'pi for ते अपि te api.

An abbreviation is indicated by the sign ॰ ; thus गतम् gatam, ॰तेन (ga)-tena.

10. When the five nasals are followed by consonants of their own class within a word, they are often, to save trouble, incorrectly replaced by the sign of Anusvāra :— e.g. अंकित aṃkita for अङ्कित aṅkita; कंपित kaṃpita for कम्पित kampita. In the same way final म् m at the end of a sentence is often wrongly written with Anusvāra; thus अहं ahaṃ for अहम् aham. In both cases the pronunciation remains unaffected by the substitution.

---

columns 1, 2, and 7 are hard (surd, voiceless), while all the rest are soft (sonant, voiced).

1. This was not originally an essential element in the letter, but represents a part of the line below which the characters were written.

11. If a consonant is followed immediately by one or more consonants they are all written in a group; — e.g. अत्क atka; कार्त्स्न्य kārtsnya. The general principle followed in the formation of these conjunct consonants, is to drop the perpendicular and horizontal lines except in the last letter. Most of these combinations, with the exception of those transliterated with thick type in the subjoined list, may be recognized without difficulty.

12. The following are the most noticeable modifications of simple consonants when written in conjunction with others:

1. The component parts are indistinguishable in ज्ञ or ज्ञ jña ज् + ञ; and in क्ष or क्ष kṣa = क् + ष.
2. A horizontal line is sometimes substituted for the distinctive portion of त t and for the loop of क k; — e.g. त्त tta = त् + त; क्त kta = क् + त.
3. श् ś is often written श् when followed by a consonant or by the vowels ŭ or ṛ̆; — e.g. श्च śca, शु śu, शृ śṛ.
4. र् r following a consonant is written with a short oblique stroke from right to left at the foot of the letter; — e.g. क्र kra, द्र dra, ष्ट्र ṣṭra, न्त्र्य ntrya.

   र् r preceding a consonant or the vowel ऋ ṛ is written with ʿ placed at the top of the letter before which it is to be sounded: — e.g. अर्क arka, वर्ष्म varṣma; निर्ऋतिः nirṛtiḥ. This sign for र् is placed to the right of any other marks at the top of the same letter; — e.g. अर्केंदु arkendu.

List of Compound Consonants

13. क्क k-ka, क्ख k-kha, क्च k-ca, क्ण k-ṇa, क्त k-ta, क्त्य k-t-ya, क्त्र k-t-ra, क्त्र्य k-t-r-ya, क्त्व k-t-va, क्न k-na, क्न्य k-n-ya, क्म k-ma, क्य k-ya, क्र or क्र k-ra, क्र्य or क्र्य k-r-ya, क्ल k-la, क्व k-va, क्व्य k-v-ya, क्ष or क्ष k-ṣa, क्ष्म k-ṣ-ma, क्ष्य k-ṣ-ya, क्ष्व k-ṣ-va —

ख्य kh-ya, ख्र kh-ra. — ग्य g-ya, ग्र g-ra, ग्र्य g-r-ya. — घ्न gh-na, घ्न्य gh-n-ya, घ्म gh-ma, घ्य gh-ya, घ्र gh-ra. — ङ्क ṅ-ka, ङ्क्त ṅ-k-ta, ङ्क्त्य ṅ-k-tya, ङ्क्य ṅ-k-ya, ङ्क्ष ṅ-k-ṣa, ङ्क्ष्व ṅ-k-ṣ-va, ङ्ख ṅ-kha, ङ्ख्य ṅ-kh-ya, ङ्ग ṅ-ga, ङ्ग्य ṅ-g-ya, ङ्घ ṅ-gha, ङ्घ्य ṅ-gh-ya, ङ्घ्र ṅ-gh-ra, ङ्ङ ṅ-ṅa, ङ्न ṅ-na, ङ्म ṅ-ma, ङ्य ṅ-ya.

च्च c-ca, च्छ c-cha, च्छ्र c-ch-ra, च्ञ c-ña, च्म c-ma, च्य c-ya. — छ्य ch-ya, छ्र ch-ra. — ज्ज j-ja, ज्झ j-jha, ज्ञ or ज्ञ j-ña, ज्ञ्य j-ñ-ya, ज्म j-ma, ज्य j-ya, ज्र j-ra, ज्व j-va. — ञ्च ñ-ca, ञ्च्म ñ-c-ma, ञ्च्य ñ-c-ya. ञ्छ ñ-cha, ञ्ज ñ-ja, ञ्ज्य ñ-j-ya.

ट्ट ṭ-ṭa, ट्य ṭ-ya. — ठ्य ṭh-ya, ठ्र ṭh-ra. — ड्ग ḍ-ga, ड्ग्य ḍ-g-ya, ड्घ ḍ-gha, ड्घ्र ḍ-gh-ra, ड्म ḍ-ma, ड्य ḍ-ya. — ढ्य ḍh-ya, ढ्र ḍh-ra. — ण्ट ṇ-ṭa, ण्ठ ṇ-ṭha, ण्ड ṇ-ḍa, ण्ड्य ṇ-ḍ-ya, ण्ड्र ṇ-ḍ-ra, ण्ड्र्य ṇ-ḍra, ण्ढ ṇ-ḍha, ण्ण ṇ-ṇa, ण्म ṇ-ma, ण्य ṇ-ya, ण्व ṇ-va.

त्क t-ka, त्क्र t-k-ra, त्त t-ta, त्त्य t-t-ya, त्त्र t-t-ra, त्त्व t-t-va त्थ t-tha, त्न t-na, त्न्य t-n-ya, त्प t-pa, त्प्र t-p-ra, त्म t-ma, त्म्य t-m-ya, त्य t-ya, त्र or त्र t-ra, त्र्य t-r-ya, त्व t-va, त्स t-sa, त्स्न t-s-na, त्स्न्य t-s-n-ya. — थ्य th-ya. — द्ग d-ga, द्ग्र d-g-ra, द्घ d-gha, द्घ्र d-gh-ra, द्द d-da, द्द्य d-d-ya. — द्ध d-dha, द्ध्य d-dh-ya, द्न d-na, द्ब d-ba, द्भ d-bha, द्भ्य d-bh-ya, द्म d-ma, द्य d-ya, द्र d-ra, द्र्य d-r-ya, द्व d-va, द्व्य d-v-ya. — ध्न dh-na, ध्न्य dh-n-ya, ध्म dh-ma, ध्य dh-ya, ध्र dh-ra, ध्र्य dh-r-ya, ध्व dh-va. — न्त n-ta, न्त्य n-t-ya, न्त्र n-t-ra, न्द n-da, न्द्र n-d-ra, न्ध n-dha, न्ध्र n-dh-ra, न्न n-na, न्प n-pa, न्प्र n-p-ra, न्म n-ma, न्य n-ya, न्र n-ra, न्स n-sa.

प्त p-ta, प्त्य p-t-ya, प्न p-na, प्प p-pa, प्म p-ma, प्य p-ya, प्र p-ra, प्ल p-la, प्व p-va, प्स p-sa, प्स्व p-s-va. — ब्घ b-gha, ब्ज b-ja, ब्द b-da, ब्ध b-dha, ब्न b-na, ब्ब b-ba, ब्भ b-bha, ब्भ्य b-bh-ya, ब्य b-ya, ब्र b-ra, ब्व b-va. — भ्न bh-na, भ्य bh-ya, भ्र bh-ra, भ्व bh-va. — म्न m-na, म्प m-pa, म्प्र m-p-ra, म्ब m-ba, म्भ m-bha, म्म m-ma, म्य m-ya, म्र m-ra, म्ल m-la, म्व m-va.

य्य y-ya, य्व y-va. — ल्क l-ka, ल्प l-pa, ल्म l-ma, ल्य l-ya, ल्ल l-la, ल्व l-va, ल्ह l-ha. — व्न v-na, व्य v-ya, व्र v-ra, व्व v-va.

श्च ś-ca, श्च्य ś-c-ya, श्न ś-na, श्य ś-ya, श्र ś-ra, श्र्य ś-r-ya, श्ल ś-la, श्व ś-va, श्व्य ś-v-ya, श्श ś-śa. — ष्ट ṣ-ṭa, ष्ट्य ṣ-ṭ-ya, ष्ट्र ṣ-ṭ-ra, ष्ट्र्य ṣ-ṭ-r-ya, ष्ट्व ṣ-ṭ-va, ष्ठ ṣ-ṭha, ष्ण ṣ-ṇa, ष्ण्य ṣ-ṇ-ya, ष्प ṣ-pa, ष्प्र ṣ-p-ra, ष्म ṣ-ma, ष्य ṣ-ya, ष्व ṣ-va. — स्क s-ka, स्ख s-kha, स्त s-ta, स्त्य s-t-ya, स्त्र s-t-ra, स्त्व s-t-va, स्थ s-tha, स्न s-na, स्न्य s-n-ya, स्प s-pa, स्फ s-pha, स्म s-ma, स्म्य s-m-ya, स्य s-ya, स्र s-ra, स्व s-va, स्स s-sa.

ह्ण h-ṇa, ह्न h-na, ह्म h-ma, ह्य h-ya, ह्र h-ra, ह्ल h-la, ह्व h-va.

14. The numerical figures in Sanskrit are —

१	२	३	४	५	६	७	८	९	०
1	2	3	4	5	6	7	8	9	0

These figures were borrowed from the Indians by the Arabs, who introduced them into Europe.

Pronunciation.

15. The following rules should be noted: —

1. The vowels are pronounced as in Italian. The short अ a, however, has rather the sound of the so-called neutral vowel in English, like the u in 'but.' It had this sound (in Sanskrit saṃvṛta, 'closed') at least as early as 300 BC.
2. The aspiration of the consonants should be heard distinctly. Thus ख = k-h in 'ink-horn'; थ = t-h in 'pot-house'; फ = p-h in 'topheavy'; घ = g-h in 'loghouse'; ध = d-h in 'madhouse'; भ = b-h in 'Hobhouse.'
3. The guttural ङ ṅ has the sound of ng in 'king'.
4. The palatals च c and ज j have the sound of ch in 'church,' and of j in 'join.'

5. The cerebrals are pronounced similarly to the so-called dentals t, d, n in English, the tongue being, however, turned rather further back against the roof of the mouth.
6. The dentals in Sanskrit are at the present day pronounced as inter-dentals, being produced by bringing the tip of the tongue against the very edge of the front teeth. In the days of the ancient Indian phoneticians they were pronounced as post-dentals, being produced at the back of the upper front teeth.
7. The dental स् s sounds like s in 'sin,' the cerebral ष् ṣ like sh in 'shun'; while the palatal श् ś is produced midway between the two, being the sibilant pronounced in the same place as the spirant in the German 'ich.'
8. The Visarga, being a final hard breathing, is in India generally pronounced as a hard h, followed by a short echo of the preceding vowel.
9. The Anusvāra, being a pure nasal unmodified by any stop, is sounded like n in the French 'bon.'
10. Since about the beginning of our era Sanskrit has been pronounced with a stress accent (instead of the earlier musical accent) much in the same way as Latin. Thus the stress is laid on a long penultimate (Kālidā́sa), on the antepenultimate when followed by a short syllable (Himā́laya), and on the fourth from the end when two short syllables follow (kā́rayati).

CHAPTER II

RULES OF SANDHI OR EUPHONIC COMBINATION OF LETTERS

16. In Sanskrit every sentence is treated as one unbroken chain of syllables. The coalescence of final and initial letters is called Sandhi ('putting together.') The rules of Sandhi are based chiefly on the **avoidance of hiatus** and on **assimilation.**

The absence of Sandhi is in many cases sufficient to mark the stops which in other languages have to be marked by punctuation.

Though both are based on the same phonetic principles, it is essential, in order to avoid confusion, to distinguish **external Sandhi**, which determines the changes of final and initial letters of *words*, from **internal Sandhi,** which applies to the final letters of *verbal roots* and *nominal stems* when followed by certain suffixes or terminations.

a. The rules of external Sandhi apply, with few exceptions (which are survivals of an earlier stage of external Sandhi), to words forming compounds, and to the final letters of nominal stems before the Pada or middle case-endings भ्याम् bhyām, भिस् bhis, भ्यस् bhyas, सु su (71), or before secondary (182, 2) suffixes beginning with any consonant except य् y.

A. External Sandhi

Classification of Vowels.

17. Vowels are divided into—

A.1. Simple Vowels: अ a, आ ā; इ i, ई ī; उ u, ऊ ū; ऋ ṛ, ॠ ṝ; ऌ ḷ.

2. Guṇa vowles : अ a, ए e, ओ o; अर् ar; अल् al.

3. Vṛddhi vowels : अ ā, ऐ ai; औ au; आर् ār[1].

1. The Vṛddhi form of ऌ ḷ, (which would be आल ā1) does not occur.

a. Guṇa ('secondary form') is the strengthening of the simple vowels by a preceding अ a (which leaves अ a itself unchanged); Vṛddhi ('increase') is the further strengthening of Guṇa vowels by means of another अ a[1].

B.1. Vowels which are liable to be changed into semivowels: इ i, ई ī; उ u; ऊ ū; ऋ ṛ, ॠ ṝ, and the diphthongs (the latter half of which is इ i or उ u): *liquid* vowels.

2. Those which are not: अ a, आ ā.

Combination of Final and Initial Vowels.

18. If the same simple vowel (short or long) occurs at the end and beginning of words, the result is a long vowel;— e.g. सा अपि ईक्षते sā api īkṣate becomes सापीक्षते sāpīkṣate; किंतु उदेति kiṃtu udeti becomes किंतूदेति kiṃtūdeti; कर्तृ ऋजु katṛ ṛju becomes कर्तॄजु kartṝju.

19. अ **a** and आ **ā** —

a. coalesce with a following simple liquid vowel to Guṇa; — e.g. तव इन्द्रः tava indraḥ = तवेन्द्रः tavendraḥ; सा उक्त्वा sā uktvā = सोक्त्वा soktvā: सा ऋद्धिः sā ṛddhiḥ = सर्द्धिः sarddhiḥ.

b. coalesce with Guṇa vowels to Vṛddhi; —e.g. तव एव tava eva = तवैव tavaiva; = सा ओषधिः sā oṣadhiḥ = सौषधिः sauṣadhiḥ.

c. are absorbed by Vṛddhi vowels; — e.g. सा औत्सुक्यवती sā autsukyavatī = सौत्सुक्यवती sautsukyavatī.

---

1. In this vowels generation, as Comparative Philosophy shows, the Guṇa vowels represents the normal stage, from which the simple vowel was reduced by loss of accent, while Vṛddhi is a lengthened variety of Guṇa. The reduction of the syllables ya, va, ra (which are parallel with the Guṇa stage) to the corresponding vowels i, u, ṛ is termed Samprasāraṇa ('distraction').

20. A simple **liquid vowel** followed by any *other* vowel or by a diphthong is changed into its semivowel; — e.g. दधि अत्र dadhi atra = दध्यत्र dadhy atra; कर्तृ उत kartṛ uta = कर्त्रुत kartar uta; मधु इव madhu iva = मध्विव madhv iva; नदी अर्थम् nadī artham = नद्यर्थम् nadyartham.

21. The Guṇa vowels ए e and ओ o —

a. remain unchanged before अ a, which is elided: ते अपि te api = तेऽपि te'pi; सो अपि so api = सोऽपि so 'pi.

b. become अ a (through अय् ay and अव् av, which drop the semivowel) before every other vowel (or diphthong): सखे इह sakhe iha = सख इह sakha iha; प्रभो एहि prabho ehi = प्रभ एहि prabha ehi.

22. The Vṛddhi vowels ऐ ai and औ au respectively become आ ā (through आय् āy) and आव् āv (the semivowel not being dropped in this case) before every vowel (or diphthong): श्रियै अर्थः śriyai arthaḥ = श्रिया अर्थः śriyā arthaḥ; तौ इति tau iti = ताविति tāv iti.

a. The (Secondary) hiatus occasioned by the dropping of य् y and व् v in the above three cases (21*b* and 22) remains.

Irregular Vowel Sandhi.

23. Vṛddhi instead of Guṇa results from the contraction of —

a. a preposition ending in अ a or आ ā with a verb beginning with ऋ ṛ; — e.g. उप ऋषति upa ṛṣati = उपार्षति upārṣati; आ ऋच्छति ā ṛcchati = आर्च्छति ārcchati.

b. the preposition प्र pra with the perfect participle passive ऊढ ūḍha (from वह् vah, 'carry'): प्रौढ prauḍha, 'lifted up.'

c. the augment अ a with an initial vowel; — e.g. अ उनत् a unat = औनत् aunat, 'he wetted' (from उद् ud, 'wet').

Absence of Vowel Sandhi.

24. Interjectional particles consisting of or ending in vowels, such as आ ā, इ i, उ u, हे he, अहो aho, are not liable to Sandhi: इ इन्द्र i indra, 'O Indra'; आ एवम् ā evam, 'is it so indeed?' अहो अपेहि aho apehi, 'Oh, go away.'

25. The vowels ई ī, ऊ ū, ए e, when dual terminations, nominal or verbal, remain unchanged before vowels (अ a not being elided after this dual ए e); they are called Pragṛhya ('separate'). The final of अमी amī, a nom. *plural* (of the pronoun असौ asau, 112), is treated in the same way.

E.g. कवी इमौ kavī imau, 'these two poets'; साधू इमौ sādhū imau, 'these two merchants'; विद्ये इमे vidye ime, 'these two sciences'; याचेते अर्थम् yācete artham, 'they two ask for money'; अमी अश्वाः amī aśvāḥ, 'those horses.'

26. In the Epics, the law-books, and other works not strictly conforming to the classical standard, vowel Sandhi is seldom applied between the first and second line (Pāda) of a hemistich.

Combination of Final and Initial Consonants.

27. The rules of Sandhi are only applicable after the final consonant of a word has been reduced to one of the eight allowable (actually occurring) consonants at the end of a word *in pausā*, viz.:

क् k,	ट् ṭ,	त् t,	प् p	} and : (Visarga)
ङ् ṅ,	न् n,	म् m		

The thirty-four consonants given in the table (6) are reduced to these eight, as follows:

A final must be hard and unaspirated, the palatals (including श् ś) and ह् h are replaced by क् k or ट् ṭ (ञ् ñ by ङ् ṅ), ष् ṣ by ट् ṭ, स् s and र् r by Visarga, while ण् ṇ, य् y, ल् l, and व् v do

not occur. Thus the second, third, and fourth columns, as well as the second line (the palatals), disappear entirely, leaving only four tenues in the first, three nasals in the fifth, and Visarga alone in the sixth and seventh.

28. No word may end in more than one consonant, except when र् r precedes a final क् k, ट् ṭ, त् t, प् p, which is radical (or substituted for a radical) and not a suffix. In the case of all other combinations the final letter or letters must be dropped till only one, in the form allowable as a final, remains. Thus भवन्त्स् bhavant-s becomes भवन् bhavan, 'being'; अबिभर्त् abibhar-t अबिभः abhibhaḥ, 'he carried' (त् t is a suffix; र् r must become Visarga); but ऊर्क् ūrk, 'strength' (क् k substituted for radical ज् j); अमार्ट् amārṭ, 'he wiped,' from मृज् mṛj (ट् ṭ substituted for radical ज् j).

Classification of Consonants.

29. Place or organ of articulation.

1. The throat, the palate, the roof of the month, the teeth, the lips, and the nose are called the places or organs of articulation.
2. By contact between the tongue and the four places — throat, palate, roof, teeth — the guttural, palatal, cerebral, and dental consonants are formed. Labial consonants are formed by contact between the lips.
3. In forming the **nasals** of the five classes, the breath partially passes through the nose while the tongue or the lips are in the position for articulating the corresponding tenuis. The real Anusvāra is formed in the nose only, while the tongue is in the position for forming the particular vowel which the Anusvāra accompanies.

4. The **semivowels** य y, र् r, ल l, व v are palatal, cerebral, dental, and labial respectively. They are described by the old Indian grammarians as produced by partial or imperfect contact of the tongue with the organ of articulation. ल l often interchanges with or is derived from र् r.
5. The three **sibilants** are hard spirants produced by partial contact of the tongue with the palate, roof, and teeth respectively. Sanskrit has not preserved any of the corresponding soft sibilants (English *z*, French *j*).
6. ह **h** and : **ḥ** are respectively soft and hard spirants produced without any contact, and articulated in the position of the vowel which precedes or follows. ह h, corresponding to the second half or the soft aspirates g-h, j-h, d-h, b-h, from which it is in fact derived, occurs only before soft letters. Visarga, corresponding to the second half of the hard aspirates (k-h, &c.), occurs only after vowels and before certain hard consonants. In India Visarga is usually articulated as a hard h, followed by a very short echo of the preceding vowel; — e.g. कः kaḥ=kah^{a}, कविः kaviḥ=kavih^{i}; ऋतुः ṛtuḥ=ṛtuh^{u}.

30. Quality of Consonants.

Consonants are —

1. either **hard** (surd, voiceless): columns I.2, 7 in the table, p. 4;
   or **soft** (sound, voiced) all the rest (columns 3, 4, 5, 6) and Anusvāra (besides all the vowels and diphthongs).
2. either **aspirated:** columns 2, 4, 7, besides ह h (in 6); or **unaspirated:** all the rest.

Hence the change of च् c to क् k is a change of place (palatal to guttural), and that of च् c to ज् j is a change of quality (hard to soft); while the change of च् c to ग् g (hard palatal to soft

guttural), or of त् t to ज् j (hard dental to soft palatal) is one of both place and quality.

31. It is essential to remember that consonant Sandhi cannot be applied till finals have been reduced to one of the eight allowable letters (27). The latter are then modified without reference to their etymological value (except partially in the case of Visarga). Only six of these finals occur at all frequently, viz. क् k, त् t, न् n, प् p, म् m, and Visarga. The changes which final consonants undergo are most conveniently treated with reference to (I) their quality, (II) their place or organ.

I. Changes of Quality.

32. Final consonants must be soft before soft initials, and hard before hard initials.

a. This rule affects only the five final hard consonants (क् k, ट् ṭ, त् t, प् p, and : ḥ), the nasals (6; 36) not being liable to changes of quality (but two of them, न् n, म् m, are liable to changes of place, like the two hard sounds त् t and Visarga: 37).

Hence final क् k, ट् ṭ, त् t, प् p before sonants become ग् g, ड् ḍ, द् d, ब् b respectively; — e.g. सम्यक् उक्तम् = सम्यगुक्तम् samyag uktam, 'well said'; दिक् गजः = दिग्गजः dig-gajaḥ), 'world-elephant.' — परिव्राट् अयम् = परिव्राडयम् parivrāḍ ayam, 'he (is) a mendicant'; परिव्राट् गच्छति = परिव्राड्गच्छति parivrāḍ gacchati, 'the mendicant goes.' — सरित् अत्र = सरिदत्र sarid atra, 'the river here'; महत् धनुः = महद्धनुः mahad-dhanuḥ, 'a large bow.' — ककुप् अत्र = ककुबत्र kakub atra, 'a region here'; अप् जः = अब्जः ab-jaḥ, 'born in water.'

33. क् k, ट् ṭ, त् t, प् p, when followed by initial न् n or म् m, may, and in practice almost invariably do, become the corresponding nasals ङ् ṅ, ण् ṇ, न् n, म् m; — e.g. दिक् नागः = दिङ्नागः or

दिङ्नाग: dig-nāgaḥ or diṅ-nāgaḥ, 'world-elephant'; जगत् नाथ: = जगद्नाथ: or जगन्नाथ: jagad-nātaḥ or jagan-nāthaḥ, 'lord of the world'; षट् मास: = षण्मास: ṣaṇ-māsaḥ, 'period of six months'; प्राक् मुख: = प्राङ्मुख: prāṇ-mukhaḥ, 'facing the east.'

34. Final त् t before ल् l becomes ल् l (through द् d); — e.g. तत् लब्धम् = तल्लब्धम् tal labdham, 'that is taken.'

35. Since the nasals have no corresponding hard latters, they remain unchanged in quality before hard letters; but in several cases a sibilant (after न् n) or cognate hard letter (after न् n or ङ् ṅ) is inserted between the two. An original palatal ञ् ñ or cerebral ण् ṇ never occurs as a final letter (27). The guttural ङ् ṅ, which is rare as a final, remains unchanged in that position, but क् k may be inserted after it before the three sibilants; — e.g. प्राङ् शेते prāṅ śete or प्राङ्क शेते prāṅk śete, 'he lies eastward.' Final म् m is liable to change before all consonants (42). Final dental न् n remains unchanged before most letters, but is modified before all palatals and cerebrals (except ष् ṣ), before the hard dentals त् t and थ् th, and before the semivowel ल् l. Its treatment requires a somewhat detailed statement.

36. A. The **dental nasal न् n** remains **unchanged**—

1. before vowels (cp. 52); — e.g. तान् उवाच tān uvāca, 'he spoke to them.'
2. before all gutturals, क् k, ख् kh, ग् g, घ् gh, as well as ह् h;— e.g. बुद्धिमान् कोऽपि buddhimān ko'pi, 'a certain wise man'; तान् हत्वा tān hatvā, 'having slain them.'
3. before all the labials, प् p, फ् ph, ब् b, भ् bh, म् m; — e.g. एतान् पाशान् etān pāśān, 'these bonds'; बान्धवान् मम bāndhavān mama, 'my relatives.'
4. before the soft dentals द् d, ध् dh, न् n; — e.g. मत्स्यान् धत्त

matsyān dhatta, 'put the fish'; राजपुत्रान् नयति rājaputrān nayati, 'he leads the princes.'

5. before the semivowels य् y, र् r, व् v; — e.g. हंसान् रक्षति haṃsān rakṣati, 'he protects the geese.'
6. before the cerebral ष् ṣ and the dental स् s, but before the latter a transitional त् t may be inserted; — e.g. तान् षट् tān ṣaṭ, 'those six'; तान् सहते tān sahate or तान्त्सहते tānt sahate, 'he endures them.'

B. The **dental nasal न् n** is **changed —**

1. before the hard palatal च् c and छ् ch; cerebral ट् ṭ and ठ् ṭh; dental त् t and थ् th, to Anusvāra, a palatal श् ś, a cerebral ष् ṣ, a dental स् s being respectively interposed[1]; — e.g. हसन् चकार hasan cakāra = हसंश्चकार hasaṃś cakāra, 'he did it laughing'; पाशान् छेत्तुम् pāśān chettum = पाशांश्छेत्तुम् pāśāṃś chettum, 'to cut the bonds'; चलन् टिट्टिभः calan ṭiṭṭibhaḥ = चलंष्टिट्टिभः calaṃṣ ṭiṭṭibhaḥ, 'a moving sandpiper'; पतन् तरुः patan taruḥ = पतंस्तरुः pataṃs taruḥ, 'a falling tree.'
2. before the soft palatals ज् j, झ् jh, and the palatal sibilant श् ś, to palatal ञ् ñ (40).
3. before the soft cerebrals ड् ḍ and ढ् ḍh to the cerebral ण् ṇ (41).
4. before the semivowel ल् l to nasalized ल् l written with Anusvāra in the form of ँ; — e.g. महान् लाभः mahān lābhaḥ = महाल्ँलाभः mahāl̐ lābhaḥ.

---

1. This seemingly inserted sibilant is really a survival of the Indo-European s of the masc. accusative plural (in -ns) and the nominative singular (in -ns: cp. 88; 89). In the oldest Vedic period this sibilant appears only where it is historically justified, but in Sanskrit its use has been extended to the Sandhi of all cases of final न् before hard palatals, cerebrals, and dentals.

II. Changes of Place.

37. The only four final consonants liable to change of place are the **dental** त् **t** and न् **n**, the labial म् **m**, and **Visarga.**

a. The dentals become palatal and cerebral before palatals and cerebrals respectively.

b. Visarga and, to a less extent, म् m adapt themselves to the organ of the following consonant.

1. Final त् t.

38. Final त् t before palatals (च c, छ् ch, ज् j, झ jh, श् ś) is changed to a palatal (च् c or ज् j); — e.g. तत् च = तच्च tac ca, 'and that'; तत् छिनत्ति = तच्छिनत्ति tac chinatti, 'he cuts that'; तत् जायते = तज्जायते taj jāyate, 'that is born'; तत् शृणोति = (तच्शृणोति tac śṛṇoti, but in practice) तच्छृणोति tac chṛṇoti[1], 'he hears that.'

39. Final त् t before ट् ṭ, ठ् ṭh, ड् ḍ, ढ् ḍh (but not before ष् ṣ) is changed to a cerebral (ड् ḍ or ढ् ḍh); — e.g. एतत् ठक्कुरः = एतट्ठक्कुरः etaṭ ṭhakkuraḥ, 'the idol of him'; तत् डयते = तड्डयते taḍ ḍayate, 'it flies'; तत् ढौकते = तड्ढौकते taḍ ḍhaukate, 'it approaches.'

2. Final न् n.

40. Final न् n before ज् j, झ् jh, and श् ś[2] becomes ञ् ñ; — e.g. तान् जयति = ताञ्जयति tāñ jayati, 'he conquers them'; तान् शार्दूलान् = ताञ्शार्दूलान् tāñ śārdūlān or ताञ्छार्दूलान् tāñ chārdūlān[1], 'those tigers.'

---

1. With the further change of the initial श् ś to the corresponding aspirate छ् ch, cp. 53
2. For the change of न् n before the hard palatals च् c and छ् ch, see 36 B 1.

41. Final न् before ड् ḍ, ढ ḍh[1] (but not ष् ṣ) is changed to ण् ṇ; — e.g. महान् डमरः = महाण्डमरः mahāṇ ḍamaraḥ, 'a great uproar.'

3. Final म् m.

42. A. Final म् m remains unchanged before vowels; — e.g. किम् अत्र = किमत्र kim atra, 'what (is) here?'

B. Final म् m is changed to Anusvāra before consonants:

1. necessarily before semivowels, sibilants, and ह् h; — e.g. तम् वेद = तं वेद taṃ veda, 'I know him'; करुणम् रोदिति = करुणं रोदिति karuṇaṃ roditi, 'he cries piteously'; मोक्षम् सेवेत = मोक्षं सेवेत mokṣaṃ seveta, 'one should devote oneself to salvation'; मधुरम् हसति = मधुरं हसति madhuraṃ hasati, 'he laughs sweetly.'

2. optionally before mutes and the nasals न् n, म् m[2] (6, cols. 1-5), where it may become the class nasal[3] (a change which is rarely made in European editions); — e.g. किम् करोषि = किं करोषि (or किङ्करोषि) kiṃ karoṣi (or kiṅ karoṣi), 'what does thou?' शत्रुम् जहि = शत्रुं जहि (or शत्रुञ्जहि) śatruṃ jahi (or śatruñ jahi), 'kill the enemy'; किम् फलम् = किं फलम् (or किम्फलम्) kiṃ phalam (or kim phalam), 'what (is) the use?' गुरुम् नमति = गुरुं नमति (or गुरुन्नमति) guruṃ namati (or gurun namati), 'he salutes the teacher'; शास्त्रम् मीमांसते = शास्त्रं मीमांसते (or शास्त्रम्मीमांसते) śāstraṃ mīmāṃsate (or śāstram mīmāṃsate), 'he studies the book.'

a. This alternative Sandhi of final म् m is identical with that

---

1. On the treatment of न् n before the hard cerebrals ट् ṭ, ठ् ṭh, and ष् ṣ, see 36 A 6 and B1.
2. Initial ङ् ṅ, ञ् ñ, ण् ṇ do not occur.
3. This assimilation was the normal Sandhi of the Vedic language.

of final न् n before the soft palatals ज् j, झ jh (40), the soft cerebral ड् ḍ and ढ् ḍh (41), and the dental न् n; and with that of final त् t before न् n (33); thus e.g. in कान्तान् न kāntān na the first word may represent the acc. pl. masc. कान्तान् kāntān (36 A 4), the abl. sing. masc. कान्तान् kāntāt (33), or the acc. sing. fem. कान्ताम् kāntām (42 B 2).

4. Final Visarga.

43. Visarga is the spirant to which the hard स् s and the corresponding soft र् r are reduced *in pausā*. If followed by a **hard letter** –

1. a palatal, cerebral, or dental (च् c, छ् ch; ट् ṭ, ठ् ṭh; त् t, थ th), it is changed to the sibilant (श् ś, ष् ṣ, स् s) of the class to which the following letter belongs; — e.g. पूर्णः चन्द्र = पूर्णश्चन्द्रः pūrṇaś candraḥ, 'the full moon'; नद्याः तीरम् = नद्यास् तीरम् nadyās tīram, 'the bank of the river.'

2. a guttural or labial (क् k, ख् kh, प् p, फ् ph), it remains unchanged[1]; — e.g. ततः कामः tataḥ kāmaḥ, 'thence love'; नद्याः पारम् nadyāḥ pāram, 'the opposite shore of the river.'

3. a sibilant, it remains unchanged or may be assimilated[2]; — e.g. सुप्तः शिशुः suptaḥ śiśuḥ or सुप्तश्शिशुः 'the child is asleep'; प्रथमः सर्गः prathamaḥ sargaḥ or प्रथमस्सर्गः prathamas sargaḥ, 'the first canto.'

44. Visarga (except when preceded by अ a or आ ā) if followed by a **soft letter** (consonant or vowel) is changed to र् r; — e.g. कविः अयम् = कविरयम् kavir ayam, 'this poet'; गौः गच्छति = गौर्गच्छति gaur gacchati, 'the cow walks'; वायुः वाति = वायुर्वाति vāyur vāti, 'the wind blows.'

---

1. Cp. the treatment of न् n before hard mutes, 36 A 2, 3; B 1.
2. This assimilation was undoubtedly the original Sandhi, and is required by some of the ancient Vedic phoneticians.

45. 1. The final syllable आः āḥ drops its Visarga before vowels or soft consonants; — e.g. अश्वाः अमी = अश्वा अमी aśvā amī, 'those horses'; आगताः ऋषयः = आगता ऋषयः āgatā ṛṣayaḥ, 'the poets have arrived'; हताः गजाः = हता गजाः hatā gajāḥ, 'the elephants (are) killed'; माः भिः = माभिः mā-bhiḥ, instr. plur. of मास् mās, 'moon.'

2. The **final syllable** अः **aḥ** —

a. drops its Visarga before vowels except अ a; — e.g. कुतः आगतः = कुत आगतः kuta āgataḥ, 'whence come?' कः एषः = क एषः ka eṣaḥ, 'who (is) he?' कः ऋषिः = क ऋषिः ka ṛṣiḥ, 'who (is) the poet?'

b. before soft consonants and before अ a, is changed to ओ o, after which अ a is elided (21 *a*); — आनीतः दीपः = आनीतो दीपः ānīto dīpaḥ, 'the lamp (has been) brought'; मनः भिः = मनोभिः mano-bhiḥ, inst. plur. 'with minds'; नरः अयम् = नरोऽयम् naro'yam, 'this man.'

46. The final syllables अः aḥ and आः āḥ, in the few instances[1] in which the Visarga represents an etymological र् r, are not subject to the exceptional rule stated in 45. In other words अः aḥ and आः āḥ, reverting to अर् ar and आर् ār, in this case follow the general rule (44). Thus पुनः अपि = पुनरपि punar api, 'even again'; भ्रातः देहि = भ्रातर्देहि bhrātar dehi, 'brother, give'; द्वाः एषा = द्वारेषा dvār eṣā, 'this door.'

47. र् r followed by र् r is always dropped, a preceding short vowel being lengthened; — e.g. विधुः राजते = विधू राजते vidhū

---

1. पुनर् punar, 'again,' प्रातर् prātar, 'early,' अन्तर् antar, 'within'; स्वर् svar, 'heaven,' अहर् ahar, 'day,' द्वार् dvār, 'door,' वार् vār, 'water'; voc. sing. of nouns in ऋ ṛ, as पितर् pitar, 'father' (101); and some forms of verbs in ऋ ṛ, as अजागर् ajāgar, 2.3. sing. imperf. of जागृ jāgṛ, 'awake.'

rājate, 'the moon shines'; पुनः रोगी = पुना रोगी punā rogī, 'ill again.'

48. The two pronouns सः saḥ, 'that,' and एषः eṣaḥ, 'this' (110 *a*), retain Visarga at the end of a sentence only, but become सो so and एषो eṣo before अ a (45, 2 *b*); — e.g. सः ददाति = स ददाति sa dadāti, 'he gives'; सः इन्द्रः = स इन्द्रः sa Indraḥ, 'that Indra'; but सः अभवत् = सोऽभवत् so'bhavat, 'he was'; मृतः सः mṛtaḥ saḥ, 'he (is) dead.'

49. भोः bhoḥ, an irregular contracted vocative (for bhavas, used as an interjection) of भवत् bhavat, 'your honour,' drops its Visarga before all vowels and soft consonants; — e.g. भोः ईशान = भो ईशान bho īśāna, 'O lord'; भोः देवाः = भो देवाः bho devāḥ, 'O gods'; but भोः छेत्तः = भोश्छेत्तः bhoś chettaḥ, 'O cutter.'

a. The same rule applies to the contracted vocative भगोः bhagoḥ (for bhagavas) from भगवत् bhagavat, 'adorable one.'

50. Nouns ending in radical र् r (82) retain the र् r before the सु su of the loc. pl.; — e.g. वार् + सु = वार्षु vār-ṣu, 'in the waters.'

a. अहर् ahar (91, 2 N.) and स्वर् svar (indeclinable) retain their र् r when compounded with पति pati: अहर्पतिः ahar-patiḥ, 'lord of day,' स्वर्पतिः svar-patiḥ, 'lord of heaven.'

Doubling of Consonants.

51. छ् ch at the beginning of a word may always be doubled after vowels; it must be so after a short vowel and after the particles आ ā and मा mā; — e.g. तव छाया = तव च्छाया tava cchāyā, 'thy shade'; आ छादयति = आच्छादयति ācchādayati, 'he covers'; मा छिदत् = मा च्छिदत् mā cchidat, 'let him not cut'; but बदरीछाया badarī-chāyā or बदरीच्छाया badarīcchāyā, 'shade of jujube trees.'

a. In the body of a word the doubling takes place after all vowels: इच्छति icchati, 'he wishes'; म्लेच्छ: mlecchaḥ, 'barbarian.'

52. Final ङ् ṅ and न् n, preceded by a **short** vowel and followed by *any* vowel (or diphthong), are doubled; — e.g. प्रत्यङ् आस्ते = प्रत्यङ्ङास्ते pratyaṅṅ āste, 'he sits westward'; धावन् अश्वः = धावन्नश्वः dhāvann aśvaḥ, 'a running horse'; but कवीन् आह्वयस्व kavīn āhvayasva, 'call the poets,' remains.

Initial Aspiration.

53. Initial श् ś, not followed by a hard consonant, may be, and in practice nearly always is, changed to the corresponding aspirate छ् ch after च् c (38) and ञ् ñ (40); — e.g. तच् श्लोकेन = तच्छ्लोकेन tac chlokena, 'by that verse'; धावन् शशः = धावञ्छशः dhāvañ chaśaḥ, 'a running hare.'

a. The same change is allowed after क् k, ट् ṭ, प् p, though not usually applied: वाक्शतम् vāk-śatam may become वाक्छतम् vāk-chatam, 'a hundred speeches.'

54. Initial ह् h, after softening a preceding क् k, ट् ṭ, त् t, प् p, is changed to the soft aspirate of the preceding letter; — e.g. वाक् हि = वाग्घि vāg ghi, 'for speech'; तत् हि = तद्धि tad dhi, 'for that.'

55. If घ् gh, ध् dh, भ् bh, or ह् h are at the end of a (radical) syllable beginning with ग् g, द् d, ब् b, and lose their aspiration as final or otherwise, the initial consonants are aspirated by way of compensation[1]; e.g. दुह् duh, 'a milker,' becomes धुक् dhuk; बुध् budh, 'wise', becomes भुत् bhut.

---

1. This is an historical survival of the original initial aspiration of such roots, which was lost (both in Greek and Sanskrit) by the operation of the later euphonic law that prohibited a syllable beginning and ending with an aspirate. Hence when the final aspirate disappeared the initial returned. Cp. Gk. nom. *θρίξ* *(=θρίκ–s)*, 'hair', besides gen. *τριχ–ός*.

B. Internal Sandhi.

56. The rules of internal Sandhi apply to the finals of nominal and verbal stems before all terminations of declension (except those beginning with consonants of the middle stem: 73 *a*) and conjugation, before primary suffixes (182, 1), and before secondary suffixes (182, 2) beginning with a vowel or य् y. They are best acquired by learning paradigms of nouns and verbs first. Many of these rules agree with those of external Sandhi; the most important of those which differ from external Sandhi are here added.

Final Vowels.

57. In many cases before a vowel (and even the same vowel) इ i and ई ī are changed to इय् iy; उ u and ऊ ū to उव् uv; ॠ ṝ to इर् ir (cp. 18 and 20); — e.g. धी dhī + इ i = धियि dhiy-i, loc. sing., 'in thought'; भू + इ i = भुवि bhuv-i, 'on earth'; युयु + उः yu-yu + uḥ = युयुवुः yu-yuv-uḥ, 'they have joined'; गॄ + अति gṝ + ati = गिरति gir-ati, 'he swallows.'

58. Final ॠ ṝ before consonant terminations is changed to ईर् īr, after labials to ऊर् ūr; while ऋ ṛ (after a single consonant) before य् y becomes रि ri (154, 3); — e.g. गॄ gṝ, passive pres. 3. sing. गीर्यते gīr-yate, 'is swallowed'; गीर्णः gīr-ṇaḥ, past pass. part., 'swallowed'; पॄ pṝ, pass. pres. पूर्यते pūr-yate, 'is filled'; past part., पूर्णः pūr-ṇaḥ, 'filled'; कृ kṛ, pass. pres. क्रियते kri-yate, 'is done.'

59. ए e, ऐ ai, ओ o, औ au are changed before suffixes beginning with vowels or य् y to अय् ay, आय् āy, अव् av, आव् āv respectively (21; 22); — e.g. ने + अन = नयन nay-ana, 'eye'; रै + ए = राये rāy-e, 'for wealth'; गो + ए = गवे gav-e, 'for a cow'; नौ + अः = नावः nāv-aḥ, 'ships'; गो + यः = गव्यः gav-yaḥ, 'relating to cows.'

Final Consonants.

60. The most notable divergence from external Sandhi is the unchangeableness of the final consonants (cp. 32) of verbal and nominal stems before terminations beginning with vowels, semivowels, and nasals[1] (while before other letters they usually follow the rules of external Sandhi); — e.g. प्राञ्चः prāñc-aḥ, 'eastern'; वचानि vac-āni, 'let me speak,' वाच्य vāc-ya, 'to be spoken,' वच्मि vac-mi, 'I speak'; but वक्ति vak-ti, 'he speaks.'

61. Nominal or verbal stems ending in consonants, and followed by terminations consisting of a single consonant, drop the termination altogether, two consonants not being tolerated at the end of a word (28). The final consonant which remains is then treated according to the rules of external Sandhi. Thus प्राञ्च् + स् prāñc + s, nom. sing., 'eastern,' becomes प्राङ् prāṅ (the स् s being first dropped, the palatals being changed to gutturals by 27, and the क् k being then dropped by 28); similarly अदोह् + त् a-doh + t = अधोक् a-dhok (55), 3. sing. imperf., 'he milked.'

62. Aspirates followed by any letters except vowels, semivowles or nasals (60) lose their aspiration; — e.g. रुन्ध् + ध्वे rundh + dhve = रुन्द्ध्वे rund-dhve[2], 'you obstruct'; लभ् + स्ये labh + sye = लप्स्ये lap-sye, 'I shall take'; but युधि yudh-i, 'in battle,' लोभ्यः lobh-yaḥ, 'to be desired.'

---

1. द् d is assimilated before the primary suffix न -na; — e.g. in अन्न an-na, 'food' (for ad-na); and त् t, द् d before the secondary suffixes मत् mat and मय maya; — e.g. विद्युन्मत् vidyun-mat, 'accompanied by lightning' (vidyut), and मृन्मय mṛn-maya, 'consisting of clay' (mṛd).
2. For Sanskrit tolerates two aspirates neither at the beginning and end of the same syllable, nor at the end of one and the beginning of the next.

a. A lost soft aspirate is, if possible, thrown back before ध्व् dhv (**not** धि dhi), भ् bh, स् s, according to 55; — e.g. अभुद्ध्वम् a-**bhud**-dhvam, 'you observed,' भुद्भिः **bhud**-bhiḥ, inst. plur., भुत्सु **bhut**su, loc. plur., but दुग्धि du**g**-dhi, 2. sing. imper., 'milk.'

b. But it is thrown forward on a following त् t and थ् th[1], which are softened; — e.g. लभ् + तः labh + taḥ = लब्धः la**b-dh**aḥ, 'taken': रुन्ध् + थः rundh + thaḥ = रुन्द्धः run**d-dh**aḥ, 'you two obstruct'; बन्ध् + तुम् bandh + tum = बन्द्धुम् ban**d-dh**um, 'to bind.'

63. Palatals. ***a.*** While च् c regularly becomes guttural before consonants (cp. 61; 27; 6, N. 1), ज् j in some cases (the majority) becomes guttural (क् k, ग् g)[2], in others cerebral (ट् ṭ, ड् ḍ, ष् ṣ);— e.g. उक्त uk-ta, 'spoken' (from वच् vac); युक्त yuk-ta, 'joined' (from युज् yuj); रुग्ण rug-ṇa, 'broken' (from रुज् ruj; cp. 65); but राट् rāṭ, nom. sing. 'king' (for राज् + स् rāj + s); मृड्ढि mṛḍḍhi, 2. sing. imper. 'wipe' (from मृज् mṛj); राष्ट्र rāṣ-ṭra, 'kingdom' (from राज् rāj; cp. 64).

b. श् ś, before ध् dh, the middle terminations (73 *a*) and the nom. स् s, usually becomes ट् ṭ or ड् ḍ (sometimes क् k or ग् g); before त् t, थ् th, it always becomes ष् ṣ (cp. 64), and before the स् s of the future and of other conjugational forms, always क् k; — e.g. from विश् viś we get विट्सु viṭ-su, 'in the settlers'; विष्ट viṣ-ṭa, 'entered'; वेक्ष्यामि ve**k**-ṣyāmi (cp. 67), 'I shall enter.'

c. च् c and ज् j (not श् ś) palatalize a following न् n; — e.g. याच् + ना yāc + nā = याच्ञा yāc-ñā, 'request'; यज् + न yaj + na = यज्ञ yaj-ña, 'sacrifice'; but प्रश्न praś-na, 'question.'

---

1. Except in the case of the root धा dhā, 'place,' which has (according to the analogy of *a*) धत् dhat before त् t and थ् th (see below, 134, third class, 1).
2. ज् j regularly becomes क् k before a conjugational स् s (cp. 144, 4).

d. The छ् ch of the root प्रछ् prach, 'ask,' is treated like श् ś: पृष्ट pṛṣ-ṭa, 'asked,' प्रक्ष्यामि prak-ṣyāmi, 'I shall ask,' प्रश्न praśna, 'question.' (In external Sandhi, i.e. when final, and before middle terminations, it becomes ट् ṭ).

64. Cerebrals change following dentals to cerebrals (cp. 39); — e.g. इष् + त iṣ + ta = इष्ट iṣ-ṭa, 'wished'; द्विष् + धि dviṣ + dhi द्विड्ढि dviḍ-ḍhi, 'hate'; षट् + नाम् ṣaṭ + nām = षण्णाम् ṣaṇ-ṇām (cp. 33), 'of six.'

a. While the cerebral silibant ष् ṣ regularly becomes a cerebral (ट् ṭ or ड् ḍ) in declension (cp. 80), and before ध dh in conjugation, it regularly becomes क् k before an स् s in conjugation (cp. 63*b* and 67); द्वेक्षि dvek-ṣi, 'ṭhou hatest,' from दिष् dviṣ.

65. Change of dental न् n to cerebral ण् ṇ:

A preceding cerebral ऋ ṛ, ॠ ṝ, र् r, ष् ṣ (even though a vowel, a guttural, a labial, य् y, व् v, ह् h, or Anusvāra intervene) changes a dental न् n (followed by a vowel or न् n, म् m, य् y, व् v) to cerebral ण् ṇ; — e.g. नृ + नाम् = नृणाम् nṛ-ṇām, 'of men'; कर्णः kar-ṇaḥ, 'ear'; दूषणम् dūṣ-aṇam, 'abuse' (a vowel intervenes); बृंहणम् bṛṃh-aṇam, 'nourishing' (Anusvāra, ह् h, vowel); अर्केण arkeṇa, 'by the sun' (guttural and vowel); क्षिप्णुः kṣip-ṇuḥ, 'throwing' (vowel and labial); प्रेम्णा premṇā, 'by love' (diphthong and labial); ब्रह्मण्यः brahmaṇ-yaḥ, 'kind of Brahmins' (vowel, ह् h, labial, vowel; न् n followed by य् y); निषण्णः niṣaṇ-ṇaḥ, 'seated' (न् n followed by न् n, which is itself assimilated to ण् ṇ); प्रायेण prāyeṇa, 'generally' (vowel, य् y, vowel).

But अर्चनम् arc-anam, 'worship' (palatal intervenes); अर्णवेन arṇavena, 'by the ocean' (cerebral intervenes); अर्धेन ardhena, 'by half' (dental intervenes); कुर्वन्ति kurvanti, 'they do' (न् n is followed by त् t); रामान् rāmān, acc. pl., 'the Rāmas' (न् n is final).

Note.— The number of intervening letters, it will be seen from the above examples, is not limited. In the word रामायण rāmāyaṇa, for instance, five letters (three vowels, a labial, and a semivowel) intervene between the र् r and the ण् ṇ.

Table showing when न् n changes to ण् ṇ.

ऋ ṛ ॠ ṝ र् r ष् ṣ	in spite of intervening vowels, guttural (including ह् h), labials (including व् v), य् y, and Anusvāra,	change न् n to ण् ṇ	if followed by vowels, न् n, म् m, य् y, व् v.

66. A. The **dental** न् n—

1. remains unchanged before य् y and व् v; — e.g. हन्यते han-yate, 'is killed'; तन्वन् tan-v-an, 'stretching.'
2. as final of a root becomes Anusvāra before स् s; — e.g. जिघांसति ji-ghāṃ-sa-ti, 'he wishes to kill' (हन् han); मंस्यते maṃ-sya-te, 'he will think' (मन् man); also when it is inserted before स् s or ष् ṣ in the neuter plural (71 *c*; 83); — e.g. यशांसि yaśāṃs-i, nom. pl. of यशस् yaśas, 'fame'; हवींषि havīṃṣ-i, neut. pl. of हविस् havis, 'oblation' (83).

B. The **dental** स् s—

1. **becomes** dental त् t as the final of roots or nominal stems:—

a. before the स् s of the verbal suffixes (future, aorist, desiderative) in the two roots वस् vas, 'dwell,' and घस् ghas, 'eat': वत्स्यति vat-syati, 'will dwell,' (151 *b* 3); अवात्सीत् a-vāt-sīt, 'has dwelt' (144, 1); जिघत्सति ji-ghat-sati, 'wishes to eat' (171, 5).

b. before the endings with initial भ् bh or स् s (and in the nom.

acc. sing. neut.) of reduplicated perfect stems (89): चकृवद्भिः cakṛ-vad-bhiḥ, चकृवत्सु cakṛ-vat-su, N.A.n. चकृवत् cakṛ-vat.

2. **disappears —**

a. between mutes; — e.g. अभक्त a-bhak-ta (for a-bhak-s-ta), 3. sing. s-aorist of भज् bhaj, 'share'; चष्टे caṣ-ṭe (for cak-ṣ-ṭe = original caś-s-te), 3. sing. pres. of चक्ष् cakṣ, 'speak.' This loss also occurs when the preposition उद् ud is compounded with the roots स्था sthā, 'stand,' and स्तम्भ् stambh, 'support'; — e.g. उत्थाय ut-thāya, 'standing up'; उत्तम्भित ut-tambhita, 'raised up.'

b. before soft dentals; — e.g. शाधि śā-dhi (for śās-dhi), 2. sing. imperat. of शास् śās, 'order'; also after becoming ष् ṣ and cerebralizing the following dental; — e.g. अस्तोढ्वम् a-sto-ḍhvam (for a-sto-ṣ-dhvam), 2. pl. aor. of स्तु stu, 'praise.'

67. Change of dental स् s to cerebral ष् ṣ:

Preceding vowels except अ a or आ ā (even though Anusvāra or Visarga intervene), as well as क् k and र् r, change dental स् s (followed by a vowel, त् t, थ् th, न् n, म् m, य् y, व् v) to cerebral ष् ṣ; — e.g. from सर्पिस् sarpis: सर्पिषा sarpiṣ-ā, 'with clarified butter'; सर्पींषि sarpīṃṣi, nom. pl.; सर्पिःषु sarpiḥṣu, loc. pl. (cp. 43, 3); from वाच् vāc: वाक्षु vāk-ṣu, loc. pl., 'in speeches'; from गिर् gir: गीर्षु gīr-ṣu (82), loc. pl., 'in speeches'; तिष्ठति tiṣṭhati, 'stands,' from स्था sthā, 'stand'; भविष्यति bhavi-ṣyati, 'will be,' from भू bhū, 'be'; सुष्वाप suṣvāpa, 'he slept,' from स्वप् svap, 'sleep'; from चक्षुस् cakṣus: चक्षुष्मत् cakṣuṣ-mat, 'possessing eyes'; but सर्पिः sarpiḥ (final); मनसा manas-ā, 'by mind' (a precedes), तमिस्रम् tamis-ram, 'darkness' (r follows).

Table showing when स् s changes to ष् ṣ.

Vowels except अ a, आ ā (in spite of intervening Anusvāra or Visarga), also क् k, र् r,	change स् s to ष् ṣ	if followed by vowels, त् t, थ् th, न् n, म् m, य् y, व् v.

Note. — The rules about the changes of the dental न् n and स् s to the corresponding cerebrals, should be thoroughly acquired, since these changes must constantly be made in declension and conjugation.

68. The **labial** म् **m** remains **unchanged** before य् y, र् r, ल् l (cp. 60 and 42 B 1); but before suffixes beginning with व् v it **becomes** न् n; — e.g. काम्यः kām-yaḥ, 'desirable,' ताम्र tām-ra, 'copper-coloured', अम्ल am-la, 'sour'; but जगन्वान् ja-gan-vān, 'having gone' (from गम् gam, 'go').

69. *a.* The (soft) **breathing** ह् **h** before स् s and, in roots beginning with द् d, before त् t, थ् th, ध् dh also, is treated like घ् gh; — e.g. लेह् + सि leh + si = लेक्षि **lek-ṣi**, 'thou lickest' (67); दह् + स्यति dah + syati = धक्ष्यति **dh**ak-ṣyati, 'he will burn' (55): दह् + त dah + ta = दग्ध dag-**dh**a, 'burnt' (62 *b*); दिह् + ध्वे dih + dhve = धिग्ध्वे **dh**ig-dhve, 'ye anoint' (62 *a*). Similarly treated are the perf. pass. participles of the roots स्निह् snih and, in one sense, मुह् muh: स्निग्ध snig-dha, 'smooth,' and मुग्ध mug-dha, 'foolish.'

b. ह् h, in all other roots, is treated like an aspirate cerebral, which, after changing a following त् t, थ् th, ध् dh to ढ् ḍh, and lengthening a preceding short vowel, is dropped; — e.g. लिह् + त lih + ta = लीढ lī**ḍh**a, 'licked'; मुह् + त muh + ta = मूढ

mūḍha, 'infatuated.' Similarly treated are the roots वह् vah and सह् sah, but with an apparent irregularity in the vowel: ऊढ ūḍha[1], 'carried' (for वह् + त vah + ta); वोढुम् voḍhum[2], 'to carry' (for वह् + तुम् vah + tum); सोढुम् soḍhum[2], 'to bear' (for सह् + तुम् sah + tum).

An exception to *b* is the root नह् nah, in which ह् h is treated as ध् dh: नद्ध **nad-dha**, 'bound.' An exception to both *a* and *b* is the root दृह् dṛh: दृढ **dṛḍha**, 'firm' (begins with द् d and has a short vowel).

CHAPTER III

DECLENSION

70. Declension, or the inflexion of nominal stems by means of endings, is most conveniently treated under the three heads of 1. nouns (including adjectives); 2. numerals; 3. pronouns.

In Sanskrit there are —

a. three genders: mesculine, feminine, and neuter;

***b.* three numbers:** singular, dual, and plural;

***c.* eight cases:** nominative, vocative, accusative, **instrumental,** dative, ablative, genitive, **locative.**[3]

---

1. The syllable व va, which is liable to Samprasāraṇa (p. 11, note 1), becomes उ u and is then lengthened.
2. Here ओ o represents the Indo-Iranian aẓh, which after cerebralizing and aspirating the following dental becomes o, just as original as (through az) becomes o; — e.g. in मनोभिः mano-bhiḥ: cp. 45*ᵇ*.
3. This is the order of the Hindu grammarians, excepting the vocative, which is not regarded by them as a case. It is convenient as the only arrangement by which such cases as are identical in form, either in the singular, the dual, or the plural, may be grouped together.

71. The normal **case-endings** added to the stem are the following:—

	SINGULAR.		DUAL.		PLURAL.	
	M. F.	N.	M. F.	N.	M.F.	N.
N.	स् s	—[b]	}	}	}	}
V.	—[a]	—	औ au	ई ī	अस् as	इ i[c]
A.	अम् am	—	}	}	}	}
I.	आ ā		}		भिस् bhis	
D.	ए e		भ्याम् bhyām		}	
Ab. }			}		भ्यस् bhyas	
G. }	अस् as		}		आम् ām	
L.	इ i		ओस् os		सु su	

a. The vocative is the same (apart from the accent) as the nominative in all numbers except the *masc. and fem. sing.* of vowel stems generally and the *masc. sing.* of consonant stems in -at, -an, -in, -as (cp. 76*a*), -yas, -vas.

b. The nom. acc. sing. neut. has the bare stem excepting the words in -a, which add म् m.

c. The nom. voc. acc. plur. neut. before the इ i insert न् n after a vowel stem and before a single final mute or sibilant of a consonant stem (modifying the न् n according to the class of the consonant).

72. An important distinction in declension (in stems ending in च् c, त् t, न् n, स् s, and ऋ ṛ) is that between the **strong** and the **weak** stem. If the stem has *two* forms, the **strong** and the **weak** stem are distinguished; if it has *three* forms, **strong, middle,** and **weakest** are distinguished.

a. Shifting of accent was the cause of the distinction. The stem, having been accented in the strong cases, here naturally preserved its full form; but it was shortened in the weak cases by the accent falling on the endings. For a similar reason the last vowel of the strong stem, if long, is regularly shortened in

the vocative, because the accent always shifted to the first syllable in that case.

73. The strong stem appears in the following cases:—

Nom. voc. acc. sing.
Nom. voc. acc. dual } of masculine nouns[1].
Nom. voc. (**not acc.**) plur.

Nom. voc. acc. **plural only** of **neuters.**

a. When the stem has *three* forms, the middle stem appears before terminations beginning with a consonant[2] (°भ्याम् -bhyām, °भिस् -bhis, °भ्यस् -bhyas, °सु -su); the weakest, before terminations beginning with a vowel in the remaining weak cases; — e.g. प्रत्यञ्चौ pratyáñc-au, nom. dual; प्रत्यग्भिः pratyág-bhiḥ, inst. plur.; प्रतीचोः pratīc-óḥ, gen. dual (93).

b. In neuters with three stems, the nom. voc. acc. sing. are middle, the nom. voc. acc. dual, weakest; — e.g. प्रत्यक् pratyák, sing., प्रतीची pratīc-í, dual, प्रत्यञ्चि pratyáñc-i, plur. (93). The other cases are as in the masculine.

NOUNS.

74. This declension may conveniently by divided into two classes:—

I. Stems ending in consonants[3]:—

A. unchangeable; B. changeable.

---

1. Excepting the stems in ऋ ṛ (101) nearly all nouns with changeable stems form their feminine with the suffix ई ī (100).
2. It is practically most convenient to name changeable stems in the middle form, since this is also the form in which they appear as prior members in compounds.
3. Some grammars begin with the vowel declension in अ a (II. A) since this contains the majority of all declined stems in the language.

II. Stems ending in vowels:— A. in अ a and आ ā; B. in इ i and उ u; C. in ई ī and ऊ ū; D. in ऋ ṛ; E. in ऐ ai, ओ o, औ au.

I. A. Unchangeable Stems.

75. The number of these stems is comparatively small, there being none ending in guttural or cerebral mutes, and none in nasals or semivowels (except र् r). They are liable to such changes only as are required by the rules of Sandhi before the consonant terminations (cp. 16 *a*). Masculines and feminines ending in the same consonant are inflected exactly alike; and the neuters differ only in the nom. voc. acc. dual and plural.

76. The final consonants of the stem retain their original sound before vowel terminations (71); but when there is no ending (nom. sing., the स् s of the m. f. being dropped), and before the loc. pl. सु su, they must be reduced to one of the letters क् k, ट् ṭ, प् p or Visarga (27), which respectively become ग् g, ड् ḍ, द् d, ब् b, or र् r, before the terminations beginning with भ् bh.

a. The voc. sing. m. f. is the same as the nom. except in stems in (derivative) अस् as (83).

b. Forms of the nom. voc. acc. plur. neut. are extremely rare in this declension; — e.g. from °भाज् -bhāj, 'sharing,' °भाञ्जि -bhāñji; nom. sing. °भाक् -bhāk.

But for practical reasons it appears preferable to begin with the consonant declension, which adds the normal endings (71) without modification; while the wide deviation of the a-declension from these endings is apt to confuse the beginner.

Stems in Dentals.

77. Paradigm सुहृद् su-hṛd, m. 'friend' (lit. 'good-hearted')

	SING.	DUAL.	PLUR.
N.V.	सुहृत् su-hṛt (27)	सुहृदौ -hṛd-au	सुहृदः -hṛd-aḥ
A.	सुहृदम् su-hṛd-am		
I.	सुहृदा su-hṛd-ā		सुहृद्भिः -hṛd-bhiḥ
D.	सुहृदे su-hṛd-e	सुहृद्भ्याम् -hṛd-bhyām	सुहृद्भ्यः -hṛd-bhyaḥ
Ab.	सुहृदः -hṛd-aḥ		
G.			सुहृदाम् -hṛd-ām
L.	सुहृदि su-hṛd-i	सुहृदोः -hṛd-oḥ	सुहृत्सु -hṛt-su (32)

a. In the paradigms of regular nouns with unchangeable stems it will be sufficient to remember the nom. sing. and the nom. inst. loc. plur.; — e.g. from ˚जित् -jit, 'conquering': ˚जित् -jit, ˚जितः -jit-aḥ, ˚जिद्भिः -jid-bhiḥ, ˚जित्सु -jit-su; from ˚मथ् -math, 'destroying': ˚मत् -mat, ˚मथः -math-aḥ, ˚मद्भिः -mad-bhiḥ, ˚मत्सु -mat-su; from ˚वृध् -vṛdh, 'increasing': ˚वृत् -vṛt, ˚वृधः -vṛdh-aḥ, ˚वृद्भिः -vṛd-bhiḥ, ˚वृत्सु -vṛt-su.

Stems in Labials.

78. Only a few ending in प p and भ bh occur. They are declined exactly like सुहृद् su-hṛd.

STEM.	NOM. SG.	NOM. PL.	INST. PL.	LOC. PL.
धर्मगुप् dharma-gup, m. 'guardian of law'	˚गुप् -gup	˚गुपः -gup-aḥ	˚गुब्भिः -gub-bhiḥ	˚गुप्सु -gup-su
ककुभ् kakubh, f. 'region'	ककुप् kakup	ककुभः kakubh-aḥ	ककुब्भिः kakub-bhiḥ	ककुप्सु kakup-su

Stems in Palatals.

79. The palatals (च् c, ज् j, श् ś) undergo a change of organ when final and before consonant terminations (cp. 63). च् c always becomes guttural (क् k or ग् g); ज् j and श् ś nearly always become guttural, but sometimes cerebral (ट् ṭ or ड् ḍ).

STEM.	NOM. SG.	NOM. PL.	INST. PL.	LOC. PL.
वाच् vāc[1],	वाक्	वाच:	वाग्भि:	वाक्षु
f. 'speech'	vā́**k**	vā́c-aḥ	vā**g**-bhíḥ	vā**k**-**ṣ**ú (67)
असृज् asṛj,	असृक्	असृञ्जि	असृग्भि:	असृक्षु
n. 'blood'	ásṛ**k**	ásṛ**ñ**j-i	ásṛ**g**-bhiḥ	ásṛ**k**-**ṣ**u
रुज् ruj,	रुक्	रुज:	रुग्भि:	रुक्षु
f. 'disease'	ru**k**	ruj-aḥ	ru**g**-bhiḥ	ru**k**-**ṣ**u
सम्राज् samrāj,	सम्राट्	सम्राज:	सम्राड्भि:	सम्राट्सु
m. 'sovereign'	samrā́**ṭ**	samrā́j-aḥ	samrā́**ḍ**-bhiḥ	sam-rā́**ṭ**su
दिश् diś,	दिक्	दिश:	दिग्भि:	दिक्षु
f. 'cardinal point'	dí**k**	díś-aḥ	di**g**-bhíḥ	di**k**-**ṣ**ú
विश् viś,	विट्	विश:	विड्भि:	विट्सु
m. 'setter'	ví**ṭ**	víś-aḥ	vi**ḍ**-bhíḥ	vi**ṭ**-sú

a. Like वाच् vāc are declined त्वच् tvac, f. 'skin,' रुच् ruc, f. 'light,' स्रुच् sruc, f. 'ladle'; जलमुच् jala-muc, m. 'cloud' (lit. 'water-shedding').

b. Like रुज् ruj are declined ऋत्विज् ṛtv-ij, m. 'priest' (lit. 'sacrificing in season'), बणिज् baṇij, m. 'merchant,' भिषज् bhiṣaj, m. 'physician'; स्रज् sraj, f. 'garland'; also ऊर्ज् ūrj, f. 'strength' (nom. ऊर्क् ūr**k**, 28).

c. Like सम्राज् samrāj is declined परिव्राज् parivrāj, m. 'mendicant'.

---

1. Stems in derivative अच् ac are changeable (93).

d. Like दिश् diś are declined °दृश् -dṛś, 'seeing,' °स्पृश् -spṛś, 'touching' (at the end of compounds).

Stems in Cerebrals.

80. The only cerebral stems are those in the sibilant ष् ṣ, which is naturally changed to cerebral ट् ṭ or ड् ḍ.

STEM.	NOM. SG.	NOM. PL.	INST. PL.	LOC. PL.
द्विष् dviṣ,	द्विट्	द्विषः	द्विड्भिः	द्विट्सु
m. 'enemy'	dvíṭ	dvíṣ-aḥ	dviḍ-bhíḥ	dviṭ-sú
प्रावृष् prā-vṛṣ	प्रावृट्	प्रावृषः	प्रावृड्भिः	प्रावृट्सु
f. 'rainy season'	prāvṛ́ṭ	prāvṛ́ṣ-aḥ	prāvṛ́ḍ-bhiḥ	prāvṛ́ṭ-su

Stems in ह् h.

81. Most of the few stems in ह् h change that letter when final or before consonant endings to a guttural, but (cp. 69 *b*) in °लिह् -lih, 'licking,' it becomes cerebral, and in उपानह् upā-nah, f. 'shoe' (that which is 'tied on'), dental:—

STEM.	NOM. SG.	NOM. PL.	INST. PL.	LOC. PL.
°दुह् -duh,	°धुक्	°दुहः	°धुग्भिः	°धुक्षु
'milking'	**-dhuk**	-duh-aḥ	**-dhug**-bhiḥ	**-dhuk**-ṣu (62 *a*)
°द्रुह् -druh,	°ध्रुक्	°द्रुहः	°ध्रुग्भिः	°ध्रुक्षु
'injuring'	**-dhruk**	-druh-aḥ	**-dhrug**-bhiḥ	**-dhruk**-ṣu
उष्णिह् uṣṇih,	उष्णिक्	उष्णिहः	उष्णिग्भिः	उष्णिक्षु
f. 'a metre'	uṣṇi**k**	uṣṇih-aḥ	uṣṇi**g**-bhiḥ	uṣṇi**k**-ṣu
मधुलिह् madhu-lih, m.	°लिट्	°लिहः	°लिड्भिः	°लिट्सु
'bee' (honey-licker')	-li**ṭ**	-lih-aḥ	-li**ḍ**-bhiḥ	-li**ṭ**-su
उपानह् upā-nah,	उपानत्	°नहः	°नद्भिः	°नत्सु
f. 'shoe'	upā-na**t**	-nah-aḥ	-na**d**-bhiḥ	-na**t**-su

Stems in र् r[1].

82. The र् r becomes Visarga only when final, that is, in the nom. sing. only, remaining before the सु su of the loc. plur. (50). A preceding इ i or उ u is lengthened when the र् r is final or followed by a consonant.

STEM.	NOM. SG.	NOM. PL.	INST. PL.	LOC. PL.
द्वार् dvār,	द्वाः	द्वारः	द्वार्भिः	द्वार्षु
f. 'door'	dvāḥ	dvār-aḥ	dvār-bhiḥ	dvār-ṣu (67)
गिर् gir,	गीः	गिरः	गीर्भिः	गीर्षु
f. 'voice'	gīḥ	gir-aḥ	gīr-bhiḥ	gīr-ṣu
पुर् pur,	पूः	पुरः	पूर्भिः	पूर्षु
f. 'town'	pūḥ	pur-aḥ	pūr-bhiḥ	pūr-ṣu

Stems in स् s.

83. These stems consist almost entirely of words formed with the derivative suffixes अस् as, इस् is, उस् us, chiefly neuters. They lengthen their final vowel (before the inserted nasal) in the nom. voc. acc. plur. neut. The masculines and feminines are nearly all adjective compounds with these stems as their final member; those in अस् as lengthen the अ a in the nom. sing.

Paradigms यशस् yaś-as, n. 'fame'; हविस् hav-is, n. 'oblation'; आयुस् āy-us, n. 'life.'

SINGULAR

N.V.A.	यशः	हविः	आयुः
	yaśaḥ	haviḥ	āyuḥ
I.	यशसा	हविषा	आयुषा
	yaśas-ā	haviṣ-ā (67)	āyuṣ-ā (67)

1. There are no stems in other semivowels.

D.	यशसे	हविषे	आयुषे
	yaśas-e	haviṣ-e	āyuṣ-e
Ab.G.	यशसः	हविषः	आयुषः
	yaśas-aḥ	haviṣ-aḥ	āyuṣ-aḥ
L.	यशसि	हविषि	आयुषि
	yaśas-i	haviṣ-i	āyuṣ-i
		DUAL	
N.V.A.	यशसी	हविषी	आयुषी
	yaśas-ī	haviṣ-ī	āyuṣ-ī
ID.Ab.	यशोभ्याम्	हविर्भ्याम्	आयुर्भ्याम्
	yaśo-bhyām (45.2)	havir-bhyām (44)	āyuṣ-bhyām
G.L.	यशसोः	हविषोः	आयुषोः
	yaśas-oḥ	haviṣ-oḥ	āyuṣ-oḥ
		PLURAL	
N.V.A.	यशांसिः	हवींषि	आयूंषि
	yaśāṃs-i (66, 2)	haviṃṣ-i	āyūṃṣ-i
I.	यशोभिः	हविर्भिः	आयुर्भिः
	yaśo-bhiḥ	havir-bhiḥ	āyur-bhiḥ
D.Ab.	यशोभ्यः	हविर्भ्यः	आयुर्भ्यः
	yaśo-bhyaḥ	havir-bhyaḥ	āyur-bhyaḥ
G.	यशसाम्	हविषाम्	आयुषाम्
	yaśas-ām	haviṣ-ām	āyuṣ-ām
L.	यशःसु	हविःषु	आयुःषु
	yaśaḥ-su	haviḥ-ṣu (67)	āyuḥ-ṣu (67)

a. सुमनस् su-manas, as an adjective, 'cheerful,' has in the nom. sing. masc. सुमनाः sumánāḥ (voc. सुमनः súmanaḥ), but neuter सुमनः sumánaḥ (but दीर्घायुः dīrghāyuḥ nom. sing. in all genders). Similarly अङ्गिरस् aṅgiras, m., उशनस् uśanas, m., names of seers, and उषस् uṣ-as, f. 'dawn,' form the nominatives अङ्गिराः áṅgirāḥ, उशनाः uśánāḥ (sometimes उशना uśánā), and उषाः uṣāḥ.

b. आशिस् ā-śis[1], f. 'blessing,' lengthens its इ i (like the stems in इर् ir) in the nom. sing. and before consonants: nom. sing. आशीः āśīḥ; pl. nom. आशिषः āśiṣ-aḥ, inst. आशीर्भिः āśīr-bhiḥ, loc. आशीःषु āśīḥ-ṣu.

c. दोस् dos, n. 'arm,' is quite regular: nom. sing. दोः doḥ, nom. dual दोषी doṣ-ī; pl. inst. दोर्भिः dor-bhiḥ, loc. दोःषु doḥ-ṣu.

I. B. Changeable Stems.

84. Regular changeable stems end in the dentals त् t, न् n, स् s, or the palatal च् c; those in त् t end in अत् at (also मत् mat, वत् vat); those in न् n end in अन् an (also मन् man, वन् van) or इन् in (also मिन् min, विन् vin); those in स् s end in यस् yas (comparatives) or वस् vas (perf. participles active); those in च् c end in अच् ac, which is properly a root meaning 'to bend.'

The stems in अत् at (85-6), इन् in (87), यस् yas (88) have two forms, strong and weak; those in अन् an (90-92), वस् vas (89), अच् ac (93) have three, strong, middle, and weakest (73).

Nouns with Two Stems.

85. 1. **Stems** in अत् **at** comprise **Present and Future Participles** (156) active (masc. and neut.)[2]. The strong stem is in अन्त् ant, the weak in अत् at[3]; — e.g. अदन्त् ad-ant and अदत् ad-at 'eating' from अद् ad, 'to eat' —

---

1. Derived not with the suffix इस् is, but from the (weakened) root शास् śās with the prefix आ ā.
2. On the formation of the feminine stem see 95.
3. In Latin and Greek the distinction was lost by normalization: gen. edentis, ἔδοντος.

MASCULINE

	SINGULAR	DUAL	PLURAL
N.V.	अदन् adán	अदन्तौ adánt-au	अदन्तः adánt-aḥ
A.	अदन्तम् adánt-am	अदन्तौ adánt-au	अदतः adat-áḥ
I.	अदता adat-á́	अद्भ्याम् adád-bhyām	अदद्भिः adád-bhiḥ
D.	अदते adat-é	अद्भ्याम् adád-bhyām	अद्भ्यः adád-bhyaḥ
Ab.	अदतः adat-áḥ	अद्भ्याम् adád-bhyām	अद्भ्यः adád-bhyaḥ
G.	अदतः adat-áḥ	अदतोः adat-óḥ	अदताम् adat-ā́m
L.	अदति adat-í	अदतोः adat-óḥ	अदत्सु adát-su

NEUTER

	SINGULAR	DUAL	PLURAL
N.A.	अदत् adát	अदती adat-í	अदन्ति adánt-i

a. महत् mah-at, 'great,' originally a present participle[1], forms its strong stem in आन्त् ānt.

N. महान् mahā́n	pl. m. महान्तः mahā́nt-aḥ	n. °हान्ति -hā́nti
A. महान्तम् mahā́nt-am	महतः mahat-áḥ	
1. महता mahat-á́	महद्भिः mahád-bhiḥ	
V. महन् máhan	L. महत्सु mahát-su	

86. The stems of the **objectives** formed with the suffixes मत् **mat and** वत् **vat**, which mean 'possessed of,' 'having,' differ from those in अत् at solely in lengthening the vowel in the nom. sing. masc.; — e.g. 1. अग्निमत् agni-mát, 'having a (sacrificial) fire' (masc. and neut.)[2] —

1. From the root मह् mah (originally magh), cp. Lat. mag-nus.
2. On the formation of the feminine stem see 95.

N.	sg. m. अग्निमान् -man	pl. °मन्तः -mánt-aḥ		n. °मन्ति -mánti
A.	अग्निमन्तम् -mánt-am		°मतः -mát-aḥ	
V.	अग्निमन् -man		L. °मत्सुः -mát-su	

2. ज्ञानवत् jñāna-vat, 'possessed of knowledge' (masc. and neut.)[1] —

N. sg. m. ज्ञानवान् jñāna-vān	pl. ज्ञानवन्तः jñāna-vant-aḥ
A. ज्ञानवन्तम् jñāna-vant-am	ज्ञानवतः jñāna-vat-aḥ

a. भवत् bháv-at, when used as the present participle of भू bhū, 'be,' is declined like अदत् adat (only the accent remains on the first syllable throughout); but when it means 'your Honour,' it is declined (as if derived with the suffix -vat) like ज्ञानवत् jñānavat: nom. भवान् bhavān, acc. भवन्तम् bhavantam. Besides भवन् bhavan there is also an irregular voc. (cp. 49) भोः **bhoḥ**, 'sir!' (a contraction of an older भवस् bhavas).

b. कियत् kí-y-at, 'how much?' and इयत् í-y-at, 'so much,' are also declined like ज्ञानवत् jñāna-vat.

N. कियान् kíyān	pl. कियन्तः kíyant-aḥ	n. कियन्ति kíyant-i
A. कियन्तम् kíyant-am	कियतः kíyat-aḥ	

87. 2. **Adjectives** formed **with** the suffix इन् **in** (masc. and neut.)[1], which means 'possessing,' are very numerous. They are derivatives from substantives in अ a; thus बल bala, 'strength,' बलिन् bal-in, 'strong.' The stem of these words is weak only before consonants and in the nom. acc. sing. neut., where it drops the न् n. In the nom. sing. masc., where (as in all regular n-stems) the न् n is dropped, and in the nom. voc. acc. pl. neut.,

1. On the formation of the feminine stem see 95.

the इ i is lengthened; — e.g. धनिन् dhan-in, 'possessing wealth.' 'rich' —

MASCULINE

	SINGULAR.	PLURAL.
N.	धनि dhan-í	धनिनः dhanín-aḥ
A.	धनिनम् dhanín-am	धनिनः dhanín-aḥ
I.	धनिना dhanín-ā	धनिभिः dhaní-bhiḥ
V.	धनिन् dhán-**in**.	

NEUTER

N.A.	धनि dhan-í	धनीनि dhaníni
V.	धनि dháni or धनिन् dhán**in**.	

a. Stems in मिन् min and विन् vin have a similar meaning and are declined in the same way; — e.g. मनस्विन् manas-vin, 'wise,' वाग्मिन् vāg-min, 'eloquent' (from वाच् vāc). स्वामिन् svā-min, m. 'lord' (lit. 'having property'), is used as a substantive only.

88. 3. **Comparatives in ईयस् īyas** (masc. and neut.)[1] form their strong stem in ईयांस् iyāṃs; — e.g. गरीयस् gár-īyas, 'heavier,' comparative of गुरु guru, 'heavy' —

MASCULINE

	SINGULAR.	PLURAL.
N.	गरीयान् gárīyā**n**	गरीयांसः gárīyāṃs-aḥ
A.	गरीयांसम् gárīyāṃs-am	गरीयसः gárīyas-aḥ
V.	गरीयन् gárīy**an**	
I.	गरीयसा gárīyas-ā	गरीयोभिः gárīy**o**-bhiḥ (45, 2)

NEUTER

N.A.	गरीयः gárīyaḥ	गरीयसी gárīyas-ī	गरीयांसि gárīyāṃs-i

1. On the formation of the feminine stem see 95.

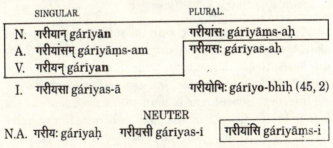

Nouns with Three Stems.

89. 1. **Participles of the reduplicated perfect in वस् vas** (mas. and neut.)[1] form their strong stem with **वांस् vāṃs**, the middle with **वत् vat**[2], the weakest with **उष् uṣ** (67; cp. 157); — e.g. **चकृवस्** cakṛ-vas[3], 'having done,' from **कृ** kṛ, 'to do' —

MASCULINE.

N.	चकृवान् cakṛ-vā́n	N.V. °वांसौ -vā́ṃs-au	°वांस: -vā́ṃs-aḥ
A.	चकृवांसम् cakṛ-vā́ṃs-am	°वांसौ -vā́ṃs-au	चक्रुष: cakr-úṣ-aḥ
V.	चकृवन् cákṛ-van		
I.	चक्रुषा cakr-úṣ-ā	°वद्भ्याम् -vád-bhyām	चकृवद्भि: -vádbhiḥ
L.	चक्रुषि cakr-úṣ-i	चक्रुषो: cakr-úṣ-oḥ	°वत्सु -vátsu

NEUTER.

N.	चकृवत् cakṛ-vát	चक्रुषी cakr-úṣ-i	चकृवांसि cakṛ-vā́ṃs-i

1. On the formation of the feminine stem see 95.
2. The change of स् s to त् t here began in the early Vedic period before भ् bh, extending thence to the loc. plur. and the nom. acc. sing. neut. उस् us is the unaccented form of वस् vas (cp. 137, 2 c).
3. Beginners sometimes confuse this *reduplicated* perf. part. active with the active participle formed by adding the suffix वत् vat to the perfect passive part.; — e.g. nom. masc. कृतवान् kṛta-vān, 'having done,' acc. कृतवन्तम् kṛta-vantam (cp. 161). The confusion is caused by both ending in °वान् -vān in the nom. sing.

a. The इ i which is inserted before the व् v in some of these participles is dropped before उष् uṣ: thus तस्थिवान् tasth-i-vā́n, but तस्थुषा tasth-ús-ā.

b. The following examples of these stems may be useful (cp. 157) :—

	NOM. SG.	NOM. PL.	ACC. PL.	INSTR. PL.
From स्था sthā,	तस्थिवान्	तस्थिवांसः	तस्थुषः	तस्थिवद्भिः
'stand'	tath-i-vā́n	tasth-i-vā́ṃs-aḥ	tasth-úṣ-aḥ	tasth-i-vád-bhiḥ
From नी nī,	निनीवान्	निनीवांसः	निन्युषः	निनीवद्भिः
'lead'	ninī-vā́n	ninī-vā́ṃs-aḥ	niny-úṣ-aḥ	ninī-vád-bhiḥ
From भू bhū,	बभूवान्	बभूवांसः	बभूवुषः	बभूवद्भिः
'be'	babhū-vā́n	babhū-vā́ṃs-aḥ	babhū-v-úṣ-aḥ	babhū-vád-bhiḥ
From तन् tan,	तेनिवान्	तेनिवांसः	तेनुषः	तेनिवद्भिः
'stretch'	ten-i-vā́n	ten-i-vā́ṃs-aḥ	ten-úṣ-aḥ	ten-i-vád-bhiḥ
From हन् han,	जघ्निवान्	जघ्निवांसः	जघ्नुषः	जघ्निवद्भिः
'kill'	jaghn-i-vā́n	jaghn-i-vā́ṃs-aḥ	jaghn-úṣ-aḥ	jaghn-i-vád-bhiḥ
From गम् gam,	जगन्वान्	जगन्वांसः	जग्मुषः	जगन्वद्भिः
'go'	jagan-vā́n[1]	jagan-vā́ṃs-aḥ	jagm-úṣ-aḥ	jagan-vád-bhiḥ
or	जग्मिवान्	जग्मिवांसः	जग्मुषः	जग्मिवद्भिः
	jagm-i-vā́n	jagam-i-vā́ṃs-aḥ	jagm-úṣ-aḥ	jagmi-vád-bhiḥ
From विद् vid,	विद्वान्[2]	विद्वांसः	विदुषः	विद्वद्भिः
'know'	vid-vā́n	vid-vā́ṃs-aḥ	vid-úṣ-aḥ	vid-vád-bhiḥ

90. 2. Nouns in अन् **an** (also मन् **man**, वन् **van**), masc. and neut.[3], form the strong stem in आन् ān, the weakest in न् n, the middle in अ a. In the nom. sing. masc. the final न् n is dropped. In the loc. sing. and the nom. voc. acc. dual the

1. On this change of म् m to न् n, see 68.
2. Without reduplication, cp. Gk. *εἰδώς*.
3. On the formation of the feminine stem see 95.

syncopation of the अ a of the suffix is optional. In the weakest cases syncope does not take place when मन् man and वन् van are immediately preceded by a consonant.

The concurrence of three consonants is here avoided, through not in stems in simple अन् an. Hence आत्मना āt-man-ā, but तक्ष्णा takṣ-ṇ-ā, मूर्ध्ना mūrdh-n-ā. Examples of the inflexion of these stems are :—

1. राजन् rā́j-an, m. 'king' —

	SING.	PLUR.
N.	राजा rā́j-ā	राजानः rā́j-ān-aḥ
A.	राजानम् rā́j-ān-am	राज्ञः rā́j-ñ-aḥ
V.	राजन् rā́j-an	
I.	राज्ञा rā́j-ñ-ā	राजभिः rā́j-a-bhiḥ
L.	राज्ञि rā́j-ñ-i or राजनि rā́j-an-i	राजसु rā́j-a-su

2. नामन् nā́-man, n. 'name' (Lat. nō-men) —

	SING.	DUAL.	PLUR.
N.A.	नाम nā́-ma	नाम्नी nā́-mn-ī or नामनी nā́-man-ī	नामानि nā́-mān-i
V.	नाम nā́ma or नामन् nā́-man		
I.	नाम्ना nā́-mn-ā	नामभ्याम् nā́-ma-bhyām	नामभिः nā́-ma-bhiḥ
L.	नाम्नि nā́-mn-i or नामनि nā́-man-i	नाम्नोः nā́-mn-oḥ	नामसु nā́-ma-su

3. ब्रह्मन् brah-mán, m. 'creator' (°मन् -man after consonant)—

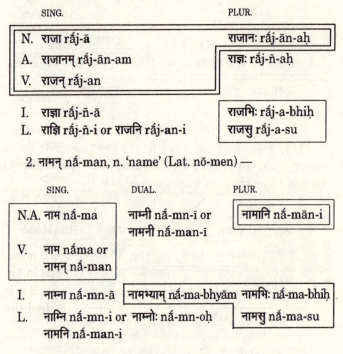

	SING.	PLUR.
N.	ब्रह्मा brah-mā́	ब्रह्माणः brah-mā́ṇ-aḥ
A.	ब्रह्माणम् brah-mā́ṇ-am (65)	ब्रह्मणः brah-máṇ-aḥ
V.	ब्रह्मन् bráh-man	
I.	ब्रह्मणा brah-máṇ-ā	ब्रह्मभिः brah-má-bhiḥ

4. ग्रावन् grā́-van, m. 'stone' —

	SING.	PLUR.
N.	ग्रावा grā́-vā	ग्रावाणः grā́-vāṇ-aḥ
A.	ग्रावाणम् grā́-vāṇ-am	ग्राव्णः grā́v-ṇ-aḥ
I.	ग्राव्णा grā́v-ṇ-ā	ग्रावभिः grā́-va-bhiḥ

2a. Irregular Stems in अन् an.

91. 1. पन्थन् pánth-an, m. 'path,' has पन्थान् pánth-ān for its strong stem, पथि path-í for its middle, and पथ् path for its weakest stem; the nom. irregularly adds स् s[1]—

	SING.	PLUR.
N.	पन्थाः pánth-ā-**ḥ**	पन्थानः pánth-ān-aḥ
A.	पन्थानम् pánth-ān-am	पथः path-áḥ
I.	पथा path-ā́	पथिभिः pathí-bhiḥ

1. This स् s is due to the fact that in the earlier language this word had two stems: the one पन्था pánthā, forming N. पन्थाः pánthā-ḥ, A. पन्थाम् pánthā-m; the other, पन्थान् pánthān, forming N. पन्था pánthā, A. पन्थानम् pánthān-am.

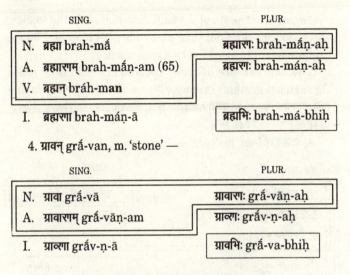

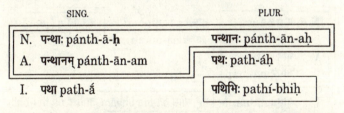

2. अहन् áh-an, n. 'day' takes अहस् áh-as as its middle stem—

	SING.	DUAL.	PLUR.
N.V.A.	अहः áh-aḥ[1]	अह्नी áhn-ī or अहनी áhan-i	अहानि áhān-i
I.	अह्ना áhn-ā	अहोभ्याम् áho-bhyām	अहोभिः áho-bhiḥ
L.	अह्नि áhn-i / अहनि áhan-i	अह्नोः áhn-oḥ	अहःसु: áhaḥ-su

3. श्वन् śv-án, m. 'dog,' forms its weakest stem, शुन् śun[2], with Samprasāraṇa. Otherwise it is declined like राजन् rājan.

	SING.		PLUR.
N.	श्वा śvā́ (κύων)	N.V.	श्वानः śvā́n-aḥ
A.	श्वानम् śvā́n-am		शुनः śún-aḥ (*κύνας*)
V.	श्वन् śván (κύον)	I.	श्वभिः śvá-bhiḥ

4. युवन् yú-van, m. 'youth' (Lat. juven-is), forms its weakest stem, यून् yūn, by Samprasāraṇa (yu-un) and contraction (cf. Lat. jūn-ior) —

	SING.		PLUR.
N.	युवा yú-vā	N.V.	युवानः yú-vān-aḥ
A.	युवानम् yú-vān-am		यूनः yū́n-aḥ
V.	युवन् yú-van	I.	युवभिः yú-va-bhiḥ

1. The Visarga is the N.V.A. sing., and when the word is the prior member of a compound (except in अहोरात्र aho-rātra, m.n. 'day and night'), is treated like an original र् r (46): hence अहरहः ahar-ahaḥ, 'day by day'; अहर्गणः ahar-gaṇaḥ, 'series of days.'
2. So also in Greek: *κυνός* = śúnaḥ.

5. मघवन् maghá-van (lit. 'bountiful'), m. a name of Indra, also forms its weakest stem, मघोन् maghón[1], by Samprasāraṇa and contraction :—

SING.	PLUR.
N. मघवा maghá-vā	N.V. मघवानः maghá-vān-aḥ
A. मघवानम् maghá-vān-am	मघोनः maghón-aḥ
V. मघवन् mágha-van	I. मघवभिः maghá-va-bhiḥ

92. The root हन् han, 'kill,' when used as a noun at the end of a compound, for the most part follows the analogy of stems in अन् an. The strong stem is हन् han (with a long vowel in the nom. sing. only), the middle ह ha, and the weakest घ्न् ghn; — e.g. ब्रह्महन् brahma-han, m. 'Brahman-killer' —

N. ब्रह्महा -hā́	N.V. ब्रह्महणः -háṇ-aḥ
A. ब्रह्महणम् -háṇ-am (65)	ब्रह्मघ्नः -**gh**n-áḥ[2]
V. ब्रह्महन् -han	
L. ब्रह्मघ्नि -**gh**n-í[2]	I. ब्रह्महभिः -há-bhiḥ
ब्रह्महणि -háṇ-i	ब्रह्महसु -há-su

3. Adjectives in अच् ac.

93. These words, the suffix[3] of which is generally expressed by '-ward,' from the strong stem in अञ्च् añc, the middle

1. Forms from मघवत् magha-vat are also sometimes found; — e.g. nom. मघवान् magha-vān, gen. मघवतः magha-vat-aḥ.
2. The cerebralization of न् n (65) does not take place here, probably because the guttural mute immediately precedes it.
3. These words are properly compounds formed with the verb अञ्च् añc, 'bend,' which has, however, practically acquired the character of a suffix.

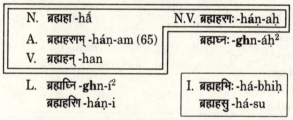

in अच् ac, and the weakest in ईच् īc or ऊच् ūc[1] (according as अच् ac is preceded by य् y or व् v); — e.g. प्रत्यच् praty-ac, m.n.[2] 'backward,' 'westward' —

MASCULINE.

	SING.	DUAL.	PLUR.
N.V.	प्रत्यङ् praty-á**ṅ** (61)	°त्यञ्चौ -tyáñc-au	°त्यञ्चः tyáñc-aḥ
A.	प्रत्यञ्चम् pratyáñc-am	°त्यञ्चौ -tyáñc-au	°तीचः -tīc-áḥ
I.	प्रतीचा pratīc-ā́	°त्यग्भ्याम् -tyá**g**-bhyām	°त्यग्भिः -tyá**g**-bhiḥ
L.	प्रतीचि pratīc-í	°तीचोः -tīc-óḥ	°त्यक्षु -tyá**k**-ṣu (30; 67)

NEUTER.

N.A.	प्रत्यक् pratyák	प्रतीची pratīc-ī́	प्रत्यञ्चि pratyáñc-i

a. Other words similarly declined are —

STRONG STEM.	MIDDLE STEM.	WEAKEST STEM.
न्यञ्च् ny-áñc, 'downward'	न्यक् ny-àk	नीच् nīc
सम्यञ्च् sam-y-áñc, 'right'	सम्यक् sam-y-ák	समीच् sam-īc
तिर्यञ्च् tir-y-áñc, 'transverse'	तिर्यक् tir-y-ák	तिरश्च् tiráś-c[3]
उदञ्च् úd-añc, 'upward'	उदक् úd-ak	उदीच् úd-īc[4]

---

1. Contractions for यच् y-ac and वच् v-ac respectively (which usually would be shortened to इच् ĭc and उच् ŭc). The apparent irregularity of the long vowel is probably due to the Samprasāraṇa here being not internal, but external, at the junction of a compound. If the vowel were short, the stem would look as if formed with a suffix च् -c added to the final vowel of the prior member; — e.g. प्रतिच् prati-c, अनुच् anu-c.
2. On the formation of the feminine see 95.
3. From तिरस् tiras (cp. Lat. trans) + अच् ac, 'going across,' 'horizontal'; as a noun, m.n., it means 'animal.'
4. ई ī, though no य् y precedes the अ a of the suffix, by analogy.

STRONG STEM.	MIDDLE STEM.	WEAKEST STEM.
अन्वञ्च् anv-áñc, 'following'	अन्वक् anv-ák	अनूच् anū́c
विष्वञ्च् víṣv-añc, 'all-pervading'	विष्वक् víṣv-ak	विषूच् víṣūc

b. पराच् párāc, 'turned away,' प्राच् prā́c, 'forward,' 'eastern, and अवाच् ávāc, 'downward,' 'southern,' have only two stems पराञ्च् párāñc, प्राञ्च् prā́ñc and अवाञ्च् ávāñc for the strong पराच् párāc, प्राच् prā́c and अवाच् ávāc for the weak :—

MASCULINE.

	SING.	PLUR.
N.V.	प्राङ् prā́ṅ (61)	प्राञ्चः prā́ñc-aḥ
A.	प्राञ्चम् prā́ñc-am	प्राचः prā́c-aḥ
I.	प्राचा prā́c-ā	प्राग्भिः prā́g-bhiḥ
L.	प्राचि prā́c-i	प्राक्षु prā́k-ṣu

94. The beginner will find it useful to remember the following points with regard to changeable stems :—

1. The vowel of the suffix is lengthened in the nom. sing. masc. except in stems in अत् at and अच् ac; — अग्निमान् agni-mā́n, ज्ञानवान् jñāna-vān; गरीयान् gár-īyān; चकृवान् cakṛ-vā́n; राजा rā́j-ā, ब्रह्मा brah-mā́, युवा yú-vā; धनी dhan-ī́, वाग्मी vāg-mī́, मनस्वी manas-vī́; but अदन् ad-án, प्रत्यङ् praty-áṅ.

2. The nom. sing. masc. ends in a nasal in all changeable stems except those in न् n (अन् an, मन् man, वन् van, इन् in, मिन् min, विन् vin), which drop it.

3. All changeable stems which lengthen the vowel in the nom. sing. masc., keep it short in the vocative, and always retain the न् n of the stem; — e.g. अग्निमन् ágni-man, ज्ञानवन् jñāna-van; गरीयन् gár-īyan; चकृवन् cákṛ-van; राजन् rā́j-an, ब्रह्मन् bráh-man, युवन् yú-van; धनिन् dhán-in, वाग्मिन् vā́g-min, मनस्विन् mánas-vin.

a. In other changeable stems the vocative differs from the nom. solely in always having the accent on the first syllable : अदन् ád-an, voc., adán, nom.; प्रत्यङ् prátyaṅ, voc., pratyáṅ, nom.

95. The **feminines** of nouns with changeable stems are formed by adding ई ī to the weak stem (when there are two stems) or the weakest (when there are three), and follow the declension of नदी nadī (100); — e.g. अदती adat-ī́; अग्निमती agni-mát-ī, ज्ञानवती jñāna-vat-ī; धनिनी dhanín-ī, वाग्मिनी vāg-mín-ī, मनस्विनी manas-vín-ī; गरीयसी gárīyas-ī; चक्रुषी cakrúṣ-ī; राज्ञी rā́jñī ('queen'); °नाम्नी -nāmn-ī (adj., 'named'); शुनी śun-ī́ ('bitch'); °घ्नी -ghn-ī ('killing'); प्रतीची pratīc-ī́, प्राची prā́c-ī.

a. The feminine of the **present participle active** of the first conjugation (125) is made from the strong masc. stem in अन्त् ant (cp. 156); that of the second conjugation from the weak stem in अत् at; — e.g. भवन्ती bhávant-ī, 'being[1];' तुदन्ती tudánt-ī[2], 'striking,' दीव्यन्ती dī́vyant-ī, 'playing,' चोरयन्ती corayant-ī, 'stealing;' but जुह्वती júhv-at-ī, 'sacrificing,' युञ्जती yuñj-at-ī́, 'joining,' सुन्वती sunv-at-ī́, 'pressing,' कुर्वती kurv-at-ī́, 'doing,' क्रीणती krīṇ-at-ī́, 'buying.'

b. The feminine of the simple future participle active is usually formed like the present part. of the first conjugation; भविष्यन्ती bhaviṣyánt-ī[2], 'about to be,' करिष्यन्ती kariṣyánt-ī, 'about to do.'

c. The few **adjectives** in वन् **-van** form their feminines in °वरी -varī; — पीवन् pī́-van (πίων), 'fat', f. पीवरी pī́-varī

---

1. But भवती bhavat-ī from भवत् bhavat, 'your Honour' (86 *a*).
2. If the verbal base, however, ends in accented अ a; — e.g. tudá, bhaviṣyá, the weak form may optionally be taken, when the ई ī receives the accent: तुदती tud-at-ī́, भविषयती bhaviṣy-at-ī́.

(πίειρα). The fem. of the irregular युवन् yú-van, 'young' (91, 4), is युवति yuva-tí or युवती yuva-tī.

Irregular Nouns with Changeable Stems.

96. 1. अप् ap, f. 'water,' which is always plural, lengthens its अ a in the strong cases (N.V.) and substitutes त् t for प् p before भ् bh :—

N. आपः ā́p-aḥ	A. अपः ap-áḥ	I. अद्भिः ad-bhíḥ	L. अप्सु ap-sú

2. अनड्वह् anaḍ-váh, m. 'ox' (lit. 'cart-drawer,' from anas + vah), has three stems: the last syllable is lengthened in the strong stem, अनड्वाह् anaḍ-vāh, and shortened by Samprasāraṇa in the weakest, अनडुह् anaḍ-uh, and in the middle अनडुत् anaḍ-ut (dissimilated, for अनडुड् anaḍ-uḍ: cp. 27). The nom. and voc. are irregularly formed, as if from a stem in वत् vat.

N. अनड्वान् anaḍvā́**n**	N.V. अनड्वाहः anaḍvā́h-aḥ
V. अनड्वन् ánaḍva**n**	
A. अनड्वाहम् anaḍvā́h-am	A. अनडुहः anaḍúh-aḥ
I. अनडुहा anaḍúh-ā	I. अनडुद्भिः anaḍú**d**-bhiḥ
L. अनडुहि anaḍúh-i	L. अनडुत्सु anaḍú**t**-su

3. पुमस् pú-maṃs[1], m. 'man,' has three forms, being lengthened in the strong stem to पुमांस् púmāṃs, shortened by syncope in the weakest to पुंस् puṃs, and in the middle to पुम् pum (with necessary loss of the स् s: cp. 28 and 16 *a*): —

1. Probably an old compound, with the second part of which the Lat. mās, 'male,' may be allied.

N. sg. पुमान् púmān (cp. 89, 1)	N.V. pl. पुमांसः púmāṃs-aḥ
V. पुमन् púman	A. पुंसः puṃs-áḥ
A. पुमांसम् púmāṃs-am	

I. पुंसा puṃs-ā́	I. पुम्भिः pum-bhíḥ
L. पुंसि puṃs-í	L. पुंसु puṃ-sú

II. Stems ending in Vowels.

97. A. Stems in अ a (masc. neut.) and आ ā[1] (fem.); — e.g.
कान्त kān-ta[2], 'beloved' (past participle of कम् kam, 'love') —

SINGULAR.

	MASC.	NEUT.	FEM.
N.	कान्तः kānta-ḥ	कान्तम् kānta-m	कान्ता kāntā
A.	कान्तम् kānta-m		कान्ताम् kāntā-m
I.	कान्तेन kāntena[3]		कान्तया kānta-y-ā[3]
D.	कान्ताय kāntāya		कान्तायै kāntā-yai[5]
Ab.	कान्तात् kāntāt[4]		कान्तायाः kāntā-yāḥ
G.	कान्तस्य kānta-sya[3]		कान्तायाः kāntā-yāḥ
L.	कान्ते kānte		कान्तायाम् kāntā-yām
V.	कान्त kānta		कान्ते kānte[6]

1. अ a = Gk. –os, –ov; Lat. -us, -um. आ ā = Gk. -α, –η; Lat. -a.
2. Certain adjectives in अः aḥ, आ ā, अम् am follow the pronominal declension (110).
3. These terminations originally came from the pronominal declension (110).
4. This termination is preserved in the Lat. ō for ōd (e.g. Gnaivōd in inscriptions), and in the Greek (Cretic) adv. τῶ–δε, 'hence.'
5. The terminations -yai (= -yā-e), -yāḥ (= -yā-as), -yām are due to the influence of the feminines in -ī (originally -yā); — e.g. nadyai, nadyāḥ, nadyām (cp. 100).
6. The voc. of अम्बा ambā, 'mother,' is अम्ब amba.

DUAL

N.A.V.	कान्तौ kāntau	कान्ते kānte	कान्ते kānte
I.D.Ab.		कान्ताभ्याम् kāntā-bhyām	
G.L.		कान्तयोः kānta-y-oḥ	

PLURAL

	MASC.	NEUT.	FEM.
N.V.	कान्ताः kāntāḥ	कान्तानि kāntā-n-i[2]	कान्ताः kāntāḥ
A.	कान्तान् kāntān[1]	कान्तानि kānt**ā**-**n**-i	कान्ताः kāntāḥ
I.	कान्तैः kānt**aiḥ**[3]		कान्ताभिः kāntā-bhiḥ
D.Ab.	कान्तेभ्यः kānt**e**-bhyaḥ		कान्ताभ्यः kāntā-bhyaḥ
G.	कान्तानाम् kāntā-**n**-ām[2]		कान्तानाम् kāntā-**n**-ām
L.	कान्तेषु kānt**e**-ṣu		कान्तासु kāntā-su

98. B. Stems in इ i and उ u (masc. fem. neut.); — शुचि śúc-i, 'pure'; मृदु mṛd-ú, 'soft' —

SINGULAR

	MASC.	FEM.	NEUT.	MASC.	FEM.	NEUT.
N.	शुचिः	शुचिः	शुचि	मृदुः	मृदुः	मृदु
	śúci-ḥ	śúci-ḥ	śúc-i	mṛdú-ḥ	mṛdú-ḥ	mṛdú
A.	शुचिम्	शुचिम्	शुचि	मृदुम्	मृदुम्	मृदु
	śúci-m	śúci-m	śúc-i	mṛdú-m	mṛdú-m	mṛdú
I.	शुचिना	शुच्या	शुचिना	मृदुना	मृद्वा	मृदुना
	śúci-**n**-ā	śúcy-ā	śúci-**n**-ā	mṛdú-**n**-ā	mṛdv-ā́	mṛdú-**n**-ā

1. The ending was originally -āns (cp. 36 B, foot-note 1), Goth. -ans, Gk. insc. *-ους*.
2. Due to the influence of the stems in अन् an: नामानि nāmāni, आत्मनाम् ātmanām.
3. This termination is preserved in such Gk. datives as ἵπποις.

	MASC.	FEM.	NEUT.	MASC.	FEM.	NEUT.
D.	शुचये	शुच्यै	शुचिने	मृदवे	मृद्वै	मृदुने
	śúc-**ay**-e	śucy-**ai**[1]	śúci-**n**-e	mṛ**dáv**-e	mṛdv-**ái**[1]	mṛdú-**n**-e
Ab.G.	शुचेः	शुच्याः	शुचिनः	मृदोः	मृद्वाः	मृदुनः
	śúc-**eḥ**	śúcy-**āḥ**	śúci-**n**-aḥ	mṛd-**óḥ**	mṛdv-**ā́ḥ**	mṛdú-**n**-aḥ
L.	शुचौ	शुच्याम्	शुचिनि	मृदौ	मृद्वाम्	मृदुनि
	śúc-**au**[2]	śúcy-**ām**	śúci-**n**-i	mṛd-**áu**	mṛdv-**ā́m**	mṛdú-**n**-i
V.	शुचे	शुचे	शुचि	मृदो	मृदो	मृदु
	śú**ce**	śú**ce**	śúci	mṛ́**do**	mṛ́**do**	mṛ́du

DUAL.

N.A.V.	शुची	शुची	शुचिनी	मृदू	मृदू	मृदुनी
	śúcī	śúcī	śúci-**n**-ī	mṛdū́	mṛdū́	mṛdú-n-ī
I.D.Ab.	शुचिभ्याम् śúci-bhyām			मृदुभ्याम् mṛdú-bhyām		
G.L.	शुच्योः	शुच्योः	शुचिनोः	मृद्वोः	मृद्वोः	मृदुनोः
	śúcy-oḥ	śúcy-oḥ	śúci-**n**-oḥ	mṛdv-óḥ	mṛdv-óḥ	mṛdú-**n**-oḥ

PLURAL.

N.V.	शुचयः	शुचयः	शुचीनि	मृदवः	मृदवः	मृदूनि
	śúc**ay**-aḥ	śúc**ay**-aḥ	śúcī-**n**-i	mṛ**dáv**-aḥ	mṛ**dáv**-aḥ	mṛdū́-**n**-i
A.	शुचीन्	शुचीः	शुचीनि	मृदून्	मृदूः	मृदूनि
	śúcīn	**śúcīḥ**	śúcī-**n**-i	**mṛdū́n**	**mṛdū́ḥ**	mṛdū́-**n**-i
I.	शुचिभिः śúci-bhiḥ			मृदुभिः mṛdú-bhiḥ		
D.Ab.	शुचिभ्यः śúci-bhyaḥ			मृदुभ्यः mṛdú-bhyaḥ		
G.	शुचीनाम् śúcī-**n**-ām			मृदूनाम् mṛdū́-**n**-ām		
L.	शुचिषु śúci-ṣu			मृदुषु mṛdú-ṣu		

---

1. Cp. 97, foot-note 5.
2. This very anomalous ending, being the Vṛddhi vowel of उ u, not इ i, seems to be due to the influence of the stems in उ u, the inflexion of which is entirely analogous.

a. Neuter adjectives (not substantive) may be declined throughout (except N.V.A. of all numbers), and fem. adjectives and substantives in the D.Ab.G.L. sing., like masculines. Thus the L. sing. of मति matí, f. 'thought,' is मत्याम् matyā́m or मतौ matáu, but वारि vāri, n. 'water,' only वारिणि vāriṇi.

b. The voc. sing. of neuters may optionally follow the masc. from; — e.g. वारि vāri or वारे vāre; मधु mádhu or मधो mádho.

c. The **feminine** of objectives in उ u is sometimes also fromed by adding ई ī; — e.g. तनु tanú or तन्वी tanv-ī, f. 'thin'; लघु laghú or लघ्वी laghv-ī, f. 'light'; पृथु pṛthú, f. 'broad,' पृथ्वी pṛthv-ī́, '(the broad) earth.'

Irregularities.

99. 1. पति pát-i (Gk. *πόσι–s*), m. 'husband,' is irregular in the weak cases of the singular: I. पत्या páty-ā, D. पत्ये páty-e Ab.G. पत्युः páty-uḥ[1], L. पत्यौ páty-**au**. When it means 'lord,' or occurs at the end of compounds, it is regular (like शुचि śuci). The fem. is पत्नी pátnī, 'wife' (Gk. *πότνια*).

2. सखि sákh-i, m. 'friend,' has the same irregularities, but in addition has a strong stem formed with Vṛddhi, सखाय् sákhāy : N. सखा sákhā, A. सखायम् sákh**āy**-am, I. सख्या sákhy-ā, D. सख्ये sákhy-e, Ab.G. सख्युः sákhy-**uḥ**[1], L. सख्यौ sákhy-**au**, V. सखे sákhe; du. N.A.V. सखायौ sákh**āy**-au; pl. N.V. सखायः sákh**āy**-aḥ, A. सखीन् sákhīn. At the end of compounds सखि sakhi is regular is the weak cases, but retains the stem सखाय् sakhāy in the strong. The fem. is सखी sakh-ī.

3. The neuters अक्षि ákṣi, 'eye,' अस्थि ásthi, 'bone,' दधि dádhi, 'curds,' सक्थि sákthi, 'thigh,' form their weakest cases from stems in अन् an (अक्षन् akṣan, &c., like नामन् nāman):—

---

1. This anomalous ending appears to be due to the influence of the Ab.G. in names of relationship (101) in ऋ ṛ, like पितुर् pitúr.

N.A.V.	अक्षि	du. अक्षिणी	pl. अक्षीणि
	ákṣi	ákṣi-ṇ-ī	ákṣī-ṇ-i
I.	अक्ष्णा	अक्षिभ्याम्	अक्षिभिः
	akṣṇ-ā́	ákṣi-bhyām	ákṣi-bhiḥ
G.	अक्ष्णः	अक्ष्णोः	अक्ष्णाम्
	akṣṇ-áḥ	akṣṇ-óḥ	akṣn-ā́m

4. द्यु dyú, f. 'sky' (originally diu, weak grade of द्यो dyo : 102*a*), retains this stem before consonant terminations (taking Vṛddhi in the N.V. sing.), but changes it to दिव् div before vowels:—

SING.		PLUR.	
N.	द्यौः dyáu-ḥ (*Zεύs = Δjεύs*)	N.	दिवः dív-aḥ
A.	दिवम् dív-am	A.	दिवः dív-aḥ
I.	दिवा div-ā́	I.	द्युभिः dyú-bhiḥ
D.	दिवे div-é	D.Ab.	द्युभ्यः dyú-bhyaḥ
Ab.G	दिवः div-áḥ (*Διϝόs*)	G.	दिवाम् div-ā́m
L.	दिवि div-í (*Διϝί*)	L.	द्युषु dyú-ṣu
V.	द्यौः dyàu-ḥ[1] (*Zεῦ*)		

100. C. Stems in ई ī and ऊ ū (**fem.**), according as they are monosyllabic or polysyllabic, show various differences of inflexion : —

1. Monosyllabic stems change ई ī and ऊ ū to इय् iy and उव् uv before vowels, the polysyllabic stems to य् y and व् v.

2. Monosyllabic stems have the normal terminations (71) throughout: they **may** take the special feminine terminations (-ai, -āḥ, -ām),[2] polysyllabic stems must.

---

1. The nom. with voc. accent, while the Greek has the proper voc.
2. These terminations started from the polysyllabic stems in ई -ī, originally या -yā, which was fused with the normal endings ए e and अस् as to यै -yai and यास् -yās, and, in the loc., with an ending अम् -am (of unknown origin) to याम् -yām.

3. Monosyllabic stems use the nom. (which takes स् s), polysyllabic stems shorten the ई ī and ऊ ū of the nom., in the voc. sing.

4. Polysyllabic stems in ई ī have no स् s in the nom. sing. except लक्ष्मीः lakṣmīḥ, 'goddess of prosperity,' तन्त्रीः tantrīḥ, 'string,' and optionally तन्द्री tandrī, 'sloth.'

5. Polysyllabic stems form the acc. sing. in ईम् īm and ऊम् ūm, the acc. pl. in ईस् īs and ऊस् ūs.

SINGULAR.

Stem	धी dhī, 'thought'	भू bhū, 'earth'	नदी nad-ī 'river'	वधू vadh-ū, 'woman'
N.V.	धीः dhī́-ḥ	भूः bhū́-ḥ	N. नदी nadī́	वधूः vadhū́-ḥ
A.	धियम् dhíy-am	भुवम् bhúv-am	नदीम् nadī́-m	वधूम् vadhū́-m
I.	धिया dhiy-ā́	भुवा bhuv-ā́	नद्या nady-ā́	वध्वा vadhv-ā́
D.	धिये dhiy-é	भुवे bhuv-é	नद्यै nady-**ái**	वध्वै vadhv-**ái**[1]
Ab.G.	धियः dhiy-áḥ	भुवः bhuv-áḥ	नद्याः nady-**ā́ḥ**	वध्वाः vadhv-**ā́ḥ**[1]
L.	धियि dhiy-í	भुवि bhuv-í	नद्याम् nady-**ā́m**	वध्वाम् vadhv-**ā́m**
			V. नदि nádi	वधु vádhu

1. The special feminine terminations in -ai, -ās, -ām are here, as in the ā declension (97), due to the influence of the polysyllabic ī declension.

DUAL.

N.V.A.	धियौ	भुवौ	नद्यौ	वध्वौ
	dhíy-au	bhúv-au	nady-àu	vadhv-àu
I.D.Ab.	धीभ्याम्	भूभ्याम्	नदीभ्याम्	वधूभ्याम्
	dhī-bhyā́m	bhū-bhyā́m	nadī́-bhyām	vadhū́-bhyām
G.L.	धियोः	भुवोः	नद्योः	वध्वोः
	dhiy-óḥ	bhuv-óḥ	nady-óḥ	vadhv-óḥ

PLURAL.

N.V.A.	धियः	भुवः	N.V. नद्यः	वध्वः
	dhíy-aḥ	bhúv-aḥ	nady-àḥ	vadhv-àḥ
			A. नदीः	वधूः
			nadī́ḥ	vadhū́ḥ
I.	धीभिः	भूभिः	नदीभिः	वधूभिः
	dhī-bhíḥ	bhū-bhíḥ	nadī́-bhiḥ	vadhū́-bhiḥ
D.Ab.	धीभ्यः	भूभ्यः	नदीभ्यः	वधूभ्यः
	dhī-bhyáḥ	bhū-bhyáḥ	nadī́-bhyaḥ	vadhū́-bhyaḥ
G.	धियाम्	भुवाम्	नदीनाम्	वधूनाम्
	dhiy-ā́m	bhuv-ā́m	nadī́-**n**-ām	vadhū́-**n**-ām
L.	धीषु	भूषु	नदीषु	वधूषु
	dhī-ṣú	bhū-ṣú	nadī́-ṣu	vadhū́-ṣu

a. स्त्री strī́, f. 'woman,' though monosyllabic, has most of the characteristics of polysyllabic stems in ई ī (100, 2-5): it **must** take the special fem. terminations, it shortens its ई ī in the voc., it has no स् s in the nom., and has an optional acc. sing. in ईम् īm and acc. plur. in ईस् īs. This is doubtless due to its originally having been a dissyllable.

N.	स्त्री strī́	N.V.	स्त्रियः stríy-aḥ
A.	स्त्रियम् stríy-am / स्त्रीम् strī́-**m**	A.	स्त्रियः stríy-aḥ / स्त्रीः strī́-**ḥ**
I.	स्त्रिया striy-ā́	I.	स्त्रीभिः strī-bhíḥ
D.	स्त्रियै striy-**ái**	D.Ab.	स्त्रीभ्यः strī-bhyáḥ
Ab.G.	स्त्रियाः striy-**ā́ḥ**	G.	स्त्रीणाम् strī-**ṇ**-ā́m
L.	स्त्रियाम् striy-**ā́m**	I.	स्त्रीषु strī-ṣú
V.	स्त्रि strí		

Dual. N.V.A. स्त्रियौ stríy-au, I.D.Ab. स्त्रीभ्याम् strī-bhyā́m, G.L. स्त्रियोः striy-óḥ.

101. D. Stems in ऋ ṛ (masc. and **fem.**), which in origin are consonant stems in अर् -ar, are closely analogous in their declension to stems in अन् -an (90). These nouns mostly end in the suffix तृ -tṛ (i.e. -tar, Gk. -τηρ, -τωρ, Lat. -tor). They distinguish a strong stem तर् -tar or तार् -tār, a middle तृ tṛ, and a weakest त्र् tr. The inflexion of masc. and fem. differs in the acc. plur. only.

In the strong stem the names of relations take the Guṇa form (ar), the names of agents take the Vṛddhi form (ār).

The sing. gen. is formed in उर् ur, the loc. in अरि ari, the voc. in अर् ar; the pl. acc. masc. in ॠन् ṝn, fem. in ॠस् ṝs, the gen. in ॠणाम् ṝṇām.

Stem	दातृ dātṛ́ m. 'giver'	पितृ pitṛ́, m. 'father'	मातृ mātṛ́, f. 'mother'
	(δωτήρ, dator)	(πάτήρ, păter)	(μήτηρ, māter)

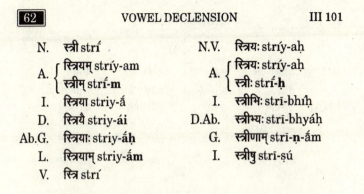

SINGULAR.

N.	दाता dātā́	पिता pitā́	माता mātā́
A.	दातारम् dātā́r-am	पितरम् pitár-am	मातरम् mātár-am
I.	दात्रा dātr-ā́	पित्रा pitr-ā́	मात्रा mātr-ā́
D.	दात्रे dātr-é	पित्रे pitr-é	मात्रे mātr-é
Ab.G.	दातुर् dāt-**úr**	पितुर् pit-**úr**	मातुर् māt-**úr**
L.	दातरि dāt-**ári**	पितरि pit-ári (*πατέρι*)	मातरि māt-ári
V.	दातर् dā́tar (*δῶτερ*)	पितर् pítar (Ju-piter)	मातर् mā́tar (*μῆτερ*)

DUAL.

N.V.	दातारौ dātā́r-au	पितरौ pitár-au	मातरौ mātár-au
I.D.Ab.	दातृभ्याम् -tṛ́-bhyām	पितृभ्याम् -tṛ́-bhyām	मातृभ्याम् -tṛ́-bhyām
G.L.	दात्रोः dātr-óḥ	पित्रोः pitr-óḥ	मात्रोः mātr-óḥ

PLURAL.

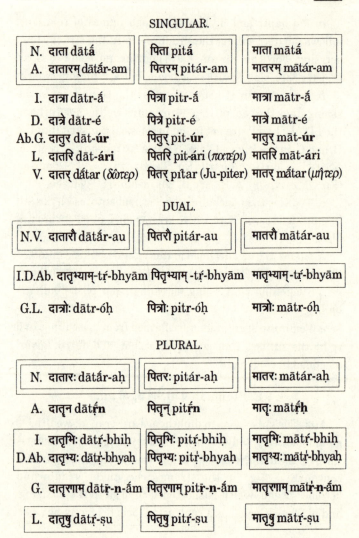

N.	दातारः dātā́r-aḥ	पितरः pitár-aḥ	मातरः mātár-aḥ
A.	दातॄन् dātṝ́n	पितॄन् pitṝ́n	मातॄः mātṝ́ḥ
I.	दातृभिः dātṛ́-bhiḥ	पितृभिः pitṛ́-bhiḥ	मातृभिः mātṛ́-bhiḥ
D.Ab.	दातृभ्यः dātṛ́-bhyaḥ	पितृभ्यः pitṛ́-bhyaḥ	मातृभ्यः mātṛ́-bhyaḥ
G.	दातॄणाम् dātṝ-**ṇ**-ā́m	पितॄणाम् pitṝ-**ṇ**-ā́m	मातॄणाम् mātṝ-**ṇ**-ā́m
L.	दातृषु dātṛ́-ṣu	पितृषु pitṛ́-ṣu	मातृषु mātṛ́-ṣu

a. नप्तृ náptṛ and भर्तृ bhartṛ́, though names of relations, follows दातृ dātṛ́, taking the Vṛddhi form in the strong stem: acc. sing. नप्तारम् náptār-am. भर्तारम् bhartā́r-am; also स्वसृ svásṛ, f. 'sister': acc. sing. स्वसारम् svásār-am, but acc. pl. स्वसॄः svásṝḥ.

b. नृ nṛ, m. 'man' (Gk. ἀ-νήρ), takes the Guṇa form in the strong stem; the gen. pl. is नृणाम् nṛṇā́m as well as नॄणाम् nṝṇām; the I.D.Ab.G. sing. are not found in classical Sanskrit (but the D. and G. in the Rig-veda are नरे nár-e, नरः nár-aḥ); — N. ना nā́, A. नरम् nár-am, L. नरि nár-i (Ep. Gk. ἀ-νέρ-ι). N. pl. नरः nár-aḥ (Ep. Gk. ἀ-νέρ-ες), A. नॄन् nṝ́n, I. नृभिः nṛ́-bhiḥ, L. नृषु nṛ́-ṣu.

c. क्रोष्टृ kroṣ-ṭṛ́, m. 'jackal' (lit. 'yeller'), substitutes क्रोष्टु kroṣṭu in the middle cases: N. pl. क्रोष्टारः kroṣṭā́r-aḥ, I. pl. क्रोष्टुभिः kroṣṭu-bhiḥ.

d. Stems in तृ tṛ, if declined in the neuter, would be inflected like the neut. of शुचि śuci: N.A. sing. धातृ dhātṛ́, du. धातृणी dhātṛ́-ṇ-ī, pl. धातृणि dhātṛ́-ṇ-i; I. sing. धातृणा dhātṛ́-ṇ-ā, pl. धातृभिः dhātṛ́-bhiḥ.

e. **Feminine** agent nouns are formed from masculines in तृ tṛ by the suffix ई ī: masc. दातृ dātṛ́, fem. दात्री dātr-ī, 'giver' (declined like नदी nadī).

E. Stems in ऐ ai, ओ o, औ au.

102. The only stems in diphthongs are रै rai, m. 'wealth,' गो go, m.f. 'bull, cow,' द्यो dyo, f. 'sky,' and नौ nau, f. 'ship.' रै rai changes the इ i of the diphthong to य् y before vowels, but drops it before consonants. गो go, in the strong cases, takes Vṛddhi and becomes गौ gau, which is shortened to गा gā in the acc. sing. and pl. The ab. gen. has a contracted form (os for av-as).

These stems form a transition between the consonant and vowel declension: they agree with the former in taking the normal endings; with the latter in adding स् s in the nom. sing. and in showing a vowel before endings with initial consonant:—

SINGULAR.

N.V.	रा:	गौ:	नौ:
	rā́-ḥ (Lat. rē-s)	**gáu**-ḥ (*βοῦs*)	náu-ḥ (*ναῦs*)
A.	रायम्	गाम्	नावम्
	rā́y-am	gā́-m (*βῶν*)	nā́v-am (*νῆϝα*)
I.	राया	गवा	नावा
	rāy-ā́	gáv-ā	nāv-ā́
D.	राये	गवे	नावे
	rāy-é (rē-ī)	gáv-e	nāv-é
Ab.G.	राय:	गो:	नाव:
	rāy-áḥ	**gó**-ḥ	nāv-áḥ (*νηϝόs*)
L.	रायि	गवि	नावि
	rāy-í	gáv-i	nāv-í (*νηϝί*)

DUAL.

N.A.V.	रायौ	गावौ	नावौ
	rā́y-au	gā́v-au	nā́v-au
I.D.Ab.	राभ्याम्	गोभ्याम्	नौभ्याम्
	rā-bhyā́m	gó-bhyām	nau-bhyā́m
G.L.	रायो:	गवो:	नावो:
	rāy-óḥ	gáv-oḥ	nāv-óḥ

PLURAL.

N.V.	राय:	गाव:	नाव:
	rā́y-aḥ	gā́v-aḥ	nā́v-aḥ (*νῆϝεs*)
A.	राय:	गा:	नाव:
	rāy-áḥ	gā́-ḥ	nā́v-aḥ (*νῆϝαs*)

I.	राभिः	गोभिः	नौभिः
	rā-bhíḥ	gó-bhiḥ	nau-bhíḥ (ναῦ–φι)
D.Ab.	राभ्यः	गोभ्यः	नौभ्यः
	rā-bhyáḥ (rē-bus)	gó-bhyaḥ	nau-bhyáḥ
G.	रायाम्	गवाम्	नावाम्
	rāy-ā́m	gáv-ām (βοῶν)	nāv-ā́m (νηϝῶν)
L.	रासु	गोषु	नौषु
	rā-śu	gó-ṣu	nau-ṣú (ναυσί)

a. द्यो dyo, 'sky,' is declined like गो go; the nom. sing. is the same as that of द्यु dyu (99, 4); in the dual and plur. the strong forms alone occur: — N. द्यौः dyáuḥ (*Ζεύς),* A. द्याम् dyā́m (Lat. diem), D. द्यवे dyáv-e, Ab.G. द्योः dyóḥ, L. द्यवि dyáv-i; Dual N.A. द्यावौ dyā́v-au, N. pl. द्यावः dyā́v-aḥ.

Degrees of Comparison.

103. 1. The **secondary** suffix of the comparative °तर -tara (Gk. *–τερο*) and that of the superlative °तम -tama (Lat. -timo) are added to the weak or middle stem of derivative adjectives (and even substantives); — e.g. शुचि śuci: शुचितर śuci-tara, शुचितम śuci-tama; प्राच् prāc: प्राक्तर prāk-tara, प्राक्तम prāktama; धनिन् dhanin: धनितर dhani-tara, धनितम dhani-tama; विद्वस् vidvas: विद्वत्तर vidvat-tara, विद्वत्तम vidvat-tama; प्रत्यच् pratyac: प्रत्यक्तर pratyak-tara, प्रत्यक्तम pratyak-tama.

a. These suffixes form their **feminine** in आ ā; but तम tama, when used as an ordinal suffix, forms its fem. in ई ī (cp.107).

2. The **primary** suffix of the comparative, इयस् īyas (Gk. *-ιων*, Lat. -ior), and that of the superlative, इष्ठ iṣṭha (Gk.*-ιστο*), are added to the root, which generally takes Guṇa (and is accented). Before them every word must be reduced to one syllable by dropping suffixes; — e.g. अणु áṇ-u, 'minute': अणीयस् áṇ-īyas,

अणिष्ठ áṇ-iṣṭha; गुरु gur-ú[1], 'heavy': गरीयस् gár-īyas, गरिष्ठ gár-iṣṭha; लघु lagh-ú, 'light': लघीयस् lágh-īyas, लघिष्ठ lághiṣṭha (Gk. *ἐ-λάχ-ιστος*); दूर dū-rá, 'far': दवीयस् dáv-īyas; वर vár-a, 'choice': वरीयस् vár-īyas, 'better'; क्षुद्र kṣud-rá, 'mean': क्षोदीयस् kṣód-īyas; युवन् yú-van, 'young': यवीयस् yáv-īyas; ह्रस्व hras-va, 'short': ह्रसीयस् hrás-īyas; with irregular radical syllable: दीर्घ dīrgh-á, 'long': द्राघीयस् drā́gh-īyas; बहुल bah-u-lá, 'abundant': बंहीयस् báṃh-īyas.

a. In some cases यस् yas is attached (instead of ईयस् īyas); — e.g. ज्यायस् jyā́-yas, 'superior,' ज्येष्ठ jyéṣṭha (root ज्या jyā); भूयस् bhū́-yas, 'more,' भूयिष्ठ bhū́-y-iṣṭha (root भू bhū); प्रेयस् pré-yas, 'dearer,' प्रेष्ठ pré-ṣṭha (root प्री prī); श्रेयस् śré-yas, 'better' (Gk. *κρείων*), श्रेष्ठ śré-ṣṭha; स्थिर sthi-rá, 'firm': स्थेयस् sthé-yas.

b. Some comparatives and superlatives belong only in sense to their positives; — e.g. नेदीयस् néd-īyas, नेदिष्ठ néd-iṣṭha, 'nearest,' to अन्तिक antiká, 'near'; कनीयस् kán-īyas, 'lesser,' कनिष्ठ kán-iṣṭha, 'least,' to अल्प álpa, 'small'; वर्षीयस् várṣ-īyas, 'older,' वर्षिष्ठ várṣ-iṣṭha, 'oldest,' to वृद्ध vṛddhá, 'old.'

NUMERALS.

104. Cardinals.

1	१ एक é-ka.	4	४ चतुर् catúr (quatour).
2	२ द्व dvá.[2]	5	५ पञ्च páñca (*πέντε*)
3	३ त्रि trí (Gk. *τρι-*, Lat. tri-)	6	६ षष् ṣáṣ (sex).
		7	७ सप्त saptá (*ἑπτά*)

1. By assimilation for original गरु gar-ú, cp. Gk. *βαρ-ύ-s*, Lat. grâv-i-s.
2. As first member of a compound द्वि dvi.

8 ८ अष्ट aṣṭá (ὀκτώ).
9 ९ नव náva (novem).
10 १० दश dáśa (δέκα).
11 ११ एकादश ékā-daśa.
12 १२ द्वादश dvā́-daśa[1] (δώδεκα).
13 १३ त्रयोदश tráyo-daśa[2].
14 १४ चतुर्दश cátur-daśa.
15 १५ पञ्चदश páñca-daśa.
16 १६ षोडश ṣóḍaśa[3].
17 १७ सप्तदश saptá-daśa.
18 १८ अष्टादश aṣṭā́-daśa.
19 १९ नवदश náva-daśa.
ऊनविंशति ūna-viṃśati.
20 २० विंशति viṃśatí (viginti).
21 २१ एकविंशति éka-viṃśati.
22 २२ द्वाविंशति dvā́-viṃśati.
23 २३ त्रयोविंशति tráyo-viṃśati[2].
28 २८ अष्टाविंशति aṣṭā́-viṃśati.
29 २९ नवविंशति náva-viṃśati.
ऊनत्रिंशत् ūna-triṃśat.
30 ३० त्रिंशत् triṃśát.
39 ३९ नवत्रिंशत् náva-triṃśat.
ऊनचत्वारिंशत् ūna-catvāriṃśat.
40 ४० चत्वारिंशत् catvāriṃśát[4].
49 ४९ नवचत्वारिंशत् náva-catvāriṃśat.
ऊनपञ्चाशत् ūna-pañcāśat.
50 ५० पञ्चाशत् pañcā-śát.
60 ६० षष्टि ṣaṣ-ṭí.
70 ७० सप्तति sapta-tí.
80 ८० अशीति aśītí.
82 ८२ द्व्यशीति dvy-aśīti.
90 ९० नवति nava-tí.
96 ९६ षण्णवति ṣáṇ-ṇavati.
100 १०० शतम् śatám (centum).
101 १०१ एकशतम् éka-śatam.
एकाधिकं शतम् ekādhikaṃ śatam.
102 १०२ द्विशतम् dví-śatam.
द्व्यधिकं शतम् dvy-adhikaṃ śatam.

---

1. Here द्वा dvā is an old dual: 'two (and) ten.'
2. Trayo for trayaḥ (45, 2) is the nom. plur. (105).
3. For ṣáṣ-daśa, through ṣáẓ-ḍaśa (cp. 69*b*, foot-note 2).
4. Catvārim for catvāri (105), neut. plur., like triṃ-śat.

103 १०३ त्रिशतम् trí-śatam.
त्र्यधिकं शतम् try-adhikaṃ śatam.
110 ११० दशशतम् dáśa-śatam.
दशाधिकं शतम् daśādhikaṃ śatam.
200 २०० द्वे शते dve śate
द्विशतम् dvi-śatám.
300 ३०० त्रीणि शतानि trīni śatāni.
त्रिशतम् tri-śatám.
1000 १००० दश शतानि daśa śatāni.
सहस्रम् sahásram.
100,000 लक्ष lakṣá (lakh).
1,000,000 नियुतम् niyutam.
10,000,000 कोटि kóṭi (crore).

a. In order to form the numbers from 20 to 100 not enumerated above, it is only necessary to remember that 2, 3, and 8 are द्वा dvā (*δύω*), त्रयः trayaḥ (*τρεῖς*), and अष्टा aṣṭā (*ὀκτώ*) before 20 and 30 (द्वात्रिंशत् dvā́-triṃśat, त्रयस्त्रिंशत् tráyas-triṃśat, अष्टात्रिंशत् aṣṭā́-triṃśat), and द्वि dvi, त्रि tri, अष्ट aṣṭa before 80; both forms may be used with 40, 50, 60, 70 and 90.

b. The alternative designations of 19, 29, &c. are formed with the old past participle ऊन ū-na, 'diminished'; — e.g. ऊनविंशति ūna-viṃśati, 'twenty diminished (by one).' By prefixing the necesary cardinal to this participle, other alternatives may be formed; — e.g. त्र्यूनत्रिंशत् try-ūna-triṃśat, 'thirty diminished by three,' i.e. 27.

c. Similarly alternatives to 101, 102, &c. are formed by means of the adjective अधिक adhi-ka, 'exceeding,' 'plus'; — e.g. द्व्यधिकं शतम् dvi-adhikaṃ śatam, 'a hundred exceeded by two.'

d. The difference of senses in द्विशतम् dvi-śatam, त्रिशतम् tri-śatam, &c. is only to be distinguished by the accent, these compounds meaning 102, 103, &c., when accented on the first member, but 200, 300 &c., when accented on the last.

Declension of Cardinals.

105. Only the first four cardinals distinguish the genders.

1. एकः ékaḥ, एका ékā, एकम् ékam, following the declension of the pronominal adjectives, is inflected like सर्व sarva (120 *b*).

2. द्व dvá, 'two,' is declined like the dual of कान्त kānta: N.A. m. द्वौ dváu, f. द्वे dvé, n. द्वे dvé; I.D.Ab. द्वाभ्याम् dvā́bhyām, G.L. द्वयोः dvá-y-oḥ.

3. त्रि trí, in the masc. and neut., is declined like the plural of शुचि śuc-i, except in the gen., which is formed as if from त्रय traya (the regular form त्रीणाम् trī-ṇ-ā́m is found in the Rig-veda). Its fem. stem is तिसृ tisṛ́, the inflexion of which differs in the N.A.G. from that of the regular stems in ऋ ṛ.

4. चतुर् catúr, 'four,' in the masc. and neut., has the strong stem चत्वार् catvā́r (cp. quatuor). The G.pl., though the stem ends in a consonant, inserts न् n before the ending (like षट् ṣaṭ). The feminine stem is चतसृ cátasṛ, which is inflected exactly like तिसृ tisṛ́.

	MASC.	NEUT.	FEM.	MASC.	NEUT.	FEM.
N.V.	त्रयः tráy-aḥ	त्रीणि trī́ṇi	तिस्रः tisr-**áḥ**	चत्वारः cat**vā́r**-aḥ	चत्वारि cat**vā́r**-i	चतस्रः cátas**r-aḥ**
A.	त्रीन् trī́n	त्रीणि trī́ṇi	तिस्रः tisr-**áḥ**	चतुरः catúr-aḥ	चत्वारि cat**vā́r**-i	चतस्रः cátas**r-aḥ**
I.	त्रिभिः tri-bhíḥ		तिसृभिः tisṛ́-bhiḥ	चतुर्भिः catúr-bhiḥ		चतसृभिः catasṛ́-bhiḥ
D.Ab.	त्रिभ्यः tri-bhyáḥ		तिसृभ्यः tisṛ́-bhyaḥ	चतुर्भ्यः catúr-bhyaḥ		चतसृभ्यः catasṛ́-bhyaḥ
G.	त्रयाणाम् **trayāṇā́m**		तिसृणाम् tisṛ-ṇā́m (cp. 101b)	चतुर्णाम् catur-**ṇā́m**		चतसृणाम् cataṣṛ-ṇā́m
L.	त्रिषु tri-ṣú (τρι-σι)		तिसृषु tisṛ́-ṣu	चतुर्षु catúr-ṣu		चतसृषु catasṛ́-ṣu

106. ***a.*** षष् ṣáṣ, 'six': N.A. षट् ṣáṭ (27), I. षड्भि: ṣaḍ-bhíḥ, D.Ab. षड्भ्य: ṣaḍ-bhyáḥ, G. षराणाम् ṣaṇ-ṇā́m (65), L. षट्सु ṣaṭ-sú.

b. पञ्च páñca, 'five,' is declined like a neuter in अन् an (90, 2) except in the gen., where it follows कान्त kānta:— N.A. पञ्च páñca, I. पञ्चभि: pañcá-bhiḥ, D.Ab. पञ्चभ्य: pañca-bhyaḥ, G. पञ्चानाम् pañcā-n-ā́m, L. पञ्चसु pañcá-su.

The numerals for 7 to 10 are declined in exactly the same way. अष्ट aṣṭá, however, has also the following alternative (older) forms: — N.A. अष्टौ aṣṭáu, I. अष्टाभि: aṣṭā-bhíḥ, D.Ab. अष्टाभ्य: aṣṭā-bhyáḥ, L. अष्टासु: aṣṭā-sú[1].

c. The cardinals 3 to 19 are used as plural adjectives, agreeing with their substantives in number and case (3 and 4 in gender also). The cardinals from 20 to 99 (which are feminine), as well as शतम् śatám and सहस्रम् sahásram, are used as singular substantives, the accompanying substantive being either in the same case or in the genitive; — e.g. शतेन दासीभि: or दासीनाम् śatena dāsībhiḥ or dāsīnām, 'with a hundred female slaves.'

Ordinals.

107. The ordinals from 'first' to 'tenth' are formed with various suffixes : थ tha (for original त ta), म ma, य ya, ईय īya, or a combination of the first with the second and fourth (थम thama, तीय t-īya); those from 'eleventh' to 'nineteenth' have the same form as the cardinals (excepting both inflexion like कान्त kānta and change to accent); while those from 'twentieth' onward either abbreviate the cardinal or add the suffix तम tama

1. अष्टौ aṣṭáu and अष्टा aṣṭā́ (ὀκτώ, Lat. octō, Gothic ahtáu) are old dual forms, meaning probably 'the two tetrads' (perhaps with reference to the fingers of the two hands).

to it. The **feminine** of all but 'first' to 'fourth' is formed with ई ī.

1st प्रथम: pra-thamáḥ, f. ā́.

2nd द्वितीय: dvi-tī́yaḥ, f. ā (from an older dvi-tá).

3rd तृतीय: tṛ-tī́yaḥ, f.ā (Lat. ter-tius).

4th चतुर्थ: catur-tháḥ, f. ī́ (*τέταρ-τος*, quar-tus);
तुरीय: tur-ī́yaḥ, f. ā (for k-tur-iya);
तुर्य: tur-yaḥ, f. ā (for k-tur-ya).

5th पञ्चम: pañca-máḥ, f. ī́.

6th षष्ठ: ṣaṣ-ṭháḥ (sex-tus).

7th सप्तम: sapta-máḥ (septimus).

8th अष्टम: aṣṭa-máḥ.

9th नवम: nava-máḥ.

10th दशम: daśa-máḥ (decimus).

11th एकादश: ekādaśáḥ.

19th { नवदश: navadaśáḥ.
ऊनविंश: ūnaviṃśaḥ.

20th { विंश: viṃśáḥ.
विंशतितम: viṃśati-tamáḥ.

30th { त्रिंश: triṃśáḥ.
त्रिंशत्तम: triṃśat-tamáḥ.

40th { चत्वारिंश: catvāriṃśáḥ.
चत्वारिंशत्तम: catvāriṃśat-tamaḥ

50th { पञ्चाश: pañcāśáḥ.
पञ्चाशत्तम: pañcāśat-tamáḥ.

60th षष्टितम: ṣaṣṭi-tamaḥ.

61st एकषष्ट: eka-ṣaṣṭáḥ.

70th सप्ततितम: saptati-tamaḥ.

71st { एकसप्ततितम: ekasaptati-tamaḥ.
एकसप्तत: eka-saptataḥ.

80th अशीतितम: aśīti-tamaḥ.

81st { एकाशीतितम: ekāśīti-tamaḥ
एकाशीत: ekāśītaḥ.

90th नवतितम: navati-tamaḥ.

91st { एकनवतितम: eka-navati-tamaḥ.
एकनवत: eka-navataḥ.

100th शततम: śata-tamáḥ.

Numeral Adverbs and other Derivatives.

108. ***a.* Multiplicative adverbs:** — सकृत् sa-kṛ́t, 'once' (lit. 'one making'); द्विः dví-ḥ, 'twice' (GK. *δί-s* Lat. bi-s); त्रिः trí-ḥ, 'thrice' (Gk. *τρί-s,* Lat. tri-s); चतुः catúḥ, 'four times' for catúr-s); पञ्चकृत्वः pañca-kṛtváḥ, 'five times' (lit. 'five makings'); षट्कृत्वः ṣaṭ-kṛtváḥ, 'six times'; &c.

***b.* Adverbs of manner :—** एकधा eka-dhā́, 'in one way'; द्विधा dvi-dhā́ or द्वेधा dve-dhā́, 'in two ways'; त्रिधा trí-dhā or त्रेधा tre-dhā́, 'in three ways'; चतुर्धा catur-dhā́, 'in four ways'; पञ्चधा pañca-dhā́, 'in five ways'; षोढा ṣo-ḍhā́, 'in six ways' (cp. 104, foot-note 3); सप्तधा sapta-dhā́, 'in seven ways'; अष्टधा aṣṭa-dhā́, 'in eight ways'; &c.

***c.* Distributive adverbs :—** एकशः eka-śaḥ, 'singly'; द्विशः dvi-śaḥ, 'in pairs'; त्रिशः tri-śaḥ, 'in threes'; पञ्चशः pañca-śaḥ, 'by fives'; &c.

***d.* Aggregative nouns :—** द्वय dvay-á, adj. 'twofold'; n. 'a pair'; त्रय tray-á, adj., f. -í́, 'threefold'; n., í́, f., and त्रितय tri-taya, n. 'triad'; चतुष्टय cátuṣ-ṭaya, adj. 'fourfold'; n. 'tetrad'; पञ्चतय pañca-taya, adj. 'fivefold'; अष्टतय aṣṭa-taya,' adj. 'eightfold'; n. 'ogdoad'; दशतय dáśa-taya, adj. 'tenfold'; n. 'decade'; &c.

PRONOUNS.

109. A. Personal Pronouns.

Stem (in composition) मद् mad (sing.) and अस्मद् asmad (plur.)	Stem (in composition) त्वद् tvad (sing.) and युष्मद् yuṣmad (plur.)

SINGULAR.

N.	अहम् ahám, 'I'	त्वम् tv-ám, 'thou'
A.	माम् mā́m, 'me'	त्वाम् tvā́m, 'thee'

I.	मया má-y-ā, 'by me'	त्वया tvá-y-ā, 'by thee'
D.	मह्यम् má-**h**yam (mi**hi**), 'to me'	तुभ्यम् tú-**bh**yam (ti**bi**), 'to thee'
Ab.	मद् **mád**, 'from me'	त्वद् tv**ád**, 'from thee'
G.	मम má-ma, 'of me'	तव táva, 'of thee'
L.	मयि má-y-i, 'in me'	त्वयि tvá-y-i, 'in thee'

DUAL.

NA.	आवाम् āvā́m, 'we or us two'	युवाम् yuvā́m, 'ye or you two'
I.D.Ab.	आवाभ्याम् āvā́-bhyām, 'by, to, or from us two'	युवाभ्याम् yuvā́-bhyām, 'by, to, or from you two'
G.I.	आवयोः āvá-y-oḥ, 'of or in us two'	युवयोः yuvá-y-oḥ, 'of or in you two'

PLURAL.

N.	वयम् vay-ám, 'we'	यूयम् yū-y-ám[1], 'ye'
A.	अस्मान् asmā́n, 'us'	युष्मान् yuṣmā́n, 'you'
I.	अस्माभिः asm**ā́**-bhiḥ, 'by us'	युष्माभिः yuṣm**ā́**-bhiḥ, 'by you'
D.	अस्मभ्यम् asmá-bhya**m**, 'to us'	युष्मभ्यम् yuṣmá-bhya**m**, 'to you'
Ab.	अस्मद् asm**ád**, 'from us'	युष्मद् yuṣm**ád**, 'from you'
G.	अस्माकम् asm**ā́ka**-m[2], 'of us'	युष्माकम् yuṣm**ā́ka**-m[2], 'of you'
L.	अस्मासु asm**ā́**-su, 'in us'	युष्मासु yuṣm**ā́**-su, 'in you'

---

1. Changed from original यूषम् yū́ṣ-ám by the the influence of वयम् vay-ám.
2. These are properly not genitives at all, but neuter singulars of possessive adjectives, meaning 'belonging to us, our,' 'belonging to you, your,' which have come to be used as genitives. Similarly in German, a case of possessive pronouns, *mein, dein, sein*, came to be employed as the gen. of personal pronouns.

a. The following unaccented forms, which are not allowed at the beginning of a sentence, are also used: Sing. A. मा mā, त्वा tvā; D.G. मे me (μοι), ते te (τοι). Dual. A.D.G. नौ nau (Gk. νῶι), वाम् vām. Plur. A.D.G. नः naḥ (Lat. nōs), वः vaḥ (Lat. vōs).

B. Demonstrative Pronouns.

110. The stem त **ta** (in composition तद् ta-d), 'that' (also = 'he, she, it'), may be taken as the type of the pronominal declension:—

	SINGULAR.			PLURAL.		
	MASC.	NEUT.	FEM.	MASC.	NEUT.	FEM.
N.	सः **sáḥ**[1]	तद् tá-**d**	सा **sá**	ते té (τοι)	तानि tā́ni	ताः tā́ḥ
A.	तम् tám	तद् tá-**d**	ताम् tā́m	तान् tā́n	तानि tā́ni	ताः tā́ḥ
I.	तेन téna		तया tá-yā	तैः táiḥ (τοῖς)		ताभिः tā́-bhiḥ
D.	तस्मै tá-**smai**		तस्यै tá-**syai**	तेभ्यः té-bhyaḥ		ताभ्यः tā́-bhyaḥ
Ab.	तस्मात् tá-**smāt**		तस्याः tá-**syāḥ** (Ab., G.)	तेषाम् té-ṣām[3] (G.)		तासाम् tā́-sām[4] (G.)
G.	तस्य tá-sya[2]					
L.	तस्मिन् tá-**smin**		तस्याम् tá-**syām**	तेषु té-ṣu		तासु tā́-su

DUAL.

N.A.m. तौ táu, f. ते té, n. ते té.

I.D.Ab.m.f.n. ताभ्याम् tā́-bhyām; G.L. तयोः tá-y-oḥ.

a. A compound of त ta, 'that,' is एत **e-tá**, 'this.' It is declined exactly like the former: Sing. N. एषः eṣá-ḥ (48, 67), एषा eṣā́, एतद् etá-d; A. एतम् etá-m, एताम् etā́-m, एतद् etá-d, &c.

---

1. Cp. 48; sá, sā, ta-d = Gk. ὁ, η, τό, Gothic sa, sō, that-a (Engl. that, Lat. is-tud).
2. Hom. Gk. τοῖο (for τόσιο).
3. Lat. is-tōrum.
4. Lat. is-tārum, Gk. τάων (for τάσων).

111. Both the pronominal roots अ **a** and इ **i** (which here in some cases show a double inflexion) are employed in the declension of अयम् **a-y-ám**, 'this' (indefinitely):—

SINGULAR.

	MASC.	NEUT.	FEM.
N.	अयम् a-y-ám	इदम् **i-d**-ám	इयम् i-y-ám
A.	इमम् **i-m**-ám	इदम् **i-d**-ám	इमाम् **i-m**-ā́m
I.	अनेन **an**-éna		अनया **an**-áyā
D.	अस्मै a-smái		अस्यै a-syái
Ab.	अस्मात् a-smā́t		अस्याः a-syā́ḥ
G.	अस्य a-syá		अस्याः a-syā́ḥ
L.	अस्मिन् a-smín		अस्याम् a-syā́m

PLURAL.

	MASC.	NEUT.	FEM.
N.	इमे **i-m**-é	इमानि **i-m**-ā́ni	इमाः **i-m**-ā́ḥ
A.	इमान् **i-m**-ā́n	इमानि **i-m**-ā́ni	इमाः **i-m**-ā́ḥ
I.	एभिः **e**-bhíḥ		आभिः ā-bhíḥ
D.Ab.	एभ्यः e-bhyáḥ		आभ्यः ā-bhyáḥ
G.	एषाम् e-ṣā́m		आसाम् ā-sā́m
L.	एषु e-ṣú		आसु ā-sú

DUAL.

N.A. m. इमौ **i-m**-áu, f. इमे **i-m**-é, n. इमे **i-m**-é.

I.D.Ab.m.f.n. आभ्याम् ā-bhyā́m; G.L. अनयोः **an**-áyoḥ.

112. The demonstrative pronoun, which in the nom. sing. has the curious form m. f. **असौ a-s-áu**, n. अदस् a-d-ás, meaning 'that,' 'you,' employs in the rest of its declension the stem **अमु a-m-u**, for which **अमू a-m-ū** is substituted in the **fem. plur.** (also acc. sing. and partly in dual) and **अमी a-m-ī** in the **masc. plur.** (except the acc.).

SINGULAR.

	MASC.	NEUT.	FEM.
N.	असौ a-s-**áu**	अदः a-d-áḥ	असौ a-s-**áu**
A.	अमुम् a-m-ú-m	अदः a-d-áḥ	अमूम् a-m-ū́-m
I.	अमुना amú-n-ā		अमुया amú-y-ā
D.	अमुष्मै amú-ṣmai		अमुष्यै amú-ṣyai
Ab.	अमुष्मात् amú-ṣmāt		अमुष्याः amú-ṣyāḥ
G.	अमुष्य amú-ṣya		अमुष्याः amú-ṣyāḥ
L.	अमुष्मिन् amú-ṣmin		अमुष्याम् amú-ṣyām

PLURAL.

	MASC.	NEUT.	FEM.
N.	अमी amī́	अमूनि amū́ni	अमूः amū́-ḥ
A.	अमून् amū́n	अमूनि amū́ni	अमूः amū́-ḥ
I.	अमीभिः amī́-bhiḥ		अमूभिः amū́-bhiḥ
D.Ab.	अमीभ्यः amī́-bhyaḥ		अमूभ्यः amū́-bhyaḥ
G.	अमीषाम् amī́-ṣām		अमूषाम् amū́-ṣām
L.	अमीषु amī́-ṣu		अमूषु amū́-ṣu

DUAL.

N.A.m.f.n. अमू amū́; I.D.Ab. अमूभ्याम् amū́-bhyām; G.L. अमुयोः amú-y-oḥ.

a. The unaccented defective pronoun of the third person, एन ena ('he, she, it'), is declined in the A. of all numbers, I. sg., and G.L. dual: A. एनम् ena-m, एनाम् enā-m, एनद् ena-d; एनौ enau, एने ene, एने ene; एनान् enā-n, एना: enā-ḥ, एनानि enāni; I.sg. एनेन enena, f. एनया ena-y-ā; G.L. du. एनयो: ena-y-oḥ.

C. Interrogative Pronoun.

113. The stem of the interrogative pronoun क **ka**, 'who, which, what?' is inflected exactly like त ta, excepting that the N.A. neuter is किम् kí-m; — e.g. N. क: káḥ, का kā́, किम् kím; plur. के ké, का: kā́ḥ, कानि kā́ni. L. sg. कस्मिन् ká-smin, f. कस्याम् ká-syām; pl. केषु ké-ṣu, f. कासु kā́-su.

a. In derivation the stems कि ki and कु ku, as well as क ka, are used; — e.g. कियत् ki-y-at, 'how great?' कुत्र ku-tra, 'where?' कदा ka-dā, 'when?' As the first member of a compound किम् kim is generally employed, sometimes कु ku: किंरूप kiṃ-rūpa, adj. 'of what form?' कुकर्मन् ku-karman, n. ('what kind of' =) 'wicked deed.'

D. Relative Pronoun.

114. The stem of the relative pronoun य **ya**, 'who,' 'which,' is declined exactly like त ta:—

	SING.			PLUR.		
N.	य: yá-ḥ	या yā́	यद् yá-d	ये yé	या: yā́ḥ	यानि yā́ni
A.	यम् yá-m	याम् yā́-m	यद् yá-d	यान् yā́n	या: yā́ḥ	यानि yā́ni
D.	यस्मै yá-smai	यस्यै yá-syai	यस्मै yá-smai	येभ्य: yé-bhyaḥ	याभ्य: yā́-bhyaḥ	येभ्य: yé-bhyaḥ

E. Reflexive Pronouns.

115. ***a.*** स्वयम् sva-y-ám, 'self,' is indeclinable (originally á nom. sing. like a-y-ám). It may express any person or number (e.g. 'myself,' 'himself,' 'yourselves'). It usually has the meaning of a nominative, but often of an instrumental, and sometimes of a genitive. It frequently also means 'spontaneously.'

b. आत्मन् ātmán, 'self,' is a masc. substantive (declined like ब्रह्मन् brahman, 90, 3). It is used in the singular as a reflexive pronoun of all persons and genders.

c. स्वः sváḥ, स्वा svā́, स्वम् svám (Lat. suus), 'own,' is a reflexive adjective (declined like सर्व sarva, 120*b*) referring to all three persons and numbers ('my, thy, his, our, your, their own'). It is also used (like आत्मन् ātman) in the oblique cases as a reflexive pronoun; — e.g. स्वं निन्दन्ति svaṃ nindanti, 'they blame themselves.'

d. निज ni-ja, properly an adjective meaning 'inborn,' 'native,' is often used in the sense of a pronominal reflexive adjective (like स्व sva).

F. Possessive Pronouns.

116. Possessives are formed with the suffix ईय īya, from the stems of the personal pronouns मद् mad, त्वद् tvad, &c.: मदीय mad-īya, 'my,' त्वदीय tvad-īya, 'thy'; अस्मदीय asmad-īya, 'our,' युष्मदीय yuṣmad-īya, 'your'; तदीय tad-īya, 'his, her, its, their.'

a. With the suffix क ka are formed from the genitives मम mama and तव tava, मामक māma-ká, 'my,' and तावक tāva-ka, 'thy' (cp. 109, foot-note 2); from भवत् bhavat, 'your Honour,' भावत्क bhāvat-ka, 'your.'

G. Compound Pronouns.

117. By adding दृश् dṛś, दृश dṛśa, or दृक्ष dṛkṣa, to certain pronominal stems, the following compound pronouns have been formed: — तादृश् tā-dṛ́ś, तादृश tā-dṛ́śa, तादृक्ष tā-dṛ́kṣa, 'such'

(lit. 'of that look'); याद्दृश् yā-dṛ́ś, यादृश yā-dṛ́śa, 'what like,' 'of what kind'; ईदृश् ī-dṛ́ś, ईदृश ī-dṛ́śa, ईदृक्ष ī-dṛ́kṣa, 'such'; कीदृश् kī-dṛ́ś, कीदृश kī-dṛ́śa, 'what like?'; मादृश mā-dṛśa, 'like me,' त्वादृश tvā-dṛśa, 'like thee.'

a. The **feminine** stem of the compounds in दृश् dṛś is the same as the masc. and neut.; — e.g. nom. sing. m. f. n. तादृक् tādṛ́k; that of the compounds in दृश dṛśa is formed with ई ī; — e.g. तादृशी tādṛśī; of those in दृक्ष dṛkṣa with आ ā; — e.g. तादृक्षा tādṛkṣā.

118. By adding वत् vat and यत् yat to certain pronominal stems, the following compounds, implying quantity, have been formed: — तावत् tā́-vat and एतावत् etā́-vat, 'so much'; यावत् yā́-vat, 'as much'; इयत् í-yat, 'so much,' कियत् kí-yat, 'how much?' These are all declined like nouns in वत् vat (86), and form their **feminines** in the same way (तावती tāvat-ī, इयती iyat-ī, &c.).

a. कति ká-ti, 'how many?' (Lat. quot), तति tá-ti, 'so many' (Lat. toti-dem), यति yá-ti, 'as many,' are uninflected in the N.A., but in the other cases are declined like शुचि śuci (98) in the plural.

119. The interrogative क ka, by the addition of चित् cit, चन cana, or अपि api, is changed to an indefinite pronoun, 'some,' 'some one': कश्चित् kaś cit, काचित् kā cit, किंचित् kiṃ cit; कश्चन kaś cana, काचन kā cana, किंचन kiṃ cana; कोऽपि ko'pi, कापि kāpi, किमपि kim api.

a. In the same manner indefinite adverbs are formed: कदा ka-dā, 'when?' कदाचित् kadā cit, कदाचन kadā cana, 'some time or other,' 'once'; क्व kva, 'where?' न क्वापि na kvāpi, 'not anywhere,' 'nowhere.'

b. The relative preceding the interrogative renders it indefinite: यः कः yaḥ kaḥ, 'whosoever'; यस्य कस्य yasya kasya, 'of

whomsoever.' Similarly यः कश्चित् yaḥ kaścit, यः कश्च yaḥ kaśca, or यः कश्चन yaḥ kaścana, 'whosoever.'

c. The relative pronoun, if doubled, assumes a distributive meaning: यो यः yo yaḥ, 'whoever, whatever in each case' (followed by a double correlative).

H. Pronominal Adjectives.

120. Several adjectives derived from, or allied in meaning to, pronouns, follow the pronominal declension (like त ta) either altogether or in part.

a. अन्य anyá, 'other,' अन्यतर anya-tará, 'either,' इतर í-tara, 'other,' कतर ka-tará, 'which of two?' कतम ka-tamá, 'which of many?' एकतम eka-tamá, 'one (of many),' follow the pronominal declension throughout, taking द् d in the N.V.A. sing. neut.; अन्यः anyá-ḥ, अन्या anyā́, अन्यद् anyá-d (cp. Lat. aliu-d); D. अन्यस्मै anyá-smai, f. अन्यस्यै anyá-syai, L. अन्यस्मिन् anyá-smin; &c.

b. सर्व sárva, 'every,' 'all,' उभय ubhá-ya, 'both' (sg. and pl.)[1], एक éka, 'one' (105), एकतर eka-tara, 'either,' differ only in taking म् m instead of द् d in the N.A. sing. neut; — e.g. सर्वः sárva-ḥ, सर्वा sárvā, सर्वम् sárva-m; D. सर्वस्मै sárva-smai, Ab. सर्वस्मात् sárva-smāt, G. सर्वस्य sárva-sya, L. सर्वस्मिन् sárva-smin; pl. N. सर्वे sárve, सर्वाः sárvāḥ, सर्वाणि sárvāṇi.

c. पूर्व pū́rva, 'prior,' 'east,' अवर áva-ra, 'posterior,' 'west,' अधर ádha-ra, 'inferior,' 'west,' उत्तर út-tara, 'subsequent,' 'north,' दक्षिण dákṣiṇa, 'south,' पर pára, 'subsequent,' 'other,' अपर ápa-ra, 'other,' 'inferior,' अन्तर ánta-ra, 'outer,' स्व svá, 'own,' besides necessarily taking म् m in the N.A. sing. neut., *may* follow the nominal declension in the Ab. L. sing. m. n.

1. But उभ ubhá, 'both,' is declined in the dual only (like कान्त kānta).

and in the N. plur. masc.; — e.g. N.A.n. पूर्वम् pū́rva-m; Ab. m.n. पूर्वस्मात् pū́rva-smāt or पूर्वात् pū́rvāt; L. पूर्वस्मिन् pū́rva-smin or पूर्वे pū́rve; N. pl. m. पूर्वे pū́rve or पूर्वाः pū́rvāḥ.

d. अर्ध ardhá, 'half,' अल्प álpa, 'little,' कतिपय kati-payá, 'some,' प्रथम prá-thama, 'first,' चरम cara-má, 'last,' द्वय dva-yá and द्वितय dví-taya, 'twofold' (and similar words in य ya and तय taya), are inflected like ordinary adjectives, except that they *may* follow the pronominal declension in the N. pl. masc.; — e.g. चरमाः caramā́ḥ or चरमे caramé.

e. द्वितीय dvitī́ya, 'second,' and तृतीय tṛtī́ya, 'third,' *may* follow the pronominal declension throughout the oblique cases of the singular; — e.g. D.m.n. तृतीयाय tṛtī́yāya or तृतीयस्मै tṛtī́ya-smai; L.f. तृतीयायाम् tṛtī́yā-yām or तृतीयस्याम् tṛtī́ya-syām; but N. pl. m. only तृतीयाः tṛtī́yāḥ.

f. Any of these pronominal words occurring at the end of possessive compounds (189) are declined like ordinary adjectives.

CHAPTER IV

CONJUGATION

121. Sanskrit verbs are inflected with either active or middle terminations. The **active** voice is called **Parasmai-pada,** i.e. transitive (lit. 'word for another'). The **middle** voice is called **Ātmane-pada,** i.e. reflexive (lit. 'word for oneself'). The **passive** takes the terminations of the Ātmanepada; with which it coincides except in the present and imperfect (where it forms its stem with the suffix य ya), and in the third sing. aorist.

a. The Sanskrit verb has in each tense and mood **three numbers,** Singular, Dual, and Plural, with three persons in each.

122. There are in Sanskrit **five tenses** conjugated in the indicative: 1. Present (with imperative and objective moods); 2. Imperfect; 3. Perfect; 4. Aorist (with a kind of optative called Benedictive or Precative); 5. Future (with the Conditional, a kind of past future).

There are also **participles** connected with three of these tenses, present, perfect, and future; and one **infinitive** (167), a verbal noun unconnected with any tense.

a. Classical Sanskrit has neither a pluperfect tense nor a subjunctive mood (excepting the survivals of it in the first persons imperative); nor has it an imperative or a proper optative of any tense except the present. There are, therefore, far fewer verbal forms in non-Vedic Sanskrit than in Greek.

The Present System.

123. While the perfect, aorist, and future tenses add the terminations directly (or after inserting a sibilant) to the root, the present group (the present with its moods and the imperfect) forms a special stem, which is made in ten different ways. Hence the native Sanskrit grammarians have divided all verbs into ten classes. The tenth class, which is really a secondary formation, retains its present stem in nearly all the other verbal forms also, as do the secondary verbs generally (causatives, desideratives, intensives, denominatives).

The Ten Classes.

124. The ten classes are divided into **two conjugations.** In the first, comprising the first, fourth, sixth, and tenth classes, the present stem ends in अ a, and remains unchanged throughout.

In the second conjugation, which comprises all the remaining classes, the terminations are added directly to the final

of the root or to the suffixes उ u, नु nu, ना nā, (नी nī, न् n), and the **present stem is changeable,** being either **strong or weak.**

A. First Conjugation.

125. 1. The **first** or **Bhū** class adds अ a to the last letter of the root, which, being accented, takes Guṇa of a final vowel (short or long) and of a short medial vowel followed by one consonant; — e.g. भू bhū, 'be,' forms the present stem भव bháv-a; बुध् budh, 'know': बोध bódh-a.

2. The **sixth** or **Tud** class adds an accented अ á to the root, which (being unaccented) has no Guṇa. Before this अ á final ॠ ṝ changes to इर् ir. Thus तुद् tud, 'strike': तुद् tud-á: कॄ kṝ, 'scatter': किर kir-a.

3. The **fourth** or **Div** class adds य ya to the last letter of the root, which is accented (but the weak form in some cases assumed by the root points to the य ya having originally been accented); — e.g. नह् nah, 'bind': नह्य náh-ya; दिव् div, 'play': दीव्य dī́v-ya (133 B).

4. The **tenth** or **Cur** class adds the suffix अय áya, before which a final vowel takes Vṛddhi, but a short medial vowel followed by one consonant takes Guṇa; — e.g. चुर् cur, 'steal': चोरय cor-áya. Short medial अ a followed by one consonant is in most cases lengthened; — e.g. कम् kam: कामय kām-áya, 'desire.'

B. Second Conjugation.

126. The strong forms are —

1. the singular present and imperfect active;
2. all first persons imperative **active and middle**;
3. the third person singular imperative active.

In these forms the vowel of the root or the affix, being accented, is strengthened; while in the weak forms it becomes short because the terminations are accented.

a. In the ninth class the accented form of the affix is ना nā́, the unaccented नी nī or न् n; in the seventh they are respectively न ná and न् n.

127. 1. The **second** or **Ad** class adds the terminations directly to the root, which in the strong forms takes Guṇa if possible (125, 1); — e.g. अद् ad, 'eat': sing. 1. अद्मि ád-mi, 2. अत्सि át-si, 3. अत्ति át-ti; इ i, 'go': एमि é-mi, एषि é-ṣi, एति é-ti; लिह् lih, 'lick': लेह्मि léh-mi, लेक्षि lé**k**-ṣi (69 *a*), लेढि lé-**ḍhi** (69 *b*).

a. This and the seventh are the most difficult classes to conjugate, because terminations beginning with various consonants come into contact with the final consonants of roots, and consequently many rules of internal Sandhi have to be applied.

2. The **third** or **Hu** class adds the terminations directly to the reduplicated root, which in the strong forms takes Guṇa if possible; — e.g. हु hu, 'sacrifice': जुहोमि ju-hó-mi, 'I sacrifice'; जुहुमः ju-hu-máḥ, 'we sacrifice.'

a. The intensives conjugated in the active (172) follow this class.

3. The **seventh** or **Rudh** class adds the terminations directly to the final consonant, before which न ná is inserted in the strong, and न् n in the weak forms; — e.g. युज् yuj, 'join': युनज्मि yu-ná-j-mi; युञ्ज्मः yuñj-máḥ.

4. The **fifth** or **Su** class adds नु nu, which takes Guṇa in the strong forms, to the root; — e.g. सु su, 'press out': सुनोमि su-nó-mi; सुनुमः su-nu-máḥ.

5. The **eighth** or **Tan** class adds उ u, which takes Guṇa in the strong forms, to the root; — e.g. तन् tan, 'stretch': तनोमि tan-ó-mi; तनुमः tan-u-máḥ.

a. All the (seven) verbs of this class end in न् n, except कृ kṛ, 'do,' which has an irregular present stem: करोमि kar-ó-mi (134 E).

6. The **ninth** or **Krī** class adds to the root ना nā́ in the strong forms, but in the weak नी nī before consonants and न् n

before vowels; — e.g. क्री krī, 'buy': क्रीणामि krī-ṇá-mi; pl. 1. क्रीणीमः krī-ṇī-máḥ, 3. क्रीणन्ति krī-ṇ-ánti.

The Augment.

128. The imperfect, the aorist, and the conditional prefix to the root accented अ á as their augment, **which forms Vṛddhi with an initial vowel** (23); — e.g. बुध् budh, 'know': 3. sing. imperf. अबोधत् á-bodha-t; उन्द् und, 'wet': उनत्ति u-ná-t-ti, 'he wets,' औनत् **áu**-na-t, 'he wetted'; ऋ ṛ, 'go': ऋच्छति ṛcchāti, 'he goes,' आर्च्छत् ā́rcchat, 'he went.'

a. The augment is dropped in the imperf. and aorist (which are then used imperatively) after the prohibitive particle मा mā́ (μή): मा कार्षीत् or करोत् mā kārṣit or karot, 'may be not do it.'

Reduplication.

129. Five verbal formations take reduplication in Sanskrit: the present stem of the third conjugational class, the perfect, one kind of aorist, the desiderative, and the intensive. Each of these five has certain peculiarities, which must be treated separately under the special rules of reduplication (130, 135, 149, 170, 173). Common to all are the following.

General Rules of Reduplication.

1. The first syllable of a root (i.e. that portion of it which ends with a vowel) is reduplicated; — e.g. बुध् budh: बुबुध् bu-budh.

2. Aspirated letters are represented by the corresponding unaspirated; — e.g. भिद् bhid, 'cut': बिभिद् bi-bhid; धू dhū, 'shake': दुधू du-dhū.

3. Gutturals are represented by the corresponding palatals. ह् h by ज् j; — e.g. कम् kam, 'love': चकम् ca-kam; खन् khan, 'dig': चखन् ca-khan; गम् gam, 'go': जगम् ja-gam; हस् has, 'laugh': जहस् ja-has.

4. If the root begins with more than one consonant, the first only is reduplicated; — e.g. क्रुश् kruś, 'shout': चुक्रुश् cu-kruś; क्षिप् kṣip, 'throw'; चिक्षिप् ci-kṣip.

5. If a root begins with a sibilant followed by a hard consonant, the latter is reduplicated; — e.g. स्तु stu, 'praise': तुष्टु tu-ṣṭu (67); स्था sthā, 'stand': तस्था ta-sthā; श्चुत् ścut, 'drip': चुश्चुत् cu-ścut; स्कन्द् skand, 'leap': चस्कन्द् ca-skand. But स्मृ smṛ, 'remember': सस्मृ sa-smṛ (m is soft).

6. If the radical vowel, whether final or medial, is long, it is shortened in the reduplicative syllable; — e.g. गाह् gāḥ, 'enter': जगाह् ja-gāḥ; क्री krī, 'buy': चिक्री ci-krī; कूज् kūj, 'hum': चुकूज् cu-kūj.

7. If the radical (not final) vowel is ए e, it is represented by इ i; if ओ o or औ au, by उ u; — e.g. सेव् sev, 'worship': सिषेव् si-ṣev (67); ढौक् ḍhauk, 'approach': डुढौक् ḍuḍhauk.

8. Roots which, according to the native Sanskrit grammarians, end in ए e, ऐ ai, ओ o are more conveniently stated to end in आ ā, and are so treated in reduplication; — e.g. गै gai, 'sing,' 3. sing. perfect जगौ ja-gau (136, 4).

Special Rule of Reduplication for the Third Class.

130. ऋ ṛ and ॠ ṝ are represented in reduplication by इ i; — भृ bhṛ, 'bear': बिभर्ति bí-bhar-ti; पॄ pṝ, 'fill': पिपर्ति pí-par-ti.

Terminations.

131. The following table gives the terminations, which are on the whole the same for all verbs, of the present system. The chief difference is in the optative, which is characterized by ए e in the first, and या yā́ and ई ī in the second conjugation. It will prevent confusion to remember that the present indicative has the primary (-mi, -si, -ti, &c.), while the imperative (with some variations)

and the optative, as well as the imperfect, have the secondary terminations (-m, -s, -t, &c.). Of the other tenses, the future takes the primary, and the aorist, with the benedictive and the conditional, takes the secondary terminations; while the perfect takes in the active (with many variations) the secondary, and in the middle, the primary endings.

In order to understand clearly the difference between the two conjugations, the following points should be noted. **In the first or a-conjugation** (as in the a-declension), **the accent** is never on the terminations, but always **on** the same syllable of **the stem** (the root in the first and fourth, the affix in the sixth and tenth classes), which therefore remains unchanged. On the other hand, in the second conjugation (as in the declension of changeable stems) the accent falls on the strong stem, which is shortened in the weak forms by the shifting of the accent to the terminations. **In the second conjugation,** therefore, **the terminations are accented** except in the strong forms (126) of the present. The same would apply to the imperfect, were it without an augment (128).

PARASMAIPADA

Present	Imperfect	Optative Ist Conj.	Optative 2nd Conj.	Imperative
1. मि mi[1]	अम् am[2]	एयम् eyam[3]	याम् yā́m	आनि āni
2. सि si	स् s	एस् es	यास् yā́s	— (1) हि hí[4] (2)
3. ति ti	त् t	एत् et	यात् yā́t	तु tu
1. वस् vas[1]	व va[1]	एव eva	याव yā́va	आव āva
2. थस् thas	तम् tam	एतम् etam	यातम् yā́tam	तम् tam
3. तस् tas	ताम् tām	एताम् etām	याताम् yā́tām	ताम् tām
1. मस mas[1]	म ma[1]	एम ema	याम yā́ma	आम āma
2. थ tha	त ta	एत eta	यात् yā́ta	त ta
3. अन्ति anti[5]	अन् an[6]	एयुर् eyur	युर् yúr	अन्तु antu[5]

ĀTMANEPADA

Present	Imperfect	Operative		Imperative
1. ए	ए इ	एय	ईय	ऐ
e	e(1) i(2)	eya[3]	īyá	ai
2. से	थास्	एथास्	ईथास्	स्व
se	thās	ethās	īthā́s	sva
3. ते	त	एत	ईत	ताम्
te	ta	eta	ītá	tām
1. वहे	वहि	एवहि	ईवहि	आवहै
vahe[1]	vahi[1]	evahi	īváhi	āvahai
2. एथे	एथाम्	एयाथाम्	ईयाथाम्	एथाम्
ethe(1)	ethām(1)	eyāthām	īyā́thām	ethām(1)
आथे	आथाम्			आथाम्
ā́the(2)	āthām (2)			ā́thām (2)
3. एते	एताम्	एयाताम्	ईयाताम्	एताम्
ete (1)	etām (1)	eyātām	īyā́tām	etām (1)
आते	आताम्			आताम्
ā́te (2)	ātām (2)			ā́tām (2)
1. महे	महि	एमहि	ईमहि	आमहै
mahe	mahi[1]	emahi	īmáhi	āmahai
2. ध्वे	ध्वम्	एध्वम्	ईध्वम्	ध्वम्
dhve	dhvam	edhvam	īdhvám	dhvam
3. अन्ते	अन्त	एरन्	ईरन्	अन्ताम्
ante (1)	anta(1)	eran	īrán	antām (1)
अते	अत			अताम्
áte (2)	ata (2)			átām (2)

1. The final अ a of the first conjugation is lengthened before म् m or व् v; — e.g. भवामि bhávā-mi, भवाव: bhavā-vaḥ.

2. Terminations beginning with vowels should be added in the first conjugation after dropping the final अ a; — e.g. अभवम् á-bhav-am, भवेत् bháv-et.

3. The terminations of the first conjugation, given in the above table as beginning with ए e, really consist of the final अ a of the base + ई i; but on practical grounds it is preferable to assume that they begin with ए e.

4. Verbs of the first conjugation take no termination in the 2. sing. imperat. Par. (being exactly parallel with the vocative singular of the a-declension). Those of the second take धि dhi (Gk. θι) after consonants, हि hi after vowels. But —

a. in the ninth class आन āna takes the place of धि dhi;— e.g. मथान math-āná[1] (but क्रीणीहि krī-ṇī-hí).

b. हि hi is dropped in the fifth and eighth classes, if the उ u is preceded by a single consonant; -- e.g. सुनु su-nú (but आप्नुहि āp-nu-hí).

c. in the third class हु hu adds धि dhi (instead of हि hi) after a vowel: जुहुधि ju-hu-**dhí**.

5. Verbs of the third class and some other reduplicated present stems (cp. 134 A 4, B; 172) drop the न् n of the 3. plur. pres. indic. and imperat. **Par.** In the **Ātm.** the whole **second conjugation rejects** the **न् n** of the **3. plur.** pres. impf. impv.

6. Verbs of the third class and some other reduplicated stems (cp. 134 A 4, B; 172) take उर् ur instead of अन् an in the 3. plur. impf. Par. Those of the second class which end in आ ā, as well as विद् vid, 'know,' and द्विष् dviṣ, -'hate,' may do so. Before this suffix a final आ ā is dropped, while ई ī, उ u, ऋ ṛ are

1. The origin of this peculiar imperative ending is uncertain. It perhaps stands for -nā-ná: ā being the reduced form (= long nasal sonant) of the class suffix -nā, and na the ending which is found in the Vedic 2. pl. impv.; — e.g. i-ta-na.

guṇated; — e.g. भी bhī, 'fear': अबिभयु: á-bi-bhay-uḥ; अजुहवु: á-ju-hav-uḥ; अयान् á-yā-n or अयु: á-y-uḥ. That the final of this ending (which also appears in the 3. plur. optative and the 3. plur. perf. active) is etymologically र् r, and not स् s, is proved by the corresponding forms in the Avesta.

Paradigms.

132. As the four classes of the first conjugation are inflected exactly alike, one paradigm will suffice for them. The same applies to the fifth and eighth classes. In the second class द्विष् dviṣ has been used for the paradigm, because it illustrates better than अद् ad both the rules of internal Sandhi and the difference between strong and weak forms.

FIRST CONJUGATION

First Class : भू bhū, 'be': Present stem भव bháv-a.

Present.

	PARASMAIPADA			ĀTMANEPADA		
	SINGULAR	DUAL	PLURAL	SINGULAR	DUAL	PLURAL
1.	भवामि	भवावः	भवामः	भवे	भवावहे	भवामहे
	bhávā-mi	bhávā-vaḥ	bhávā-maḥ	bháv-e	bhávā-vahe	bhávā-mahe
2.	भवसि	भवथः	भवथ	भवसे	भवेथे	भवध्वे
	bháva-si	bháva-thaḥ	bháva-tha	bháva-se	bháv-ethe	bháva-dhve
3.	भवति	भवतः	भवन्ति	भवते	भवेते	भवन्ते
	bháva-ti	bháva-taḥ	bháv-anti	bháva-te	bháv-ete	bháv-ante

Imperfect.

1.	अभवम्	अभवाव	अभवाम	अभवे	अभवावहि	अभवामहि
	á-bhav-am	á-bhavā-va	á-bhavā-ma	á-bhava-e	á-bhavā-vahi	á-bhavā-mahi
2.	अभवः	अभवतम्	अभवत	अभवथाः	अभवेथाम्	अभवध्वम्
	á-bhava-ḥ	á-bhava-tam	á-bhava-ta	á-bhava-thāḥ	á-bhav-ethām	á-bhava-dhvam
3.	अभवत्	अभवताम्	अभवन्	अभवत	अभवेताम्	अभवन्त
	á-bhava-t	á-bhava-tām	á-bhav-an	á-bhava-ta	á-bhav-etām	á-bhav-anta

Imperative.

1.	भवानि	भवाव	भवाम	भवै	भवावहै	भवामहै
	bháv-āni	bháv-āva	bháv-āma	bháv-ai	bháv-āvahai	bháv-āmahai
2.	भव	भवतम्	भवत	भवस्व	भवेथाम्	भवध्वम्
	bháva	bháva-tam	bháva-ta	bháva-sva	bháv-ethām	bhava-dhvam
3.	भवतु	भवताम्	भवन्तु	भवताम्	भवेताम्	भवन्ताम्
	bháva-tu	bháva-tām	bháv-antu	bháva-tām	bháv-etām	bháv-antām

Optative.

1.	भवेयम्	भवेव	भवेम	भवेय	भवेवहि	भवेमहि
	bháv-eyam	bháv-eva	bháv-ema	bháv-eya	bháv-evahi	bháv-emahi
2.	भवेः	भवेतम्	भवेत	भवेथाः	भवेयाथाम्	भवेध्वम्
	bháv-eḥ	bháv-etam	bháv-eta	bháv-ethāḥ	bháv-eyāthām	bháv-edhvam
3.	भवेत्	भवेताम्	भवेयुः	भवेत	भवेयाताम्	भवेरन्
	bháv-et	bháv-etām	bháv-eyuḥ	bháv-eta	bháv-eyātām	bháv-eran

SECOND CONJUGATION

Second Class : **द्विष्** dviṣ, 'hate': Present stem **द्वेष्** dveṣ, **द्विष्** dviṣ.

Present.

	PARASMAIPADA.			ĀTMANEPADA.		
	SINGULAR	DUAL	PLURAL	SINGULAR	DUAL	PLURAL
1.	**द्वेष्मि** dvéṣ-mi	**द्विष्वः** dviṣ-váḥ	**द्विष्मः** dviṣ-máḥ	**द्विषे** dviṣ-é	**द्विष्वहे** dviṣ-váhe	**द्विष्महे** dviṣ-máhe
2.	**द्वेक्षि** dvé**k**-**ṣ**i (64*a*)	**द्विष्ठः** dviṣ-ṭháḥ	**द्विष्ठ** dviṣ-ṭhá	**द्विक्षे** dvi**k**-**ṣ**é	**द्विषाथे** dviṣ-ā́the	**द्विड्ढ्वे** dvi**ḍ**-**ḍh**vé (64)
3.	**द्वेष्टि** dvéṣ-ṭi (64)	**द्विष्टः** dviṣ-ṭáḥ	**द्विषन्ति** dviṣ-ánti	**द्विष्टे** dviṣ-ṭé	**द्विषाते** dviṣ-ā́te	**द्विषते** dviṣ-**áte**

Imperfect.

	SINGULAR	DUAL	PLURAL	SINGULAR	DUAL	PLURAL
1.	**अद्वेषम्** á-dveṣ-am	**अद्विष्व** á-dviṣ-va	**अद्विष्म** á-dviṣ-ma	**अद्विषि** á-dviṣ-i	**अद्विष्वहि** á-dviṣ-vahi	**अद्विष्महि** á-dviṣ-mahi
2.	**अद्वेट्** á-dveṭ (28)	**अद्विष्टम्** á-dviṣ-ṭam	**अद्विष्ट** á-dviṣ-ṭa	**अद्विष्ठाः** á-dviṣ-ṭhāḥ	**अद्विषाथाम्** á-dviṣ-āthām	**अद्विड्ढ्वम्** á-dvi**ḍ**-**ḍh**vam
3.	**अद्वेट्** á-dveṭ (28)	**अद्विष्टाम्** á-dviṣ-ṭām	**अद्विषन्** á-dviṣ-an	**अद्विष्ट** á-dviṣ-ṭa	**अद्विषाताम्** á-dviṣ-ātām	**अद्विषत** á-dviṣ-**ata**

Imperative.

1.	द्वेषाणि dvéṣ-āṇi (65)	द्वेषाव dvéṣ-āva	द्वेषाम dvéṣ-āma	द्वेषै dvéṣ-ai	द्वेषावहै dvéṣ-āvahai	द्वेषामहै dvéṣ-āmahai
2.	द्विड्ढि dviḍ-ḍhí (64)	द्विष्टम् dviṣ-ṭám	द्विष्ट dviṣ-ṭá	द्विक्ष्व dvi**k**-**ṣ**vá (64*a*)	द्विषाथाम् dviṣ-ā́thām	द्विड्ढ्वम् dvi**ḍ**-**ḍh**vám (64)
3.	द्वेष्टु dvéṣ-ṭu	द्विष्टाम् dviṣ-ṭā́m	द्विषन्तु dviṣ-ántu	द्विष्टाम् dviṣ-ṭā́m	द्विषाताम् dviṣ-ā́tām	द्विषताम् dviṣ-**átām**

Optative.

1.	द्विष्याम् dviṣ-yām	द्विष्याव dviṣ-yā́va	द्विष्याम dviṣ-yā́ma	द्विषीय dviṣ-īyá	द्विषीवहि dviṣ-īváhi	द्विषीमहि dviṣ-īmáhi
2.	द्विष्याः dviṣ-yā́ḥ	द्विष्यातम् dviṣ-yā́tam	द्विष्यात dviṣ-yā́ta	द्विषीथाः dviṣ-īthā́ḥ	द्विषीयाथाम् dviṣ-īyā́thām	द्विषीध्वम् dviṣ-īdhvám
3.	द्विष्यात् dviṣ-yā́t	द्विष्याताम् dviṣ-yā́tām	द्विष्युः dviṣ-yúḥ	द्विषीत dviṣ-ītá	द्विषीयाताम् dviṣ-īyā́tām	द्विषीरन् dviṣ-īrán

Third Class : हु hu, 'sacrifice': Present stem जुहो ju-hó, जुहु ju-hu.

Present.

	PARASMAIPADA			ĀTMANEPADA		
	SINGULAR	DUAL	PLURAL	SINGULAR	DUAL	PLURAL
1.	जुहोमि juhó-mi	जुहुवः juhu-váḥ	जुहुमः juhu-máḥ	जुह्वे júhv-e	जुहुवहे juhu-váhe	जुहुमहे juhu-máhe
2.	जुहोषि juhó-ṣi	जुहुथः juhu-tháḥ	जुहुथ juhu-thá	जुहुषे juhu-ṣé	जुह्वाथे júhv-āthe	जुहुध्वे juhu-dhvé
3.	जुहोति juhó-ti	जुहुतः juhu-táḥ	जुह्वति júhv-**ati**	जुहुते juhu-té	जुह्वाते júhv-āte	जुह्वते júhv-**ate**

Imperfect.

1.	अजुहवम् á-juhav-am	अजुहुव á-juhu-va	अजुहुम á-juhu-ma	अजुह्वि á-juhv-i	अजुहुवहि á-juhu-vahi	अजुहुमहि á-juhu-mahi
2.	अजुहोः á-juho-ḥ	अजुहुतम् á-juhu-tam	अजुहुत á-juhu-ta	अजुहुथाः á-juhu-thāḥ	अजुह्वाथाम् á-juhv-āthām	अजुहुध्वम् á-juhu-dhvam
3.	अजुहोत् á-juho-t	अजुहुताम् á-juhu-tām	अजुहवुः á-juh**av-uḥ**	अजुहुत á-juhu-ta	अजुह्वाताम् á-juhv-ātām	अजुह्वत á-juhv-**ata**

Imperative.

1.	जुहवानि juháv-āni	जुहवाव juháv-āva	जुहवाम juháv-āma	जुहवै juháv-ai	जुहवावहै juháv-āvahai	जुहवामहै juháv-āmahai
2.	जुहुधि juhu-**dhí**	जुहुतम् juhu-tám	जुहुत juhu-tá	जुहुष्व juhu-ṣvá	जुह्वाथाम् júhv-āthām	जुहुध्वम् juhu-dhvám
3.	जुहोतु juhó-tu	जुहुताम् juhu-tā́m	जुह्वतु júhv-atu	जुहुताम् juhu-tā́m	जुह्वाताम् júhv-ātām	जुह्वताम् júhv-**atām**

Optative.

1.	जुहुयाम् juhu-yā́m	जुहुयाव juhu-yā́va	जुहुयाम juhu-yā́ma	जुह्वीय juhv-īyā	जुह्वीवहि juhv-īváhi	जुह्वीमहि juhv-īmáhi
2.	जुहुयाः juhu-yā́ḥ	जुहुयातम् juhu-yā́tam	जुहुयात juhu-yā́ta	जुह्वीथाः juhv-īthā́ḥ	जुह्वीयाथाम् juhv-īyāthām	जुह्वीध्वम् juhv-īdhvám
3.	जुहुयात् juhu-yā́t	जुहुयाताम् juhu-yā́tām	जुहुयुः juhu-yúḥ	जुह्वीत juhv-ītá	जुह्वीयाताम् juhv-īyā́tām	जुह्वीरन् juhv-īrán

Fifth Class : सु su, 'press out': Present stem सुनो su-nó, सुनु su-nu.

Present.

	PARASMAIPADA			ĀTMANEPADA		
	SINGULAR	DUAL	PLURAL	SINGULAR	DUAL	PLURAL
1.	सुनोमि sunó-mi	सुनुवः sunu-váḥ	सुनुमः sunu-máḥ	सुन्वे sunv-é	सुनुवहे sunu-váhe	सुनुमहे sunu-máhe
2.	सुनोषि sunó-ṣi	सुनुथः sunu-tháḥ	सुनुथ sunu-thá	सुनुषे sunu-ṣé	सुन्वाथे sunv-ā́the	सुनुध्वे sunu-dhvé
3.	सुनोति sunó-ti	सुनुतः sunu-táḥ	सुन्वन्ति sunv-ánti	सुनुते sunu-té	सुन्वाते sunv-ā́te	सुन्वते sunv-**áte**

Imperfect.

	SINGULAR	DUAL	PLURAL	SINGULAR	DUAL	PLURAL
1.	असुनवम् á-sunav-am	असुनुव á-sunu-va	असुनुम á-sunu-ma	असुन्वि á-sunv-i	असुनुवहि á-sunu-vahi	असुनुमहि á-sunu-mahi
2.	असुनोः á-suno-ḥ	असुनुतम् á-sunu-tam	असुनुत á-sunu-ta	असुनुथाः á-sunu-thāḥ	असुन्वाथाम् á-sunv-āthām	असुनुध्वम् á-sunu-dhvam
3.	असुनोत् á-suno-t	असुनुताम् á-sunu-tām	असुन्वन् á-sunv-an	असुनुत á-sunu-ta	असुन्वाताम् á-sunv-ātām	असुन्वत á-sunv-ata

Imperative.

1.	सुनवानि sunáv-āni	सुनवाव sunáv-āva	सुनवाम sunáv-āma	सुनवै sunáv-ai	सुनवावहै sunáv-āvahai	सुनवामहै sunáv-āmahai
2.	सुनु sunú	सुनुतम् sunu-tám	सुनुत sunu-tá	सुनुष्व sunu-ṣvá	सुन्वाथाम् sunv-ā́thām	सुनुध्वम् sunu-dhvám
3.	सुनोतु sunó-tu	सुनुताम् sunu-tā́m	सुन्वन्तु sunv-ántu	सुनुताम् sunu-tā́m	सुन्वाताम् sunv-ā́tām	सुन्वताम् sunv-átām

Optative.

1.	सुनुयाम् sunu-yā́m	सुनुयाव sunu-yā́va	सुनुयाम sunu-yā́ma	सुन्वीय sunv-īyá	सुन्वीवहि sunv-īváhi	सुन्वीमहि sunv-īmáhi
2.	सुनुयाः sunu-yā́ḥ	सुनुयातम् sunu-yā́tam	सुनुयात sunu-yā́ta	सुन्वीथाः sunv-īthā́ḥ	सुन्वीयाथाम् sunv-īyā́thām	सुन्वीध्वम् sunv-īdhvám
3.	सुनुयात् sunu-yā́t	सुनुयाताम् sunu-yā́tām	सुनुयुः sunu-yúḥ	सुन्वीत sunv-ītá	सुन्वीयाताम् sunv-īyā́tām	सुन्वीरन् sunv-īrán

Seventh Class : रुध् rudh, 'obstruct': Present stem रुणध् ru-ṇá-dh, रुन्ध् ru-n-dh.

Present.

	PARASMAIPADA			ĀTMANEPADA		
	SINGULAR	DUAL	PLURAL	SINGULAR	DUAL	PLURAL
1.	रुणध्मि ru-ṇá-dh-mi (65)	रुन्ध्वः rundh-váḥ	रुन्ध्मः rundh-máḥ	रुन्धे rundh-é	रुन्ध्वहे rundh-váhe	रुन्ध्महे rundh-máhe
2.	रुणत्सि ru-ṇá-t-si (62)	रुन्द्धः rund**-dh**áḥ (62*b*)	रुन्द्ध rund**-dh**á	रुन्त्से runt**-s**é	रुन्धाथे rundh-ā́the	रुन्द्ध्वे rund-dhvé
3.	रुणद्धि ru-ṇá**-d-dhi** (62*b*)	रुन्द्धः rund**-dh**áḥ	रुन्धन्ति rundh-ánti	रुन्द्धे rund**-dh**é	रुन्धाते rundh-ā́te	रुन्धते rundh**-áte**

Imperfect.

1.	अरुणधम् á-ru-ṇa-dh-am	अरुन्ध्व á-rundh-va	अरुन्ध्म á-rundh-ma	अरुन्धि á-rundh-i	अरुन्ध्वहि á-rundh-vahi	अरुन्ध्महि á-rundh-mahi
2.	अरुणत् á-ru-ṇa-**t** (27, 28)	अरुन्द्धम् á-rund**-dh**am	अरुन्द्ध á-rund**-dh**a	अरुन्द्धाः á-rund**-dh**āḥ	अरुन्धाथाम् á-rundh-āthām	अरुन्द्ध्वम् á-rund-dhvam
3.	अरुणत् á-ru-ṇa-**t** (27, 28)	अरुन्द्धाम् á-rund**-dh**ām	अरुन्धन् á-rundh-an	अरुन्द्ध á-rund**-dh**a	अरुन्धाताम् á-rundh-ātām	अरुन्धत á-rundh**-ata**

Imperative.

1.	रुणधानि	रुणधाव	रुणधाम	रुणधै	रुणधावहै	रुणधामहै
	ru-ṇá-dh-āni	ru-ṇá-dh-āva	ru-ṇá-dh-āma	ru-ṇá-dh-ai	ru-ṇá-dh-āvahai	ru-ṇá-dh-āmahai
2.	रुन्द्धि	रुन्द्धम्	रुन्द्ध	रुन्त्स्व	रुन्धाथाम्	रुन्द्ध्वम्
	run**d**-dhí (62)	run**d-dh**ám	run**d-dh**á	run**t**-svá	rundh-ā́thām	run**d**-dhvám
3.	रुणद्धु	रुन्द्धाम्	रुन्धन्तु	रुन्द्धाम्	रुन्धाताम्	रुन्धताम्
	ru-ṇá-**d-dh**u (62*b*)	run**d-dh**ā́m	rundh-ántu	run**d-dh**ā́m	rundh-ā́tām	rundh-**átām**

Optative.

1.	रुन्ध्याम्	रुन्ध्याव	रुन्ध्याम	रुन्धीय	रुन्धीवहि	रुन्धीमहि
	rundh-yā́m	rundh-yā́va	rundh-yā́ma	rundh-īyá	rundh-īváhi	rundh-īmáhi
2.	रुन्ध्याः	रुन्ध्यातम्	रुन्ध्यात	रुन्धीथाः	रुन्धीयाथाम्	रुन्धीध्वम्
	rundh-yā́ḥ	rundh-yā́tam	rundh-yā́ta	rundh-īthā́ḥ	rundh-īyā́thām	rundh-īdhvám
3.	रुन्ध्यात्	रुन्ध्याताम्	रुन्ध्युः	रुन्धीत	रुन्धीयाताम्	रुन्धीरन्
	rundh-yā́t	rundh-yā́tām	rundh-yúḥ	rundh-ītá	rundh-īyā́tām	rundh-īrán

Ninth Class : क्री krī, 'buy': Present stem क्रीणा krī-ṇā́, क्रीणी krī-ṇī, क्रीण् krī-ṇ.

Present.

	PARASMAIPADA SINGULAR	DUAL	PLURAL	ĀTMANEPADA SINGULAR	DUAL	PLURAL
1.	क्रीणामि krī-ṇā́-mi	क्रीणीवः krī-ṇī-váḥ	क्रीणीमः krī-ṇī-máḥ	क्रीणे krī-ṇ-é	क्रीणीवहे krī-ṇī-váhe	क्रीणीमहे krī-ṇī-máhe
2.	क्रीणासि krī-ṇā́-si	क्रीणीथः krī-ṇī-tháḥ	क्रीणीथ krī-ṇī-thá	क्रीणीषे krī-ṇī-ṣé	क्रीणाथे krī-ṇ-ā́the	क्रीणीध्वे krī-ṇī-dhvé
3.	क्रीणाति krī-ṇā́-ti	क्रीणीतः krī-ṇī-táḥ	क्रीणन्ति krī-ṇ-ánti	क्रीणीते krī-ṇī-té	क्रीणाते krī-ṇ-ā́te	क्रीणते krī-ṇ-**áte**

Imperfect.

	PARASMAIPADA SINGULAR	DUAL	PLURAL	ĀTMANEPADA SINGULAR	DUAL	PLURAL
1.	अक्रीणाम् á-krī-ṇā-m	अक्रीणीव á-krī-ṇī-va	अक्रीणीम á-krī-ṇī-ma	अक्रीणि á-krī-ṇ-i	अक्रीणीवहि á-krī-ṇī-vahi	अक्रीणीमहि á-krī-ṇī-mahi
2.	अक्रीणाः á-krī-ṇā-ḥ	अक्रीणीतम् á-krī-ṇī-tam	अक्रीणीत á-krī-ṇī-ta	अक्रीणीथाः á-krī-ṇī-thāḥ	अक्रीणाथाम् á-krī-ṇ-āthām	अक्रीणीध्वम् á-krī-ṇī-dhvam
3.	अक्रीणात् á-krī-ṇā-t	अक्रीणीताम् á-krī-ṇī-tām	अक्रीणन् á-krī-ṇ-an	अक्रीणीत á-krī-ṇī-ta	अक्रीणाताम् á-krī-ṇ-ātām	अक्रीणत á-krī-ṇ-**ata**

Imperative.

1.	क्रीणानि krī-ṇ-ā́ni	क्रीणाव krī-ṇā́-va	क्रीणाम krī-ṇā́-ma	क्रीणै krī-ṇ-aí	क्रीणावहै krī-ṇā́-vahai	क्रीणामहै krī-ṇā́-mahai
2.	क्रीणीहि krī-ṇī-hí	क्रीणीतम् krī-ṇī-tám	क्रीणीत krī-ṇī-tá	क्रीणीष्व krī-ṇī-ṣvá	क्रीणाथाम् krī-ṇ-ā́thām	क्रीणीध्वम् krī-ṇī-dhvám
3.	क्रीणातु krī-ṇā́-tu	क्रीणीताम् krī-ṇī-tā́m	क्रीणन्तु krī-ṇ-ántu	क्रीणीताम् krī-ṇī-tā́m	क्रीणाताम् krī-ṇ-ā́tām	क्रीणताम् krī-ṇ-átām

Optative.

1.	क्रीणीयाम् krī-ṇī-yā́m	क्रीणीयाव krī-ṇī-yā́va	क्रीणीयाम krī-ṇī-yā́ma	क्रीणीय krī-ṇ-īyá	क्रीणीवहि krī-ṇ-īváhi	क्रीणीमहि krī-ṇ-īmáhi
2.	क्रीणीयाः krī-ṇī-yā́ḥ	क्रीणीयातम् krī-ṇī-yā́tam	क्रीणीयात krī-ṇī-yā́ta	क्रीणीथाः krī-ṇ-īthā́ḥ	क्रीणीयाथाम् krī-ṇ-īyā́thām	क्रीणीध्वम् krī-ṇ-īdhvám
3.	क्रीणीयात् krī-ṇī-yā́t	क्रीणीयाताम् krī-ṇī-yā́tām	क्रीणीयुः krī-ṇī-yúḥ	क्रीणीत krī-ṇ-ītá	क्रीणीयाताम् krī-ṇ-īyā́tām	क्रीणीरन् krī-ṇ-īrán

Irregularities of the Present Stem.

First Conjugation.

133. A. First or Bhū Class, 1. क्रम् kram, 'step,' आ-चम् ā-cam, 'sip,' गुह् guh, 'conceal,' ष्ठिव् ṣṭhiv, 'spit,' lengthen their vowel:— क्राम krắm-a, आचाम ā-cắm-a, गूह gū́h-a, ष्ठीव ṣṭhī́v-a. — मृज् mṛj, 'cleanse,' takes Vṛddhi: मार्ज mắrj-a. — सद् sad, 'sink,' substitutes ई ī for अ a: सीद् sī́d-a (for si-s[a]da: Lat. sīdo).

2. गम् gam, 'go,' and यम् yam, 'restrain,' form the present stem with छ cha (Gk. σκ): गच्छ् gá-ccha, यच्छ् yá-ccha (see below, C 2).

3. घ्रा ghrā, 'smell,' पा pā, 'drink,' स्था sthā, 'stand,' reduplicate with इ i: जिघ्र jí-ghra, पिब pí-ba (Lat. bi-bo), तिष्ठ tí-ṣṭha (Gk. ἵ-στη-μι, Lat. sisto). These verbs originally belonged to the third (reduplicating) class (cp. सद् sad above, A 1).

4. दंश् daṃś, 'bite,' मन्थ् manth, 'churn,' सञ्ज् sañj, 'adhere,' drop the nasal: — दश dáś-a, मथ máth-a, सज sáj-a.

5. दृश् dṛś, 'see,' ध्मा dhmā, 'blow,' म्ना mnā, 'study,' substitute पश्य páś-ya, धम dhám-a, मन mán-a.

B. Fourth or Div Class. 1. तम् tam, 'languish,' भ्रम् bhram, 'roam,' शम् śam, 'cease,' श्रम् śram, 'be weary,' मद् mad, 'rejoice,' दिव् div, 'play,' lengthen their vowel:— ताम्य tắm-ya माद्य mắd-ya, दीव्य dī́vya, &c.

2. भ्रंश् bhraṃś, 'fall,' drops its nasal: भ्रश्य bhráś-ya. — व्यध् vyadh, 'pierce,' takes Samprasāraṇa: विध्य vīdh-ya. — जन् jan. 'be born,' substitutes जा jā: जाय jắ-ya (cp. 154 *a*, 1).

C. Sixth or Tud Class. 1. कृत् kṛt, 'cut,' मुच् muc, 'loosen,' लुप् lup, 'break,' लिप् lip, 'paint,' विद् vid, 'find,' सिच् sic, 'sprinkle,' insert a nasal: — कृन्त kṛnt-á, मुञ्च muñc-á, लुम्प lump-á, लिम्प limp-á, विन्द vind-á, सिञ्च siñc-á.

2. इष् iṣ, 'wish,' substitutes छ् ch for ष् ṣ, and ऋ ṛ, 'go,' adds छ् ch: — इच्छ् i-cchá, ऋच्छ् ṛ-cchá (cp. A 2).

3. प्रछ् prach, 'ask,' भ्रज्ज् brajj, 'fry,' व्रश्च् vraśc, 'cut,' take Samprasāraṇa: — पृच्छ pṛcch-á, भृज्ज bhṛjj-á, वृश्च vṛśc-á.

Second Conjugation.

134. A Second or Ad Class.

1. The root is irregularly **strengthened** in the following verbs: —

a. यु yu, 'join,' and all other roots ending in उ u, take Vṛddhi instead of Guṇa in the strong forms before terminations beginning with consonants; — यौमि **yaú**-mi, but अयवम् á-yav-am.

b. मृज् mṛj, 'cleanse,' takes Vṛddhi instead of Guṇa: 3. sing. मार्ष्टि **márṣ**-ṭi (cp. 63), 3. pl. मृजन्ति mṛj-ánti.

c. शी śī, 'lie down,' Ātm., takes Guṇa throughout its weak forms, besides inserting र् r before the terminations in the 3. plur. pres., impv., impf.: — 3. sg. शेते **śé**-te (Gk. *κεῖ-ται*), 3. pl. शेरते śé-**r**-ate, शेरताम् śé-**r**-atām, अशेरत á-śe-**r**-ata.

2. The root is irregularly **weakened** in the following verbs:—

a. वश् vaś, 'desire,' takes Samprasāraṇa in the weak forms: 3. sg. वष्टि váṣ-ṭi (63 *b*), 3. pl. उशन्ति uś-ánti.

b. अस् as, 'be,' drops its initial अ a in the optative and all the weak forms of the pres. and imperative; — e.g. 3. sg. opt. स्यात् s-yā́t; 3. pl. pres. सन्ति s-ánti (sunt). The 2. sing. impv. is एधि e-dhí (for az-dhí, Avestic zdī). In the imperfect it inserts ई ī before the endings of the 2.3. sing.: आसीः ās-ī-ḥ, आसीत् ās-ī-t.

c. हन् han, 'kill,' Par., drops its न् n before त् t and थ् th in the weak forms: 3. sg. हन्ति hán-ti, but 2. pl. हथ ha-thá. In the 3. pl. pres., impv., impf. the radical अ a is dropped and the ह h becomes घ् gh: घ्नन्ति **ghn**-ánti, घ्नन्तु **ghn**-ántu, अघ्नन् á-**ghn**-an. The 2. sg. impv. is जहि **ja-hí** (for झहि jha-hí, with palatalized initial, instead of घहि gha-hí).

3. A **vowel** or semivowel is irregularly **inserted** in the following verbs:—

a. **अन्** an, 'breathe,' **जक्ष्** jakṣ, 'eat,' **रुद्** rud, 'weep,' **श्वस्** śvas, 'breathe,' **स्वप्** svap, 'sleep,' insert **इ** i before terminations beginning with consonants except **य्** y; but **ई** ī or **अ** a before the **स्** s and **त्** t of the 2.3. sg. impf. Par.; — e.g. **रोदिमि** ród-i-mi, but **रुदन्ति** rud-ánti, **रुद्याम्** rud-yā́m; impf. 3. sg. **अरोदीत्** á-rod-**ī**-t or **अरोदत्** á-rod-**a**-t.

b. **ईड्** īḍ, 'praise,' and **ईश्** īś, 'rule,' both Ātm., insert **इ** i before terminations beginning with **स्** s and **ध्** dh (i.e. 2. sg. pl. pres. and impv.): — **ईशिषे** īś-i-ṣe, **ईशिध्वे** īś-i-dhve; **ईशिष्व** īś-i-ṣva, **ईशिध्वम्** īś-i-dhvam.

c. **ब्रू** brū, 'speak,' inserts **ई** ī in the strong forms before terminations beginning with consonants:— **ब्रवीमि** bráv-ī-mi (but **ब्रूमः** brū-máḥ), **अब्रवीत्** á-brav-ī-t.

d. **इ** i preceded by **अधि** adhi, 'read' (Ātm. only), resolves **ई** ī in the pres. and **ऐ** ai (augm. a + i) in the impf. before vowels into **ईय्** īy and **ऐय्** aiy:— pres. sg. 1. **अधीये** adhī-**y**-é, 2. **अधीषे** adhī-ṣé; impf. sg. 1. **अध्यैयि** adhy-ái-**y**-i, 2. **अध्यैथाः** adhy-ái-thāḥ.

4. The **reduplicated verbs** **चकास्** ca-kās, 'shine,' **जक्ष्** ja-kṣ (for ja-gh[a]s, from ghas), 'eat,' **जागृ** jā-gṛ, 'wake' (intensive of **गृ** gṛ), **दरिद्रा** dari-drā (intensive of **द्रा** drā, 'run'), 'be poor,' though accounted verbs of the second class, follow those of the third in taking **अति** **ati** and **अतु** **atu** in the 3. pl. pres. and impv., and **उर्** **ur** for **अन्** an in the 3. pl. impf.: — 3. sg. **दरिद्राति** dári-drā-ti, 3. pl. **दरिद्रति** dáridr-**ati**; 3. pl. impf. **अजक्षुः** á-jakṣ-**uḥ**.

a. **शास्** śās, 'rule,' follows the same analogy; it also takes **शिष्** śiṣ as its weak stem before consonants: — 3. sg. **शास्ति** śā́s-ti, du. **शिष्टः** śiṣ-ṭáḥ, pl. **शासति** śā́s-**ati**.

B. Third or Hu Class. 1. दा dā, 'give,' and धा dhā, 'place,' use दद् dad and दध् dadh as their stems in the weak forms. दध् dadh (against 62 *b*) becomes धत् dhat before त् t and थ् th: दधामि da-dhā́-mi, but du. 1. दध्वः dadh-váḥ, 2. धत्थः **dhat-th**áḥ. The 2. sg. impv. Par. is देहि d**e**-hí (for da-z-dhí) and धेहि dh**e**-hí (for dha-z-dhí).

2. मा mā, 'measure,' and हा hā, 'depart,' both Ātm., have मिमी mi-mī and जिही ji-hī as their present stems, dropping the ई ī before vowels: — pres. sg. 1. जिहे jíh-e, 2. जिहीषे jíhī-ṣe, pl. 3. जिहते jíh-ate; impf. sg. 1. अजिहि á-jih-i, 2. अजिहीथाः á-jihī-thāḥ, pl. 3. अजिहत á-jih-ata.

a. हा hā, 'abandon,' Par., has जही jahī in the weak forms, dropping ई ī before vowels and य् y: — 3. sg. जहाति jáhā-ti, but du. जहीतः jahī-taḥ, pl. जहति jah-**ati**; impv. 2. sg. जहीहि jahī-hi; opt. 1. sg. जह्याम् jah-yām.

C. Fifth or Su Class. 1. Roots ending in vowels may drop the उ u before व् v or म् m: — सुनोमि su-nó-mi, but सुन्वः sun-váḥ or सुनुवः su-nu-váḥ.

2. Roots ending in consonants change उ u to उव् uv before vowels: — शक्नुवन्ति śak-n**uv**-ánti.

3. श्रु śru, 'hear,' and धू dhū, 'shake,' form the present stems शृणु śṛ-ṇu and धुनु dh**u**-nu.

D. Seventh or Rudh Class. अञ्ज् añj, 'anoint,' भञ्ज् bhañj, 'break,' हिंस् hiṃs, 'injure,' drop their nasal before inserting न na:— अनज्मि a-ná-j-mi, भनज्मि bha-ná-j-mi, हिनस्मि hi-na-s-mi.

E. Eighth or Tan Class. कृ kṛ, 'do,' takes करो **kar**-ó as its strong stem, and as its weak कुरु **kur**-u, the उ u of which must be dropped before म् m, य् y, व् v: — करोमि karó-mi, कुरुथः kuru-tháḥ; but कुर्वः kur-váḥ, कुर्मः **kur**-máḥ; कुर्याम् **kur**-yā́m. Other verbs of this class may drop the उ u before व् v and म् m

as in the fifth. When compounded with the prepositions परि pari and सम् sam, the verb कृ kṛ has an initial स् s: परिष्कृत pári-ṣkṛta, 'adorned,' संस्कृत sáṃ-skṛta, 'put together.' This स् s is not original.

F. Ninth or Krī Class. 1. धू dhū, 'shake,' पू pū, 'purify,' लू lū, 'cut,' shorten their vowel: — धुनामि dhu-nā́-mi, पुनामि pu-nā́-mi, लुनामि lu-nā́-mi.

2. ज्ञा jñā, 'know,' and ग्रह् grah, 'seize,' are shortened to जा jā and गृह् gṛh: — जानामि jā-nā́-mi; गृह्णामि gṛh-ṇā́-mi (65).

3. बन्ध् bandh, 'bind,' and मन्थ् manth, 'churn,' drop the nasal:— बध्नामि badh-nā́-mi, मथ्नामि math-nā́-mi.

The Perfect Tense.

135. This tense is formed either by reduplication or periphrastically. Roots follow the former method, derivative verbs (chiefly causatives) the latter. There are also four roots with a prosodically long initial vowel (140 *a*, 1) which take the periphrastic perfect.

Special Rules of Reduplication.

1. ऋ ṛ, ॠ ṝ, ऌ ḷ are represented by अ a in the reduplicative syllable; — e.g. कृ kṛ, 'do': चकार ca-kā́r-a; तॄ tṝ, 'cross': ततार ta-tā́r-a; क्लृप् kḷp, 'be able': चक्लृपे ca-kḷp-é.

2. Initial अ a or आ ā becomes आ ā; — e.g. अद् ad, 'eat': आद ā́d-a; आप् āp, 'obtain': आप ā́p-a (cp. 140 *a*, 1).

3. Roots beginning with इ i contract इ i + इ i to ई ī; but if the radical इ i takes Guṇa or Vṛddhi, य् y is inserted between the reduplicative syllable and the root; — e.g. इष् iṣ, 'desire,' 3. pl. ईषुः īṣ-úḥ (for i-iṣ-uḥ), but 1. sg. इयेष i-y-éṣ-a.

4. Roots beginning with or containing य ya or व va, and liable to Samprasāraṇa (cp. 137, 2 *c*), reduplicate with इ i and उ u:—

यज् yaj, 'sacrifice': इयाज i-yáj-a; वच् vac, 'speak': उवाच u-vác-a.

136. The singular perfect active is strong, like the singular active present and imperfect, the root being accented; the remaining forms are weak, the terminations being accented. The endings are the following :—

PARASMAIPADA

	SINGULAR	DUAL	PLURAL
1.	अ a	(इ)व (i)-vá	(इ)म (i)má
2.	(इ)थ (i)-tha	अथुर् á-th**ur**[1]	अ á
3.	अ a	अतुर् á-t**ur**[1]	उर् **úr** (131, 6)

ĀTMANEPADA

1.	ए é	(इ)वहे (i)-váhe	(इ)महे (i)-máhe
2.	(इ)षे (i)-ṣé	आथे áthe	(इ)ध्वे (i)-dhvé
3.	ए é	आते áte	**इरे i-ré**

a. The terminations with initial consonant are added with the **connecting vowel** इ i[2] except in the eight verbs: द्रु dru, 'run,' श्रु śru, 'hear,' स्तु stu, 'praise,' स्रु sru, 'flow,' कृ kṛ, 'do,' भृ bhṛ, 'bear,' वृ vṛ, 'choose,' सृ sṛ, 'go,' **where it must be omitted.** The 3. pl. Ātm. retains the इ i even in these verbs. In 2. sg. Par. it is omitted by many other verbs also, and is optional in verbs ending in आ ā, as well as in most of those ending in इ i, ई ī, उ u.

1. In these two dual forms उर् ur has been borrowed from the 3. pl., the two endings थुर् thur and तुर् tur corresponding to the 2.3. du. pres. थस् thas and तस् tas.
2. This इ i was in origin probably the reduced form of the final आ ā of roots like दा dā, 'give,' and became the starting-point of इ i as a connecting vowel in other verbs.

The Strong Stem.

1. Short vowels followed by a single consonant take Guṇa throughout the singular; — e.g. इष् iṣ, 'wish': इयेष् i-y-éṣ बुध् budh, 'wake': बुबोध् bu-bódh; but जीव् jīv, 'live': जिजीव् ji-jīv.

2. Final vowels like Vṛddhi or Guṇa in the first person singular, Guṇa in the second, Vṛddhi only in the third; — e.g. इ i, 'go'. 1. इयाय i-y-ấy-a or इयय i-y-áy-a; 2. इयेथ i-y-é-tha; 3. इयाय i-y-ấy-a; कृ kṛ, 'do': 1. चकार ca-kấr-a or चकर ca-kár-a; 2. चकर्थ ca-kár-tha; 3. चकार ca-kấr-a.

3. Medial अ a followed by a single consonant takes Vṛddhi in sg. 3. and optionally in 1.; — e.g. हन् han, 'kill': 1. जघान jaghấn-a or जघन jaghán-a, 3. जघान jaghấn-a.

4. Roots ending in आ ā (or diphthongs: 129, 8) take औ au in 1.3. sg., and may retain आ ā before थ tha in 2. sg. (cp. 136 *a*); — e.g. धा dhā, 'place': 1.3. दधौ da-dháu, 2. दधाथ dadhấ-tha or दधिथ dadh-i-thá.

But ह्वा hvā or ह्वे hve, 'call,' is treated as हू hū: — 3. sg. जुहाव ju-hāv-a (cp. 154 *a*, 3).

The Weak Stem.

137. 1. In roots containing the wovels ĭ, ŭ, ṛ, the **radical syllable** remains **unchanged,** except by Sandhi; — e.g. बुध् budh: बुबुधिम bu-budh-i-ma; कृ kṛ: चकृम ca-kṛ-má; स्तु stu: तुष्टुम tu-ṣṭu-má.

a. Before terminations beginning with vowels final इ i, ई ī, ऋ ṛ if preceded by one consonant become य् y, र् r, if by more than one. इय् iy, अर् ar; while उ u, ऊ ū, and ॠ ṝ **always** become उव् uv and अर् ar: — e.g. नी nī, 'lead': निन्युः ni-ny-úḥ; श्रि śri, 'resort': शिश्रियुः śi-śriy-úḥ; कृ kṛ, 'do': चक्रुः ca-kr-úḥ; स्तृ stṛ,

'strew': तस्तरुः ta-st**ar**-úḥ; यु yu, 'join': युयुवुः yu-y**uv**-úḥ; कृ kṛ, 'scatter': चकरुः ca-k**ar**-úḥ.

2. In roots containing a medial अ a or a final आ ā, the **radical syllable is weakened.**

a. Roots in which अ a is preceded and followed by a single consonant (e.g. पत् pat), and which reduplicate the intial consonant unchanged (this excludes roots beginning with aspirates, gutturals, and for the most part व् v), contract the two syllables to one with the diphthong ए e (cp. Lat. făc-iō, fēc-ī).[1] This contraction takes place even in 2. sg. Par. when थ tha is added with इ i (the strong form being used when थ tha is added without इ i); — e.g. पच् pac, 'cook': 2. sg. पेचिथ pec-i-thá (but पपक्थ papák-tha), 3. pl. पेचुः pec-úḥ; तन् tan, 'stretch': तेनिथ ten-i-thá, तेनुः ten-úḥ.

b. जन् jan (139, 2), 'be born,' and four roots with medial अ a beginning with gutturals, viz. खन् khan, 'dig,' गम् gam, 'go,' घस् ghas, 'eat,' हन् han, 'kill,' weaken the root by dropping the radical vowel: — 3. sg. Ātm. जज्ञे ja-**jñ**-é; 3. sg. Par. जगाम ja-gā́m-a, but 3. pl. जग्मुः ja-**gm**-úḥ; जघास ja-ghā́s-a, but जक्षुः ja-**kṣ**-úḥ; जघान ja-**gh**ā́n-a, but जघ्नुः ja-**ghn**-úḥ (cp. 134, 2 *c*).

c. Five roots beginning with व va, viz. वच् vac, 'speak,' वद् vad, 'speak,' वप् vap, 'strew,' वस् vas, 'dwell,' वह् vah, 'carry'; also यज् yaj, 'sacrifice,' व्यध् vyadh, 'pierce,' स्वप् svap, 'sleep,' ग्रह् grah, 'seize,' take Samprasāraṇa. In the first five उ u + उ u (cp. 135, 4) contract to ऊ ū, in the sixth इ i + इ i to ई ī: — 3. sg. उवाच u-vā́c-a, but pl. ऊचुः **ū**c-úḥ (for u-uc-úḥ); इयाज i-yā́j-a, but ईजुः ī̇j-úḥ (for i-ij-úḥ); सुष्वाप su-ṣvā́p-a (67), but सुषुपुः su-ṣ**u**p-úḥ; जग्राह ja-grā́h-a, but जगृहुः ja-gṛh-úḥ.

---

1. This vowel spread from contracted forms like sa-z-d (Avestic hazd), weak perfect stem of sad, 'sit' (az becoming e; cp. 134; 2 *b* and 133 A 1).

d. Roots ending in आ ā drop it in all the weak forms, and optionally in 2. sg. Par. (see 136 *a* and 138, 3).

Paradigms of the Reduplicated Perfect.

138. 1. तुद् tud, 'strike': strong stem तुतोद् tu-tód; weak तुतुद् tu-tud.

PARASMAIPADA

1.	तुतोद tu-tód-a	तुतुदिव tu-tud-i-vá	तुतुदिम tu-tud-i-má[1]
2.	तुतोदिथ tu-tód-i-tha	तुतुदथुः tu-tud-áthuḥ	तुतुद tu-tud-á
3.	तुतोद tu-tód-a	तुतुदतुः tu-tud-átuḥ	तुतुदुः tu-tud-úḥ

ĀTMANEPADA

1.	तुतुदे tu-tud-é[2]	तुतुदिवहे tu-tud-i-váhe	तुतुदिमहे tu-tud-i-máhe
2.	तुतुदिषे tu-tud-i-ṣé	तुतुदाथे tu-tud-ā́the	तुतुदिध्वे tu-tud-i-dhvé
3.	तुतुदे tu-tud-é	तुतुदाते tu-tud-ā́te	तुतुदिरे tu-tud-iré

2. कृ kṛ, 'do': strong चकर् ca-kár, चकार् ca-kā́r; weak चकृ cakṛ, चक्र् cakr.

PARASMAIPADA

1.	चकर ca-kár-a[3]	चकृव ca-kṛ-vá	चकृम ca-kṛ-má
2.	चकर्थ ca-kár-tha	चक्रथुः ca-kr-áthuḥ	चक्र ca-kr-á
3.	चकार ca-kā́r-a	चक्रतुः ca-kr-átuḥ	चक्रुः ca-kr-úḥ

ĀTMANEPADA

1.	चक्रे ca-kr-é	चकृवहे ca-kṛ-váhe	चकृमहे ca-kṛ-máhe
2.	चकृषे ca-kṛ-ṣé	चक्राथे ca-kr-ā́the	चकृध्वे ca-kṛ-dhvé
3.	चक्रे ca-kr-é	चक्राते ca-kr-ā́te	चक्रिरे ca-kr-iré

1. Lat. tu-tud-i-mus. 2. Lat. tu-tud-ī. 3. Or चकार ca-kā́r-a.

3. धा dhā, 'place': strong दधा da-dhā́; weak दध् da-dh.

PARASMAIPADA

1.	दधौ da-dh**áu**	दधिव da-dh-i-vá	दधिम da-dh-i-má
2.	दधाथ dh-dhā́-tha[1]	दधथुः da-dh-áthuḥ	दध da-dh-á
3.	दधौ da-dh**áu**	दधतुः da-dh-átuḥ	दधुः da-dh-úḥ

ĀTMANEPADA

1.	दधे da-dh-é	दधिवहे da-dh-i-váhe	दधिमहे da-dh-i-máhe
2.	दधिषे da-dh-i-ṣé	दधाथे da-dh-ā́the	दधिध्वे da-dh-i-dhvé
3.	दधे da-dh-é	दधाते da-dh-ā́te	दधिरे da-dh-iré

4. नी nī, 'lead': strong निने ni-né, निनै ni-nái; weak निनी ni-nī.

PARASMAIPADA

1.	निनय ni-náy-a[2]	निन्यिव ni-ny-i-vá	निन्यिम ni-ny-i-má
2.	निनेथ ni-né-tha[3]	निन्यथुः ni-ny-áthuḥ	निन्य ni-ny-á
3.	निनाय ni-nā́y-a	निन्यतुः ni-ny-átuḥ	निन्युः ni-ny-úḥ

ĀTMANEPADA

1.	निन्ये ni-ny-é	निन्यिवहे ni-ny-i-váhe	निन्यिमहे ni-ny-i-máhe
2.	निन्यिषे ni-ny-i-ṣé	निन्याथे ni-ny-ā́the	निन्यिध्वे ni-ny-i-dhvé
3.	निन्ये ni-ny-é	निन्याते ni-ny-ā́te	निन्यिरे ni-ny-iré

5. स्तु stu, 'praise': strong तुष्टो tu-ṣṭó, तुष्टौ tu-ṣṭáu; weak तुष्टु tu-ṣṭu.

PARASMAIPADA

1.	तुष्टव tu-ṣṭáv-a[4]	तुष्टुव tu-ṣṭu-vá	तुष्टुम tu-ṣṭu-má
2.	तुष्टोथ tu-ṣṭó-tha	तुष्टुवथुः tu-ṣṭu-v-áthuḥ	तुष्टुव tu-ṣṭu-v-á
3.	तुष्टाव tu-ṣṭā́v-a	तुष्टुवतुः tu-ṣṭu-v-átuḥ	तुष्टुवुः tu-ṣṭu-v-úḥ

ĀTMANEPADA

1.	तुष्टुवे tu-ṣṭu-v-é	तुष्टुवहे tu-ṣṭu-váhe	तुष्टुमहे tu-ṣṭu-máhe
2.	तुष्टुषे tu-ṣṭu-ṣé	तुष्टुवाथे tu-ṣṭu-v-ā́the	तुष्टुध्वे tu-ṣṭu-dhvé
3.	तुष्टुवे tu-ṣṭu-v-é	तुष्टुवाते tu-ṣṭu-v-ā́te	तुष्टुविरे tu-ṣṭu-v-iré

1. Or दधिथ da-dh-i-thá.
2. Or निनाय ni-nā́y-a
3. Or निनयिथ ni-náy-i-tha.
4. Or तुष्टाव tu-ṣṭā́v-a.

6. तन् tan, 'stretch': strong ततन् ta-tán, ततान् ta-tā́n; weak तेन् ten.

PARASMAIPADA

1.	ततन ta-tán-a[1]	तेनिव ten-i-vá	तेनिम ten-i-má
2.	ततन्थ ta-tán-tha[2]	तेनथुः ten-áthuḥ	तेन ten-á
3.	ततान ta-tā́n-a	तेनतुः ten-átuḥ	तेनुः ten-úḥ

ĀTMANEPADA

1.	तेने ten-é	तेनिवहे ten-i-váhe	तेनिमहे ten-i-máhe
2.	तेनिषे ten-i-ṣé	तेनाथे ten-ā́the	तेनिध्वे ten-i-dhvé
3.	तेने ten-é	तेनाते ten-ā́te	तेनिरे ten-iré

7. गम् gam, 'go': strong जगम् ja-gám, जगाम् ja-gā́m; weak जग्म् ja-gm.

PARASMAIPADA

1.	जगम ja-gám-a[3]	जग्मिव ja-gm-ivá	जग्मिम ja-gm-imá
2.	जगन्थ ja-gán-tha	जग्मथुः ja-gm-áthuḥ	जग्म ja-gm-á
3.	जगाम ja-gā́m-a	जग्मतुः ja-gm-átuḥ	जग्मुः ja-gm-úḥ

ĀTMANEPADA

1.	जग्मे ja-gm-é	जग्मिवहे ja-gm-i-váhe	जग्मिमहे ja-gm-i-máhe
2.	जग्मिषे ja-gm-iṣé	जग्माथे ja-gm-ā́the	जग्मिध्वे ja-gm-i-dhvé
3.	जग्मे ja-gm-é	जग्माते ja-gm-ā́te	जग्मिरे ja-gm-iré

8. वच् vac, 'speak': strong उवच् u-vác, उवाच् u-vā́c; weak ऊच् ūc.

PARASMAIPADA

1.	उवच u-vác-a[4]	ऊचिव ūc-i-vá	ऊचिम ūc-i-má
2.	उवचिथ u-vác-i-tha[5]	ऊचथुः ūc-áthuḥ	ऊच ūc-á
3.	उवाच u-vā́c-a	ऊचतुः ūc-átuḥ	ऊचुः ūc-úḥ

ĀTMANEPADA

1.	ऊचे ūc-é	ऊचिवहे ūc-i-váhe	ऊचिमहे ūc-i-máhe
2.	ऊचिषे ūc-i-ṣé	ऊचाथे ūc-ā́the	ऊचिध्वे ūc-i-dhvé
3.	ऊचे ūc-é	ऊचाते ūc-ā́te	ऊचिरे ūc-iré

---

1. Or ततान ta-tā́n-a. 2. Or तेनिथ ten-i-thá. 3. Or जगाम ja-gā́m-a.
4. Or उवाच u-vā́c-a. 5. Or उवक्थ u-vák-tha.

Irregularities.

139. 1. भज् bhaj, 'share,' though beginning with an aspirate, follows the analogy of the contracting verbs with ए e (137, 2 *a*): 3. sg. बभाज ba-bhā́j-a, but 3. pl. भेजुः bhej-úḥ. Similarly राज् rāj, 'shine' (medial ā), and optionally त्रस् tras, 'tremble' (two initial consonants), and भ्रम् bhram, 'wander' (initial aspirate, two consonants): — 3. sg. A. रेजे rej-e; 3. pl. P. तत्रसुः ta-tras-uḥ or त्रेसुः tres-uḥ; बभ्रमुः ba-bhram-uḥ or भ्रेमुः bhrem-uḥ.

2. यम् yam, 'reach,' and वम् vam, 'vomit,' though beginning with य ya and व va, do not take Samprasāraṇa, but follow 137, 2 *a*:— ययाम ya-yā́ma, but येमे yem-é; ववाम va-vām-a, but वेमुः vem-uḥ; while वस् vas, 'wear,' Ātm., does not weaken the root at all:— ववसे va-vas-e.

3. विद् vid, 'know,' forms an unreduplicated perfect with present meaning: वेद véd-a, 'I know' (Gk. *οἶδα*, Germ. weiss), वेत्थ vét-tha (*οἶσ-θα*), वेद véd-a (*οἶδε*); विद्म vid-má (*ἴδ-μεν*, wissen), विद vid-á, विदुः vid-úḥ.

4. चि ci, 'gather,' जि ji, 'conquer,' हि hi, 'impel,' हन् han, 'kill,' revert to their original guttural in the radical syllable: — चिकाय ci-**k**ā́y-a, जिगाय ji-**g**ā́y-a, जिघाय ji-**gh**ā́y-a, जघान ja-**gh**ā́n-a (cp. 137, 2*b*).

5. अह् ah, 'say,' is defective, forming only 2. sg. dual and 3. sg. dual pl.: — आत्थ ā́**t**-tha, आह ā́h-a; आहथुः āh-áthuḥ, आहतुः āh-átuḥ; आहुः āh-úḥ.

6. अंश् aṃś, 'reach,' reduplicates with the syllable आन् ān, in which the radical nasal is repeated with the initial vowel (cf. Gk. aor. inf. *ἐν-εγκ-εῖν*); on the other hand, the radical nasal is dropped in the weak forms: 3. sg. P. आनंश ān-áṃśa, 3. pl. Ā. आनशिरे ān-aś-ire. The analogy of this verb is followed by अर्च् arc, 'praise': — 3. sg. आनर्च ān-árc-a.

7. भू bhū, 'be,' has the double irregularity of reduplicating with अ a and retaining its ऊ ū throughout (cp. *Gk.* πε-φύ-ᾱσι):—

बभूव ba-bhū́-v-a	बभूविव ba-bhū-v-i-vá	बभूविम ba-bhū-v-i-má
बभूथ ba-bhū́-tha बभूविथ ba-bhū́-v-i-tha	बभूवथुः ba-bhū-v-áthuḥ	बभूव ba-bhū-v-á
बभूव ba-bhū́-v-a	बभूवतुः ba-bhū-v-átuḥ	बभूवुः ba-bhū-v-úḥ

Periphrastic Prefect.

140. The verbs which cannot reduplicate, from their perfect by making an abstract feminine noun in the accusative, आम् ā́m, and adding to this the reduplicated perfect of कृ kṛ, 'do,' अस् as, 'be,' or भू bhū, 'be.' This formation started with the employment of the transitive verb कृ kṛ, e.g. गमयां चकार gamayā́ṃ cakāra, 'he did going,' i.e. 'he did go'; but in classical Sanskrit the priphrastic perfect is usually formed with अस् as, the other two auxiliaries occurring only exceptionally. The periphrastic perfect is almost entirely limited to the derivative verbs in अय aya (tenth class, causatives, and denominatives); — e.g. बोधयामास bodhayā́m āsa, 'he awakened.' Hardly any examples of desideratives or intensives are found in this tense.

a. The following are the few primary verbs taking the periphrastic perfect:—

1. four roots beginning with a prosodically long vowel: आस् ās, 'sit,' ईक्ष् īkṣ, 'see,' उज्झ् ujjh, 'forsake,' एध् edh, 'thrive';— e.g. आसां चक्रे ās-ā́ṃ cakre, 'he sat.'

2. the reduplicated roots चकास् ca-kās, 'shine,' and जागृ jā-gṛ, 'awake' (properly an intensive, 134 A4): — चकासां चकार cakās-āṃ cakāra, जागरामास jāgar-ām-āsa.

3. The roots भृ bhṛ, 'bear,' and, in the Epics, नी nī, 'lead,' and ह्वे hve, 'call,' optionally: — बिभरां बभूव bibhar-āṃ babhūva or

बभार ba-bhār-a, 'he bore'; (आ)नयामास (ā-)nayām āsa or निनाय ni-nấy-a, 'he brought'; ह्वयामास hvay-ām āsa or जुहाव ju-hấv-a, he called.'

Paradigm of the Periphrastic Perfect.

PARASMAIPADA

बोधयामास bodhayấm ās-a	बोधयामासिव bodhayấm ās-i-va	बोधयामासिम bodhayấm ās-i-ma
बोधयामासिथ bodhayấm ās-i-tha (ἠσ-θα)	बोधयामासथुः bodhayấm ās-athuḥ	बोधयामास bodhayấm ās-a
बोधयामास bodhayấm ās-a	बोधयामासतुः bodhayấm ās-atuḥ	बोधयामासुः bodhayấm ās-uḥ

Aorist.

141. There are two kinds of aorists in Sanskrit, as in Greek. The First is formed by inserting a sibilant between root and termination, the Second by adding the terminations to the root with or without the connecting vowel अ a. Both aorists take the augment (which is accented) and the secondary terminations. There are four forms of the First Aorist, and three of the Second.

First Aorist.

a. The **first form** is made by adding to the augmented root the suffix **स sa**, and is **inflected like an imperfect of the first conjugation** (á-bhava-t) except in the Ātm. 1. sg., 2.3. dual (where it follows the impf. of द्विष् dviṣ). It is taken by only a few roots ending in श् ś and ह् h (which become क् k before स् s: 63 *b*; 69 *a*), and containing the vowels इ i, उ u, or ऋ ṛ, which remain unchanged; — e.g. दिश् diś, 'point': 3. sg. अदिक्षत् á-dik-sa-t. This form corresponds to the Greek First Aorist (ἔ-δειξε, Lat. dixi-t).

PARASMAIPADA

1.	अदिक्षम् á-dik-ṣ-am	अदिक्षाव á-dikṣā-va	अदिक्षाम á-dikṣā-ma
2.	अदिक्षः á-dik-ṣa-ḥ	अदिक्षतम् á-dikṣa-tam	अदिक्षत á-dikṣa-ta
3.	अदिक्षत् á-dik-ṣa-t	अदिक्षताम् á-dikṣa-tām	अदिक्षन् á-dikṣ-an

ĀTMANEPADA

1.	अदिक्षि á-dikṣ-i	अदिक्षावहि á-dikṣā-vahi	अदिक्षामहि á-dikṣā-mahi
2.	अदिक्षथाः á-dikṣa-thāḥ	अदिक्षाथाम् á-dikṣ-āthām	अदिक्षध्वम् á-dikṣa-dhvam
3.	अदिक्षत á-dikṣa-ta	अदिक्षाताम् á-dikṣ-ātām	अदिक्षन्त á-dikṣ-anta

b. Similarly inflected is the aorist of दुह् duh, 'milk,' the stem of which is á-**dhuk-ṣa** (55): — Par. 1. sg. अधुक्षम् á-**dhuk-ṣa**-m, Ātm. अधुक्षि á-**dhukṣ**-i.

142. The **other three forms** of the First Aorist are made by adding to the augmented root the suffixes स् **s**, इष् **i-ṣ**, सिष् **s-i-ṣ** respectively, and are **inflected like imperfects of the second conjugation** (á-dveṣ-am). The siṣ-form is used, in the Par. only, by a few roots ending in आ ā, which remains unchanged throughout. The s-form and iṣ-form are used by roots ending in other vowels than आ ā, or in consonants; both have Vṛddhi throughout the Parasmaipada (a medial vowel has only Guṇa in the iṣ-form) and Guṇa throughout the Ātmanepada (a medial vowel and final ऋ ṛ remain unchanged in the s-form). All three forms have the peculiar endings ईस् **īs**, ईत् īt in the 2.3. sing. Par., and must take उर् ur in the 3. plur.

Second of s-form.

143. 1. नी nī, 'lead,' as an example of a root ending in a vowel:—

PARASMAIPADA

1.	अनैषम्	अनैष्व	अनैष्म
	á-nai-ṣ-am	á-nai-ṣ-va	á-nai-ṣ-ma
2.	अनैषी:	अनैष्टम्	अनैष्ट
	á-nai-ṣ-**īḥ**	á-nai-ṣ-ṭam	á-nai-ṣ-ṭa
3.	अनैषीत्	अनैष्टाम्	अनैषु:
	á-nai-ṣ-**īt**	á-nai-ṣ-ṭām	á-nai-ṣ-**uḥ**

ĀTMANEPADA

1.	अनेषि	अनेष्वहि	अनेष्महि
	á-ne-ṣ-i	á-ne-ṣ-vahi	á-ne-ṣ-mahi
2.	अनेष्ठा:	अनेषाथाम्	अनेढ्वम् (66 B 2)
	á-ne-ṣ-ṭhāḥ	á-ne-ṣ-āthām	á-ne-**ḍh**vam
3.	अनेष्ट	अनेषाताम्	अनेषत
	á-ne-ṣ-ṭa	á-ne-ṣ-ātām	á-ne-ṣ-ata

2. छिद् chid, 'cut off,' as an example of a root ending in a consonant:—

PARASMAIPADA

1.	अच्छैत्सम्	अच्छैत्स्व	अच्छैत्स्म
	á-cchait-s-am	á-cchait-s-va	á-cchait-s-ma
2.	अच्छैत्सी:	अच्छैत्तम् (66 B 2)	अच्छैत्त (66 B 2)
	á-cchait-s-**īḥ**	á-cchai**t**-**tam**	á-cchai**t**-**ta**
3.	अच्छैत्सीत्	अच्छैत्ताम् (66 B 2)	अच्छैत्सु:
	á-cchait-s-**īt**	á-cchai**t**-**tām**	á-cchait-**s**-**uḥ**

ĀTMANEPADA

1.	अच्छित्सि	अच्छित्स्वहि	अच्छित्स्महि
	á-cchit-s-i	á-cchit-s-vahi	á-cchit-s-mahi
2.	अच्छित्था: (66 B 2)	अच्छित्साथाम्	अच्छिद्ध्वम् (66 B 2)
	á-cchi**t**-**th**āḥ	á-cchit-s-āthām	á-cchi**d**-dhvam
3.	अच्छित्त (66 B 2)	अच्छित्साताम्	अच्छित्सत
	á-cchi**t**-**t**a	á-cchit-s-ātām	á-cchit-s-ata

a. कृ kṛ, 'do,' as ending in ऋ ṛ, is similarly inflected: — Par. अकार्षम् á-kār-ṣ-am, अकार्षीः á-kār-ṣ-īḥ, अकार्षीत् á-kār-ṣ-īt, &c. Ātm. अकृषि á-kṛ-ṣ-i, अकृथाः á-kṛ-**th**āḥ, अकृत á-kṛ-**t**a, &c. The last two forms do not properly belong to the s-aorist, being borrowed from the second form of the root aorist (148) which is not otherwise inflected in the Ātm.

Irregularities of the s-form.

144. 1. Before the suffix स् s final radical (*a*) न् n as well as म् m becomes Anusvāra (cp. 66 A 2); — e.g. अमंस्त á-mam̩-sta, from मन् man, 'think,' as well as अरंस्त á-ram̩-sta, from रम् ram, 'be glad' (cp. 42 B 1); (*b*) स् s in the verb वस् vas, 'dwell,' becomes त् t: अवात्सीत् a-vā**t**-sīt (66 B 1).

2. The termination ध्वम् dhvam (before which the स् s of the aorist is always lost) becomes ढ्वम् ḍhvam when the स् s would have been cerebralized (cp. 66 B 2); — e.g. अनेढ्वम् á-ne-ḍhvam (for á-ne-ṣ-dhvam), अकृढ्वम् á-kṛ-ḍhvam (for á-kṛ-ṣ-dhvam).

3. दा dā, 'give,' धा dhā, 'place,' स्था sthā, 'stand' (which takes the second aorist in the Par., 148), weaken their vowel to इ i (cp. 136 *a*, note 2) before the terminations of the Ātmanepada:— अदिषि á-di-ṣ-i, अदिथाः á-di-thāḥ (cp. 143 *a*), अदित á-di-ta (ἔ-δο-το), अदिष्वहि á-di-ṣ-vahi, &c.

4. दृश् dṛś, 'see,' सृज् sṛj, 'create,' स्पृश् spṛś, 'touch,' take Vṛddhi with metathesis in the Par.; — e.g. 3. sg. अस्राक्षीत् á-s**rāk**-ṣīt (63 *a*, note 2), du. अस्राष्टाम् á-srāṣ-ṭām (63 *a*; 66 B 2), pl. अस्राक्षुः á-s**rāk**-**ṣuḥ**; Ā. असृक्षि á-sṛ**k**-**ṣi**, असृष्ठाः á-sṛ**ṣ**-**ṭh**āḥ, असृष्ट á-sṛ**ṣ**-**ṭ**a, &c.

5. The aorist of दह् dah, 'burn,' and रुध् rudh, 'hinder,' is difficult owing to the Sandhi (69 *a*; 62 *b*): — sg. अधाक्षम् á-**dhāk**-ṣam,

अधाक्षीः á-**dhāk-ṣ**ī**ḥ**, अधाक्षीत् á-**dhāk-ṣ**ī**t**; du. अधाक्ष्व á-**dhāk-ṣ**va, अदाग्धम् á-dā**g-dh**am, अदाग्धाम् á-dā**g-dh**ām; pl. अधाक्ष्म á-**dhāk-ṣ**ma, अदाग्ध á-dā**g-dh**a, अधाक्षुः á-**dhāk-ṣ**uḥ; Ā. sg. अधक्षि á-**dhak-ṣ**-i, अदग्धाः á-da**g-dh**āḥ, अदग्ध á-da**g-dh**a; अधक्ष्वहि á-**dhak-ṣ**vahi, अधक्षाथाम् á-**dhak-ṣ**āthām, अधक्षाताम् á-**dhak-ṣ**-ātām; pl. अधक्ष्महि á-**dhak-ṣ**mahi, अधग्ध्वम् á-**dhag**-dhvam (62 *a*), अधक्षत á-**dhak-ṣ**-ata; अरौत्सम् á-rau**t**-sam; du. 2. अरौद्धम् á-rau**d-dh**am (62 *b*), pl. 2. अरौद्ध á-rau**d-dh**a; Ātm. sing. 1. अरुत्सि á-ru**t**-s-i, 2. अरुद्धाः á-ru**d-dh**āḥ, 3. अरुद्ध á-ru**d-dh**a; pl. 2. अरुद्ध्वम् á-ru**d**-dhvam, 3. अरुत्सत á-ru**t**-s-ata.

Third or iṣ-form.

145. This form differs from the preceding merely in adding the स् s with the connecting vowel इ i (which changes it to ष् ṣ 67). The endings of the 2.3. sg. are **ईस् īs, ईत् īt** (for iṣ-s, iṣ-t; cp 28; 150). Hardly any Parasmaipada forms of iṣ-aorists from roots ending in vowels occur in classical Sanskrit, but one such, formed from पू pū, 'purify,' in the older language and inflected in both voices, may be taken as a paradigm for the active as well as the middle:—

PARASMAIPADA

1.	अपाविषम् á-pāv-iṣ-am	अपाविष्व á-pāv-iṣ-va	अपाविष्म á-pāv-iṣ-ma
2.	अपावीः á-pāv-**īḥ**	अपाविष्टम् á-pāv-iṣ-ṭam	अपाविष्ट á-pāv-iṣ-ṭa
3.	अपावीत् á-pāv-**īt**	अपाविष्टाम् á-pāv-iṣ-ṭām	अपाविषुः á-pāv-iṣ-**uḥ**

ĀTMANEPADA

1.	अपविषि	अपविष्वहि	अपविष्महि
	á-pav-iṣ-i	á-pav-iṣ-vahi	á-pav-iṣ-mahi
2.	अपविष्ठाः	अपविषाथाम्	अपविढ्वम्
	á-pav-iṣ-ṭhāḥ	á-pav-iṣ-āthām	á-pav-i-**ḍh**vam (144, 2)
3.	अपविष्ट	अपविषाताम्	अपविषत
	á-pav-iṣ-ṭa	á-pav-iṣ-ātām	á-pav-iṣ-ata

a. बुध् budh, 'awake,' as an example of a root ending in a consonant, does not take Vṛddhi in the Par. (142):—

PARASMAIPADA

1.	अबोधिषम्	अबोधिष्व	अबोधिष्म
	á-bodh-iṣ-am	á-bodh-iṣ-va	á-bodh-iṣ-ma
2.	अबोधीः	अबोधिष्टम्	अबोधिष्ट
	á-bodh-**īḥ**	á-bodh-iṣ-ṭam	á-bodh-iṣ-ṭa
3.	अबोधीत्	अबोधिष्टाम्	अबोधिषुः
	á-bodh-**īt**	á-bodh-iṣ-ṭām	á-bodh-iṣ-**uḥ**

ĀTMANEPADA

1.	अबोधिषि	अबोधिष्वहि	अबोधिष्महि
	á-bodh-iṣ-i	á-bodh-iṣ-vahi	á-bodh-iṣ-mahi
2.	अबोधिष्ठाः	अबोधिषाथाम्	अबोधिढ्वम् (144, 2)
	á-bodh-iṣ-ṭhāḥ	á-bodh-iṣ-āthām	á-bodh-i-**ḍh**vam
3.	अबोधिष्ट	अबोधिषाताम्	अबोधिषत
	á-bodh-iṣ-ṭa	á-bodh-iṣ-ātām	á-bodh-iṣ-ata

b. मद् mad, 'exhilarate,' and वद् vad, 'speak,' take Vṛddhi in the Par.: अमादिषुः á-mād-iṣ-**uḥ**; अवादीत् á-vād-**īt**.

Fourth or siṣ-form.

146. This form differs from the preceding one simply in prefixing an additional स् s to the suffix. It is conjugated in the Parasmaipada only, and is used by not more than six roots, all ending in आ ā. या yā, 'go,' may serve as an example:—

PARASMAIPADA

1.	अयासिषम् á-yā-siṣ-am	अयासिष्व á-yā-siṣ-va	अयासिष्म á-yā-siṣ-ma
2.	अयासीः á-yā-sī**ḥ**	अयासिष्टम् á-yā-siṣ-ṭam	अयासिष्ट á-yā-siṣ-ṭa
3.	अयासीत् á-yā-sī**t**	अयासिष्टाम् á-yā-siṣ-ṭām	अयासिषुः á-yā-siṣ-**uḥ**

Second Aorist.

147. This aorist is like an imperfect formed directly from the root, the terminations being added with or without the connecting vowel अ a.

The **first form** is like an imperfect of the sixth class, the stem being formed by adding अ a to the unmodified root. It corresponds to the Second Aorist of the first conjugation in Greek (*ἔ-τυπ-ο-ν*). The inflexion of this aorist formed from सिच् sic, 'sprinkle,' is as follows:—

PARASMAIPADA

1.	असिचम् á-sic-am	असिचाव á-sicā-va	असिचाम á-sicā-ma
2.	असिचः á-sica-ḥ	असिचतम् á-sica-tam	असिचत á-sica-ta
3.	असिचत् á-sica-t	असिचताम् á-sica-tām	असिचन् á-sic-an

ĀTMANEPADA

1. असिचे á-sic-e	असिचावहि á-sicā-vahi	असिचामहि á-sicā-mahi
2. असिचथाः á-sica-thāḥ	असिचेथाम् á-sic-ethām	असिचध्वम् á-sica-dhvam
3. असिचत á-sica-ta	असिचेताम् á-sic-etām	असिचन्त á-sic-anta

Irregularities.

***a.* 1.** ख्या khyā, 'tell,' substitutes अ a for आ ā: अख्यत् á-khy**a**-t. — 2. दृश् dṛś, 'see,' takes Guṇa: अदर्शत् á-d**ar**ś-a-t. — 3. अस् as, 'throw,' adds थ् th to the root: आस्थत् ā́s-**th**-a-t[1]. — 4. पत् pat, 'fall,' and वच् vac, 'speak,' form contracted reduplicated aorists:— अपप्तम् á-pa-**pt**-am, अवोचम् á-**voc**-am (for á-va-uc-am, cp. Gk. ἔ-ειπ-ον).

Second Form.

148. The imperfect terminations of the second conjugation are attached to the root. This form corresponds to the Second Aorist of the second conjugation in Greek:— अधाम् á-dhā-m, 'I placed' (*ἔ-θη-ν*); अस्थात् á-shtā-t, 'he stood' (*ἔ-στη*); अगात् á-gā-t, 'he went' (*ἔ-βη*); अभूत् á-bhū-t, 'he became' (*ἔ-φῡ*). A few verbs ending in आ ā (as well as भू bhū, 'be') take this form. This आ ā is retained throughout except before the उर् ur of the 3. pl. There is no Ātmanepada (cp. 143*a*; 144, 3).

1. दा dā, 'give':— PARASMAIPADA

1. अदाम् á-dā-m	अदाव á-dā-va	अदाम á-dā-ma
2. अदाः á-dā-ḥ	अदातम् á-dā-tam	अदात á-dā-ta
3. अदात् á-dā-t	अदाताम् á-dā-tām	अदुः á-d-**uḥ**

---

1 The root of this aorist is, however, probably स्था sthā, 'stand,' with the vowel shortened as in अख्यत् á-khyat.

2. भू bhū, 'be':— PARASMAIPADA

1. अभूवम् á-bhū-v-am	अभूव á-bhū-va	अभूम á-bhū-ma
2. अभूः á-bhū-ḥ	अभूतम् á-bhū-tam	अभूत á-bhū-ta
3. अभूत् á-bhū-t	अभूताम् á-bhū-tām	अभूवन् á-bhū-v-an

Third or Reduplicated Form.

149. Excepting the primary verbs द्रु dru, 'run,' and श्रि śri, 'go,' this aorist has attached itself to the secondary conjugation in अय aya (tenth class and causatives). The stem is formed by a peculiar reduplication of the root, to which अ a is attached. The inflexion is like that of an imperfect of the first conjugation. Upwards of forty verbs take this aorist in classical Sanksrit.

Special Rules of Reduplication.

1. अ a, आ ā, ऋ ṛ, ॠ ṝ, ऌ ḷ are represented in the reduplicative syllable by इ i.

2. The vowel of the reduplicative syllables unless already long by position, is lengthened.

The quantity of the first three syllables of the stem is thus almost invariably ⏑ – ⏑: ă-jī-jăn-at, ă-ji-grăh-at, ă-śi-śrĭ-y-at, ă-vī-vĭś-at, ă-dī-dṛ̆ś-at, ă-dī-dăr-at (from dṝ), ă-du-drŭ-v-at, ă-mū-mŭc-at, ă-cī-kḷ̆p-at.

मुच् muc, 'release': stem अमूमुच a-mū-muc-a:—

PARASMAIPADA

1. अमूमुचम् a-mūmuc-am	अमूमुचाव a-mūmucā-va	अमूमुचाम a-mūmucā-ma
2. अमूमुचः a-mūmuca-ḥ	अमूमुचतम् a-mūmuca-tam	अमूमुचत a-mūmuca-ta
3. अमूमुचत् a-mūmuca-t	अमूमुचताम् a-mūmuca-tām	अमूमुचन् a-mūmuc-an

ĀTMANEPADA

1. अमूमुचे a-mūmuc-e	अमूमुचावहि a-mūmucā-vahi	अमूमुचामहि a-mūmucā-mahi
2. अमूमुचथाः a-mūmuca-thāḥ	अमूमुचेथाम् a-mūmuc-ethām	अमूमुचध्वम् a-mūmuca-dhvam
3. अमूमुचत a-mūmuca-ta	अमूमुचेताम् a-mūmuc-etām	अमूमुचन्त a-mūmuc-anta.

Irregularities.

a. 1. राध् rādh, 'succeed,' and व्यध् vyadh, 'pierce,' shorten their radical syllable, so as to produce the prevailing rhythm: अरीरधत् ă-rī-rădh-a-t, अवीविधत् ă-vī-vĭdh-a-t (cp. 133 B 2).

2. दीप् dīp, 'shine,' and मील् mīl, 'wink,' retaining their long radical vowel, do not lengthen the reduplicative syllable, thus inverting the usual quantity of these two syllables: अदिदीपत् a-didīp-a-t, अमिमीलत् a-mimīl-a-t.

Benedictive or Precative.

150. The active of this form is very rare, while the middle does not occur at all, in classical Sanskrit. It is an aorist optative, being formed by adding the terminations directly to the root. The terminations are those of the optative of the second conjugation, with स् s inserted between या yā and the personal inflexions. The endings of the 2.3. sing. are यास् yās (for yā-s-s), यात् yāt (for yās = yā-s-t: cp. 28; 145), being thus identical in form with those of the optative present (131). The Benedictive Par. of बुध् budh, 'awake,' would be formed as follows:—

1. बुध्यासम् budh-yā́-s-am	बुध्यास्व budh-yā́-s-va	बुध्यास्म budh-yā́-s-ma
2. बुध्याः budh-yā́-ḥ	बुध्यास्तम् budh-yā́-s-tam	बुध्यास्त budh-yā́-s-ta
3. बुध्यात् budh-yā́-t	बुध्यास्ताम् budh-yā́-s-tām	बुध्यासुः budh-yā́-s-uḥ

Simple Future.

151. The future is formed by adding to the stem the suffix स्य syá, or, with the connecting vowel इ i, इष्य i-ṣyá, and is inflected like a present of the first conjugation (bhávāmi). Most roots ending in vowels (except ऋ ṛ) take स्य sya, more than half of those ending in consonants take इष्य iṣya. Derivative verbs regularly take the latter.

a. Final vowels and prosodically short medial vowels take Guṇa:— e.g. इ i, 'go': एष्यति e-ṣyá-ti; बुध् budh, 'awake': भोत्स्यते bho**t**-sya-te (55); रुध् rudh, 'hinder': रोत्स्यति ro**t**-sya-ti; कृ kṛ, 'do': करिष्यति kar-i-ṣyá-ti; भू bhū, 'be': भविष्यति bhav-i-ṣyá-ti.

1. Several roots take both forms; — e.g. दह् dah, 'burn': धक्ष्यति **dhak**-ṣyá-ti (55) and दहिष्यति dah-i-ṣya-ti.

2. Derivatives in अय aya retain their present stem, dropping only their final अ a; — e.g. चोरय cor-aya, 'steal': चोरयिष्यति coray-i-ṣya-ti.

दा dā, 'give': — PARASMAIPADA

1. दास्यामि dā-syā́-mi	दास्यावः dā-syā́-vaḥ	दास्यामः dā-syā́-maḥ
2. दास्यसि dā-syá-si	दास्यथः dā-syá-thaḥ	दास्यथ dā-syá-tha
3. दास्यति dā-ṣyá-ti	दास्यतः dā-syá-taḥ	दास्यन्ति dā-sy-ánti

ĀTMANEPADA

1. दास्ये dā-sy-é	दास्यावहे dā-syā́-vahe	दास्यामहे dā-syā́-mahe
2. दास्यसे dā-syá-se	दास्येथे dā-sy-éthe	दास्यध्वे dā-syá-dhve
3. दास्यते dā-syá-te	दास्येते dā-sy-éte	दास्यन्ते dā-sy-ánte

Irregularities.

b. 1. Several verbs have र् ra instead of अर् ar before स्य sya (cop. 144, 4): — दृश् drś, 'see,' सृज् srj, emit,' सृप् srp, 'creep,' स्पृश् sprś, 'touch': द्रक्ष्यति **drak-**ṣyá-ti (63 *b*), स्रक्ष्यति **srak-ṣya-ti** (63 *a*), स्रप्स्यति **srap-**sya-ti, स्प्रक्ष्यति sp**rak-**ṣya-ti.

2. A few verbs strengthen the root with a nasal before स्य sya:— नश् naś, 'be lost': नङ्क्ष्यति na**ṅk-**ṣyati as well as नशिष्यति naś-i-ṣya-ti; मज्ज् majj, 'sink': मङ्क्ष्यति ma**ṅk-**ṣya-ti.

3. वस् vas, dwell, changes its स् s to त् t before स्य sya: वत्स्यति va**t-**sya-ti (66 B 1).

4. ग्रह् grah, 'seize,' takes ई ī instead of इ i as its connecting vowel: ग्रहीष्यति grah-ī-ṣya-ti (cp. 160, 3 *a*).

Periphrastic Future.

152. It is formed by adding the present of the verb अस् as, 'be,' to the nom. masc. of an agent noun in तृ -tr (101). The nom. sing. is used in all forms except the third persons dual and plural, in which the nom. dual and plural appear. The auxiliary is omitted in the third persons. The Parasmaipada only is found in use. About forty verbs, chiefly in the Epics, take this form of the future.

a. तृ tr is added, with or without इ i, to the gunated root, much in the same way as स्य sya. But roots ending in ऋ r, as well as गम् gam, 'go,' and हन् han, 'kill,' reject the connecting vowel:— कृ kr: कर्तास्मि kartāsmi (but करिष्यामि kar-i-ṣyā́-mi); गन्तास्मि gantā́smi (but गमिष्यामि gam-i-ṣyā-mi).

भू bhū, 'be':—

PARASMAIPADA

1.	भवितास्मि bhav-i-tā́smi	भवितास्वः bhav-i-tā́-svaḥ	भवितास्मः bhav-i-tā́-smaḥ

2	भवितासि	भवितास्थः	भवितास्थ
	bhav-i-tā́si	bhav-i-tā́-sthaḥ	bhav-i-tā́-stha
3.	भविता	भवितारौ	भवितारः
	bhav-i-tā́	bhav-i-**tā́rau**	bhav-i-**tā́raḥ**

इ i, 'go':—

PARASMAIPADA

1.	एतास्मि	एतास्वः	एतास्मः
	e-tā́smi	e-tā́-svaḥ	e-tā́-smaḥ
2.	एतासि	एतास्थः	एतास्थ
	e-tā́si	e-tā́-sthaḥ	e-tā́-stha
3.	एता	एतारौ	एतारः
	e-tā́	e-**tā́rau**	e-**tā́raḥ**

Conditional.

153. This is a past tense of the future, meaning 'would have.' It is formed by turning the simple future into a past, which is inflected like an imperfect of the first conjugation (ábhavam). Extremely rare even in the Par., it is still rare in the Ātm. It is to be met with cheifly in the Epics and the dramas. Examples are:— from भू bhū, 'be': (fut. भविष्यामि bhav-i-ṣyā́mi) अभविष्यम् á-bhaviṣy-am, अभविष्यः á-bhaviṣya-ḥ, अभविष्यत् á-bhaviṣya-t, &c.; Ātm. अभविष्ये á-bhaviṣy-e, &c.; इ i, 'go': (fut. एष्यामि e-ṣyā́-mi) ऐष्यम् áiṣy-am, ऐष्यः áiṣya-ḥ, ऐष्यत् áiṣya-t, &c.; Ātm. ऐष्ये áiṣy-e, &c.

Passive.

154. The passive, which takes the terminations of the Ātmanepada, differs from the latter only in the forms made from the present stem and in 3. sg. aor. From the Ātm. of verbs of the fourth class it differs in accent only: नह्यते náh-ya-te, 'he binds'; नह्यते nah-yá-te, 'he is bound.'

Before adding य ya, the root undergoes the following changes:—

1. Final आ ā (or diphthongs: 129, 8) remains or becomes ई ī; — e.g. ज्ञा jñā, 'know': ज्ञायते jñā-yá-te; पा pā, 'drink': पीयते pī-yá-te; गा gā, 'sing' (or गै gai): गीयते gī-yá-te.

2. Final इ i and उ u are lengthened; — e.g. इ i, 'go': ईयते ī-yá-te; चि ci, 'collect': चीयते cī-yá-te; श्रु śru, 'hear': श्रूयते śrū-yá-te.

3. Final ऋ ṛ after a single consonant becomes रि ri, after two consonants, अर् ar; — e.g. कृ kṛ, 'do' : क्रियते kri-yá-te; but स्मृ smṛ, 'remember': स्मर्यते samr-yá-te.

4. Final ॠ ṝ is changed to ईर् īr and, after labials, to ऊर् ūr; — e.g. कॄ kṝ, 'scatter': कीर्यते kīr-yá-te; स्तॄ stṝ, 'strew': स्तीर्यते stīr-yá-te; but पॄ pṝ, 'fill' (the only example): पूर्यते pūr-yá-te.

5. Roots ending in a consonant preceded by a nasal, lose the nasal; — e.g. भञ्ज् bhañj, 'break': भज्यते bhaj-yá-te.

6. Roots liable to Samprasāraṇa (137, 2 *c*) take it; — e.g. यज् yaj: इज्यते ij-yá-te; वच् vac: उच्यते uc-yá-te; ग्रह् grah: गृह्यते gṛh-yá-te; स्वप् svap: सुप्यते sup-yá-te.

7. Derivative verbs in अय aya drop the suffix while retaining the strong radical vowel; — e.g. चोरय cor-aya: चोर्यते cor-yate; कारय kār-aya (from कृ kṛ): कार्यते kār-ya-te.

The passive of भू bhū, 'be,' would be inflected as follows:—

PRESENT

1.	भूये bhū-y-é	भूयावहे bhū-yā́-vahe	भूयामहे bhū-yā́-mahé
2.	भूयसे bhū-yá-se	भूयेथे bhū-y-éthe	भूयध्वे bhū-yá-dhve
3.	भूयते bhū-yá-te	भूयेते bhū-y-éte	भूयन्ते bhū-y-ánte

IMPERFECT

1.	अभूये á-bhū-y-e	अभूयावहि á-bhū-yā-vahi	अभूयामहि á-bhū-yā-mahi
2.	अभूयथाः á-bhū-ya-thāḥ	अभूयेथाम् á-bhū-y-ethām	अभूयध्वम् á-bhū-ya-dhvam
3.	अभूयत á-bhū-ya-ta	अभूयेताम् á-bhū-y-etām	अभूयन्त á-bhū-y-anta

IMPERATIVE

1.	भूयै bhūy-ái	भूयावहै bhū-yā́-vahai	भूयामहै bhū-yā́-mahai
2.	भूयस्व bhū-yá-sva	भूयेथाम् bhū-y-éthām	भूयध्वम् bhū-yá-dhvam
3.	भूयताम् bhū-yá-tām	भूयेताम् bhū-y-étām	भूयन्ताम् bhū-y-ántām

OPTATIVE

1.	भूयेय bhū-y-éya	भूयेवहि bhū-y-évahi	भूयेमहि bhū-y-émahi
2.	भूयेथाः bhū-y-éthāḥ	भूयेयाथाम् bhū-y-éyāthām	भूयेध्वम् bhū-y-édhvam
3.	भूयेत bhū-y-éta	भूयेयाताम् bhū-y-éyātām	भूयेरन् bhū-y-éraṇ

Irregularities.

a. 1. खन् khan, 'dig,' has either खन्यते khan-yá-te or खायते khā-yá-te; तन् tan, 'stretch': तन्यते tan-yá-te or तायते tā-yá-te; जन् jan, 'beget,' has जायते jā́-ya-te, 'is born' (properly an Ātm. of the fourth class: cp. 133 B 2).

2. शास् śās, 'command,' has either शास्यते śās-ya-te or शिष्यते śiṣ-ya-te (cp. 134, 4 *a*).

3. ह्वा hvā, 'call' (or ह्वे hve), has हूयते hū-yáte (cp. 136, 4); वा vā (or वे ve), 'weave,' ऊयते ū-yá-te.

Aorist Passive.

155. The Ātm. of this tense supplies the place of the passive except in the **third person singular,** which has a special form. Here the augmented root adds the suffix इ i, which requires Vṛddhi of a final vowel and Guṇa of a medial vowel (but अ a is lengthened) followed by a single consonant; after आ ā, a य् y is inserted; — e.g. श्रु śru, 'hear': अश्रावि á-śrāv-i; कृ kṛ, 'do': अकारि á-kār-i; पद् pad, 'walk': अपादि á-pād-i; विश् viś, 'enter': अवेशि a-veś-i; मुच् muc, 'release': अमोचि á-moc-i; ज्ञा jñā, 'know': अज्ञायि á-jñā-**y**-i.

a. The following are peculiarities or **irregularities** in this formation:— 1. रभ् rabh, 'seize,' shows the nasalized form of the root: अरम्भि a-ra**m**bh-i. — 2. पॄ pṝ, 'fill,' has अपूरि a-**pūr**-i (cp. 154, 4). — 3. गम् gam, 'go,' रच् rac, 'fashion,' वध् vadh, 'slay,' do not lengthen their अ a: अगमि a-gam-i, अरचि a-rac-i, अवधि a-vadh-i. — 4. Verbs in अय aya drop the suffix (cp. 154, 7): रोपय **rop**-aya, causative of रुह् ruh, 'mount': अरोपि a-rop-i.

PARTICIPLES, GERUNDS, AND INFINITIVE

I. Active participles.

156. The stem of the **present** and **future** participles Par. is formed with the suffix अत् at (cp. 85). The strong stem is obtained by dropping the इ i of the 3. pl. pres. and fut. Par.: hence **verbs of the third class and other reduplicated verbs** (134 A 4) **have no nasal** in the strong stem of the **pres.** part., while the **fut.** part. **always** has अन्त् **ant** as its strong stem. Thus :—

PRES. 3. pl.	PRES. PART. (Strong).	FUT. 3.pl.	FUT. PART. (Strong)
भवन्ति	भवन्त्	भविष्यन्ति	भविष्यन्त्
bhávanti-i (1)	bhávant	bhav-iṣyánt-i	bhaviṣyánt
क्रीणन्ति	क्रीणन्त्	क्रेष्यन्ति	क्रेष्यन्त्
krī-ṇ-ánt-i (9)	krīṇánt	kre-ṣyánt-i	kreṣyánt
जुह्वति	जुह्वत्	होष्यन्ति	होष्यन्त्
júhv-at-i (3)	júhv**at**	ho-ṣyánt-i	hoṣyánt

a. The strong stem of the pres. part. of अस् as, 'be,' is सन्त् sánt (3. pl. सन्ति s-ánt-i); that of हन् han, 'slay,' is घ्नन्त् ghn-ánt (3. pl. घ्नन्ति ghn-ant-i).[1]

157. The **reduplicated perfect** participle (89) is most easily formed by taking the 3. pl. Par., with which the weakest stem is practically identical (only that र् r[2] must be changed to स् s which, being always followed by a vowel, appears as ष् ṣ). In forming the middle and strong stems from this, the final vowel of the root (changed to a semivowel before उस् us) must be restored, and in verbs which, after dropping उर् ur, become monosyllabic, इ i must be inserted :—

3. PLUR	WEAKEST STEM	STRONG STEM	MIDDLE STEM
चक्रुः	चक्रुषा	चकृवांसम्	चकृवद्भिः
ca-kr-úḥ	cakr-úṣ-ā	cakṛ-vā́ṃsam	cakṛ-vád-bhiḥ
बभूवुः	बभूवुषा	बभूवांसम्	बभूवद्भिः
babhū-v-úḥ	babhū-v-úṣ-ā	babhū-vā́ṃs-am	babhū-vád-bhiḥ
तेनुः	तेनुषा	तेनिवांसम्	तेनिवद्भिः
ten-úḥ	ten-úṣ-ā	ten-i-vā́ṃs-am	ten-i-vád-bhiḥ
ईजुः	ईजुषा	ईजिवांसम्	ईजिवद्भिः
īj-úḥ	īj-úṣ-ā	īj-i-vā́ṃs-am	īj-i-vád-bhiḥ

1. On the declension of participles in अत् at, see 85; on the formation of their feminine stems, 95 *a*.

2. Cp. 131, 6.

a. The participle of the present perfect of विद् vid, 'know' (3. pl. विदुः vid-úḥ), does not take the intermediate इ i: — inst. sg. विदुषा vidúṣ-ā; acc. विद्वांसम् vid-vā́ṃs-am; inst. pl. विद्वद्भिः vidvád-bhiḥ.

II. Ātmanepada and Passive Participles.

158. Present and **Future** Participles Ātmanepada and Passive are formed with the suffix मान māna, which is added after dropping the 3. pl. termination °न्ते -nte: — Ātm. pres. भवमान bháva-māna, fut. भविष्यमाण bhaviṣyá-māṇa; Pass. pres. भूयमान bhūyá-māna.

a. The **second conjugation** takes **आन āná** in the **pres. Ātm.**: जुह्वान júhv-**āna** (but fut. होष्यमाण hoṣyá-māṇa, Pass. pres. हूयमान hūyá-māna). The root आस् ās, 'sit,' takes the anomalous suffix ईन īna: आसीन ā́s-īna, 'sitting.'

159. The **Perfect Ātm.** would be formed with the suffix आन āná, which is added after dropping the termination इरे ire of the 3. pl. Ātm.; — e.g. बभूविरे babhūv-iré: बभूवान babhūv-āná. It has, however, become obsolete, only a few instances of it surviving in the sense of substantives or adjectives; — e.g. अनूचान anu͜ūc-āná (from anu-vac, 'having repeated' =) 'learned.'

160. The **Perfect Passive** Participle is formed with the suffixes न **ná** and the much commoner त **tá**.

1. न **na**, which is taken by primary verbs only, and is attached immediately to the root, is used by a good many roots ending in the long vowels आ ā, ई ī, ऊ ū, ॠ ṝ (which becomes ईर् īr or ऊर् ūr) and especially in द् d; — e.g. म्ला mlā, 'fade': म्लान mlā-na; ली lī, 'cling': लीन lī-na; लू lū, 'cut': लून lū-na; स्तॄ stṝ, 'strew': स्तीर्ण stīr-ṇá; पॄ pṝ, 'fill': पूर्ण pūr-ṇá (cp. 154, 4); भिद् bhid, 'cleave': भिन्न bhin-ná.

a. नुद् nud, 'push,' and विद् vid, 'find,' optionally take त ta:— नुन्न nun-na or नुत्त nut-tá; विन्न vin-na or वित्त vit-tá.

b. The final of a few roots in ज् j that take न na reverts to the original guttural; — e.g. भञ्ज् bhañj, 'break': भग्न bha**g**-na; भुज् bhuj, 'bend': भुग्न bhu**g**-na; मज्ज् majj, 'sink': मग्न ma**g**-na; विज् vij, 'tremble': विग्न vi**g**-na.

2. त **ta** is attached to the root with or without the connecting vowel इ i; — e.g. जित ji-tá, 'conquered'; पतित pat-i-ta, 'fallen.' When attaching the suffix immediately, the root has a tendency to be weakened in the usual way: verbs liable to Samprasāraṇa (137, 2*c*) take it, आ ā is in some cases weakened to ई ī or even इ i, a final nasal is in several cases lost[1]; — e.g. यज् yaj, 'sacrifice': इष्ट iṣ-ṭá (63*a*; 64); वच् vac, 'speak': उक्त uk-tá; स्वप् svap, 'sleep': सुप्त sup-tá; पा pā, 'drink': पीत pī-tá; स्था sthā, 'stand': स्थित sthi-tá (Gk. *στα-τό-ς* Lat. sta-tu-s); गम् gam, 'go': गत ga-tá; हन् han, 'kill': हत ha-tá.

a. धा dhā, 'put,' is doubly weakened: हित hi-tá (for dhi-tá).

b. दा dā, 'give,' uses its weak present stem दद् dad: दत्त dat-**tá**. After certain verbal prepositions दत्त dattá is weakened to त्त t-ta; — e.g. आत्त ā-tta (for ā-datta), 'taken.'

c. Several roots in अम् am, instead of dropping the nasal, retain it, and lengthen the preceding vowel; — e.g. कम् kam, 'love': कान्त kān-ta.

d. ध्वन् dhvan, 'sound,' follows the analogy of कम् kam, &c.: ध्वान्त dhvān-tá; while a few others in अन् an use a collateral forms of the root in आ ā; — e.g. खन् khan, 'dig': खात khā-tá; जन् jan, 'be born': जात jā-tá.

3. इत **i-ta** is taken by a considerable number of primary verbs which end either in double consonants or in single consonants

---

1. On the peculiar Sandhi of roots ending in ह् h, cp. 69.

not easily combining with त् t, and by all derivative verbs (which drop the final अ a or अय aya before it); — e.g. शङ्क् śaṅk, 'doubt': शङ्कित śaṅk-i-ta; लिख् likh, 'scratch': लिखित likh-i-tá; ईप्स īp-sa, desiderative of आप् āp, 'obtain': ईप्सित īps-i-tá; कारय kār-aya, causative of कृ kṛ, 'do': कारित kār-i-ta.

a. The full form of the root is usually retained before इत ita; but वद् vad, 'speak,' and वस् vas, 'dwell,' usually take Samprasāraṇa: — उदित ud-i-tá, उषित uṣ-i-ta; while ग्रह् grah, 'seize,' always takes Samprasāraṇa and the connecting vowel ई ī instead of इ i: गृहीत gṛh-ī-tá (cp. 151 *b* 4).

161. By adding the possessive suffix वत् **vat** to the past pass. part., a new form of very common occurrence is made, which has the value of a **perfect active** participle; — e.g. कृत kṛ-tá, 'done': कृतवत् kṛta-vat, 'having done.' It is generally used as a finite verb, the copula being omitted; — e.g. स तत् कृतवान् sa tat kṛtavān, 'he (has) done it'; सा तत् कृतवती sā tat kṛtavatī, 'she (has) done it' (cp. 89, foot-note 3).

162. The **Future Passive** Participle is formed with the suffix य ya, तव्य tav-yá, and अनीय an-ī́ya. They correspond in sense to the Lat. gerundive in -ndus.

1. Before the suffix य **ya**—

a. final आ ā becomes ए e; — e.g. दा dā: देय dé-ya, 'to be given.'

b. final इ i, ई ī take Guṇa, उ u, ऊ ū Guṇa or Vṛddhi, ऋ ṛ, ॠ ṝ Vṛddhi; — e.g. जि ji: जेय je-ya, 'to be conquered'; नी nī: नेय ne-ya, 'to be led'; हु hu: हव्य hav-yá, 'to be offered'; भू bhū: भाव्य bhāv-ya, 'about to be'; कृ kṛ: कार्य kār-yà, 'to be done.'

c. medial इ i and उ u followed by a single consonant generally take Guṇa, अ a is sometimes lengthened, ऋ ṛ remains unchanged; — e.g. भिद् bhid: भेद्य bhed-ya, 'to be split'; युज् yuj:

योज्य yoj-ya, 'to be joined'; शक् śak: शक्य śak-ya, 'possible'; but वच् vac: वाच्य vắc-ya, 'to be said'; दृश् dṛś: दृश्य dṛ́ś-ya, 'to be seen.'

2. Before the suffix तव्य **tavya**, the root, if possible, takes Guṇa, being treated in the same way as before the ता tā of the periphrastic fut. (152); — जि ji: जेतव्य je-tavya, 'to be conquered'; भू bhū: भवितव्य bhav-i-tavyá, 'that must be'; गम् gam: गन्तव्य gan-tavyá, 'to be gone'; दा dā: दातव्य dā-tavya, 'to be given'; भिद् bhid: भेत्तव्य bhet-tavya, 'to be split.'

3. Before the suffix अनीय **an-īya**, the root takes Guṇa; — e.g. चि ci: चयनीय cay-anīya, 'to be gathered'; भू bhū: भवनीय bhav-anīya, 'that must be'; कृ kṛ: करणीय kar-aṇīya, 'to be done': लुभ् lubh: लोभनीय lobh-anīya, 'to be desired.'

a. The अय aya of the causative is rejected; — भावय bhāv-aya: भावनीय bhāv-anīya, 'to be supposed.'

III. Gerund of Indeclinable Participle.

163. The suffix used for forming this participle from the **simple** verb is त्वा **tv-ā́** (an old instrumental singular of a stem in तु tu). It is most easily attached to the root by being substituted for the त tá of the passive participle; — e.g. कृत kṛ-tá, 'done': कृत्वा kṛ-tvā́, 'having done'; उक्त uk-tá, 'spoken': उक्त्वा uk-tvā, 'having spoken'; गत ga-tá, 'gone': गत्वा ga-tvā́, 'having gone.'

a. The suffix of the causative, अय aya, is, however, retained: चोरित cor-i-ta, 'stolen,' but चोरयित्वा cor-ay-i-tvā, 'having stolen.'

164. If the verb is **compounded** with a preposition it takes य **ya** instead of त्वा tvā: from भू bhū, 'be,' भूत्वा bhū-tvā́, but संभूय saṃ-bhū́-ya; from वच् vac, 'speak,' उक्त्वा uk-tvā, but प्रोच्य

pra͡uc-ya; from तॄ tṝ, cross,' अवतीर्य ava-tīr-ya, 'having descended,; from पॄ pṝ, 'fill,' संपूर्य saṃ-pūr-ya.

a. The suffix of the causative, अय aya, is retained (excepting the final अ a) before य ya if the radical vowel is short[1]; — e.g. संगमय्य saṃ-gam-ay-ya from संगमय saṃ-gam-aya, 'cause to assemble'; but विचार्य vi-cār-ya from विचारय vi-cār-aya, 'consider.'

165. त्य **tya** is added, instead of य ya, to compound verbs ending in a short vowel; — e.g. जित्वा ji-tvā́, but विजित्य vi-jí-tya.

a. The analogy of these verbs is optionally followed by roots ending in न् n or म् m, preceded by अ a, which may drop the nasal if it is dropped in the perfect participle passive (160, 2); — e.g. गम् gam, 'go': आगम्य ā-gam-ya or आगत्य ā-ga-tya (part. गत ga-tá); नम् nam, 'bend': प्रणम्य pra-ṇam-ya (65) or प्रणत्य pra-**ṇ**a-tya (part. नत na-tá); मन् man, 'think': °मन्य -man-ya or °मत्य -ma-tya (part. मत ma-tá); हन् han, 'kill': °हन्य -han-ya or °हत्य -ha-tya (part. हत ha-tá); तन् tan, 'stretch': °ताय -tā-ya (cp. 154 *a* 1) oı °तत्य -ta-tya (part. तत ta-tá). But क्रम् kram, 'stride,' has only °क्रम्य -kram-ya (part. क्रान्त krānta); खन् khan, 'dig,' only °खाय -khā-ya (part. खात khā-tá; cp. 154 *a* 1).

166. There is also a rare indeclinable participle in अम् **am.** It is most easily formed by adding the suffix to that form which the root assumes before the इ i of the 3. sg. aor. passive (155); — e.g. श्रु śru (अश्रावि á-śrāv-i, 'it was heard'): श्रावम् śrāv-am, 'having heard.'

IV. Infinitive.

167. The infinitive (= Lat. supine) is formed by adding तुम् **tu-m** (originally the acc. sg. of a verbal noun) to the form which

1. Otherwise the gerunds of the simple and the causative verb would be identical.

the verb assumes before the ता tā of the periphrastic future (152), or the तव्य tavya (162, 2) of the future part. pass.; — e.g. स्था sthā: स्थातुम sthā́-tum (Lat. sta-tum), 'to stand'; बुध् budh: बोधितुम् bodh-i-tum, 'to awake'; भू bhū: भवितुम् bháv-i-tum, 'to be'; कृ kṛ: कर्तुम् kár-tum, 'to do'; दृश् dṛś: द्रष्टुम् drás-ṭum (151 *b* 1), 'to see'; वह् vah: वोढुम् vó**ḍh**um (69 *b*), 'to carry'; सह् sah: सोढुम् so**ḍh**um (69 *b*), 'to bear'; चुर् cur: चोरयितुम् coray-i-tum, 'to steal.'

DERIVATIVE VERBS

I. Causatives.

168. This, the commonest class of derivative verbs, is formed with the suffix अय aya in the same way as the tenth class (125, 4), and is similarly inflected; — e.g. नी nī, 'lead': नायय nāy-aya, 'cause to lead'; कृ kṛ, 'make': कारय kār-aya, 'cause to make'; विद् vid, 'know': वेदय ved-áya, 'cause to know'; सद् sad, 'sit': सादय sād-áya, 'set.'

a. Most of the verbs in आ ā insert प् p before the causative suffix; — e.g. दा dā, 'give': दापय dā-p-aya; स्था sthā, 'stand': स्थापय sthā-p-aya.

b. The causative suffix is retained (as in the tenth class) throughout the conjugation excepting the (reduplicated) aorist (which is connected with the causative in sense only: cp. 149).

Irregularities.

1. ज्ञा jñā, 'know,' ग्ला glā, 'languish,' म्ला mlā, 'fade,' स्ना snā, 'wash,' optionally shorten the radical vowel before पय paya: ज्ञापय jñā-p-aya or ज्ञपय jña-p-aya, &c.

2. A few roots ending in other vowels than आ ā take पय paya:— जि ji, 'conquer': जापय **jā-p**aya, 'cause to win'; इ i with अधि adhi, 'read': अध्यापय adhy-**āpa**ya, 'teach'; ऋ ṛ, 'go': अर्पय

ar-**p**aya, 'put'; रुह् ruh, 'grow': रोपय ro-**p**aya, as well as रोहय roh-áya, 'raise.'

3. धू dhū, 'shake,' makes धूनय dhū-**n**-aya, 'shake'; प्री prī, 'love': प्रीणय prī-**ṇ**-aya, 'delight'; भी bhī, 'fear': भीषय bhī-**ṣ**-aya, as well as the regular भायय bhāy-aya, 'frighten.'

4. लभ् labh, 'take,' inserts a nasal: लम्भय la**m**bh-aya; while दंश् daṃś, 'bite,' retains its nasal: दशय da**ṃ**ś-aya (cp. 133 A 4).

5. हन् han, 'kill,' substitutes the denominative stem घातय ghāta-ya, 'make slaughter of.'

II. Desideratives.

169. Desiderative stems are formed by adding to the root, reduplicated in a peculiar way, the suffix स sa, directly in about seventy cases, but with the connecting vowel इ i (i.e. इष i-ṣa) in nearly thirty others. Thus भू bhū, 'be,' becomes बुभूष bú-bhū-ṣa, 'desire to be,' but जीव् jīv, 'live,' जिजीविष ji-jīv-iṣa, 'desire to live.' Desideratives are inflected like verbs of the first conjugation (p. 92).

The accent being on the reduplicative syllable, the **root** as a rule remains unchanged, but—

1. before स sa, final इ i and उ u are lengthened, while ऋ ṛ and ॠ ṝ becomes ईर् īr or, after labials, ऊर् ūr; — e.g. चि ci, 'gather': चिचीष ci-cī-ṣa; स्तु stu, 'praise': तुष्टूष tu-ṣṭū-ṣa; तॄ tṝ, 'cross': तितीर्ष ti-tīr-ṣa; मृ mṛ, 'die': मुमूर्ष mu-mūr-ṣa.

2. before इष iṣa, final ई ī, उ u, ॠ ṝ must take Guṇa; medial ऋ ṛ takes it also, medial उ u does so in one case, and medial इ i not at all; — e.g. शी śī, 'lie': शिशयिष śi-śay-iṣa; शॄ śṝ, 'crush': शिशरिष śi-śar-iṣa; नृत् nṛt, 'dance': निनर्तिष ni-nart-iṣa; शुभ् śubh, 'beautify': शुशोभिष śu-śobh-iṣa; विद् vid, 'know': विविदिष vi-vid-iṣa, as well as विवित्स vi-vit-sa.

Special Rules of Reduplication.

170. 1. अ a, आ ā, and ऋ ṛ are represented by इ i in the reduplicative syllable (but ऊर् ūr, standing for ऋ ṛ after labials, reduplicates with उ u); — e.g. दह् dah, 'burn': दिधक्ष di-**dhak-ṣ**a (55; 69*a*); स्था sthā, 'stand': तिष्ठास ti-ṣṭhā-sa; सृज् sṛj, 'create': सिसृक्ष si-sṛ**k-ṣ**a (63 *a*); भृ bhṛ, 'bear': बुभूर्ष bu-bh**ū**r-ṣa.

a. The reduplication of roots containing इ i and उ u is normal; — e.g. विश् viś, 'enter': विविक्ष vi-vi**k-ṣ**a (63 *b*); बुध् budh, 'know': बुभुत्स bu-**bhut**-sa (55); दुह् duh, 'milk': दुधुक्ष du-**dhuk-ṣ**a (55; 69 *a*); रुह् ruh, 'grow': रुरुक्ष rú-ru**k-ṣ**a. Thus all desideratives, except those from roots containing उ u, ऊ ū, redpulicate with इ i.

2. The two or three roots with initial vowel that take the desiderative reduplicate internally with इ i: अश् aś, 'eat,' अशिशिष áś-iś-iṣa; ईक्ष् īkṣ, 'see': ईचिक्षिष īc-ikṣ-iṣa. आप् āp, 'optain,' forms its stem by contraction: ईप्स **íp**-sa.

Irregularities.

171. 1. गम् gam, 'go,' and हन् han, 'kill,' lengthen their radical vowel; while मन् man, 'think,' lenghtens the reduplicative vowel as well:— जिगांस ji-gām̐-sa (beside जिगमिष jí-gam-iṣa); जिघांस jí-**ghām̐**-sa (66 A 2); मीमांस **mī-mām̐**-sa (66 A 2), 'reflect.'

2. ग्रह grah, 'seize,' प्रछ् prach, 'ask,' स्वप् svap, 'sleep,' take Samparasāraṇa: — जिघृक्ष ji-**ghṛk**-ṣa (55; 69 *a*), पिपृच्छिष pi-pṛcch-iṣa, सुषुप्स su-ṣ**up**-sa.

3. दा dā, 'give,' धा dhā, 'place,' मा mā, 'measure,' पद् pad, 'go,' रभ् rabh, 'grasp,' लभ् labh, 'take,' शक् śak, 'be able,' contract the first two syllables of the stem in such a way as to retain only the reduplication and one consonant of the root: दित्स dí-**t**-sa, धित्स **dhí-t**-sa (for dí-dh(ā)-sa: 55), मित्स mi-**t**-sa, पित्स pi-**t**-sa, रिप्स ri-**p**-sa, लिप्स lí-**p**-sa, शिक्ष śí-k-ṣa.

4. चि ci, 'gather,' जि ji, 'conquer,' हन् han, 'kill' (cp. 171, 1), revert to their original guttural: **चिकीष** ci-**kī**-ṣa (beside **चिचीष** ci-cī-ṣa); **जिगीष** jí-**gī**-ṣa; **जिघांस** jí-**ghā**ṃ-sa.

5. **घस्** ghas, 'eat,' changes its **स्** s to **त्** t: ji-gha**t**-sa, 'be hungry.'

III. Intensives (Frequentatives).

172. These verbs are meant to convey an intensification or frequent repetition of the action expressed by the simple root. Only monosyllabic verbs beginning with a consonant are liable to be turned into intensives. Hence neither verbs of the tenth class nor roots like **अद्** ad can form this derivative. About sixty roots (less than half the number found in Vedic literature) take the intensive in Sanskrit, but forms of it rarely occur.

The stem, which takes a peculiar kind of strong reduplication, has **two forms.** The one adds the personal endings immediately to the reduplicated stem (accented on the first syllable in strong forms), being conjugated in the Parasmaipada only, like a verb of the third or reduplicated class (p. 96); — e.g. **बोभोति** bó-bho-ti from **भू** bhū, 'be.' The other adds accented **य** ya, in the same way as the passive (154), to the reduplicated stem, being conjugated in the Ātmanepada only, like the passive (p. 130); — e.g. **बोभूयते** bo-bhū-yá-te from **भू** bhū.

a. The first intensive may optionally insert **ई** ī before terminations beginning with consonants in the strong forms. Stems ending in consonants do not take Guṇa either before this **ई** ī or before terminations beginning with vowels; — e.g. **विद्** vid, 'know'; **वेवेद्मि** vé-ved-mi or **वेविदीमि** vé-vid-ī-mi, **वेविद्मः** ve-vidmáḥ, imper. **वेविदानि** vé-vid-āni; but **हू** hū, 'call': **जोहोमि** jó-ho-mi or **जोहवीमि** jó-hav-ī-mi, **जोहवानि** jó-hav-āni.

Special Rules of Reduplication.

173. The reduplicative syllable takes Guṇa and lengthens अ a; — e.g. निज् nij, 'cleanse': नेनेक्ति né-nek-ti; नी nī, 'lead': नेनीयते ne-nī-yá-te; बुध् budh, 'know': बोबुधीति **bo**-budh-ī-ti; प्लु plu, 'float': पोप्लूयते po-plū-ya-te; तप् tap, 'be hot': तातप्यते tā-tap-ya-te.

a. Roots ending in अम् am repeat the nasal instead of lengthening the vowel; — e.g. क्रम् kram, 'stride': चङ्क्रमीति ca**ṅ**-kram-ī-ti, चङ्क्रम्यते ca**ṅ**-kram-yá-te.

b. Roots containing ऋ ṛ insert ई ī between the reduplication and the root; — e.g. मृ mṛ, 'die': मरीमर्ति mar-**ī**-mar-ti; दृश् dṛś, 'see': दरीदृश्यते dar-ī-dṛś-ya-te; नृत् nṛt, 'dance': नरीनृत्यते nar-ī-nṛt-ya-te.

Irregularities.

174. गृ gṛ, 'awake,' reduplicating with आ ā (as from गर् gar), forms the stem जागृ jā-gṛ, which has almost assumed the character of a root (134 A 4) and is used as the only present stem of the verb: 3. sg. जागर्ति jā-gar-ti, 3. pl. जाग्रति já-gr-ati.

a. दह् dah, 'burn,' and जभ् jabh, 'snap at,' reduplicate with a nasal, while चर् car, 'move,' changes its radical vowel as well: दन्दहीति da**n**-dah-ī-ti and दन्दह्यते da**n**-dah-ya-te; जञ्जभ्यते ja**ñ**-jabh-yá-te; चञ्चूर्यते ca**ñ**-c**ū**r-yá-te.

b. पद् pad, 'go,' besides reduplicating with a nasal, inserts ई ī after it: पनीपद्यते pa-**n**-**ī**-pad-ya-te; while द्रा drā, 'run' reduplicates as if (173 *b*) it contained ऋ ṛ (only that the inserted vowel is इ i, which, however, is long by position): दरिद्राति **dár-i**-drā-ti (cp. 143 A 4).

IV. Denominatives.

175. A large number of verbs, inflected like those of the a-conjugation (p. 92), are derived, with the suffix य yá, from nouns, to which they express some such relation as 'be or act like,' 'treat as,' 'make,' 'desire.' Before the suffix, final इ i and उ u are lengthened; अ a often is also, but sometimes becomes ई ī (cp. 154, 1). Examples are: — नमस्य namas-yá, 'pay homage (names) to'; स्वामीय svāmī-ya, 'regard as a master' (svāmi); गोपाय gopā-yá, 'be like a herdsman (go-pā) to,' 'protect'; राजाय rājā-ya, 'play the king' (rāja); द्रुमाय drumā-ya, 'rank as a tree' (druma); पुत्रीय putrī-ya, 'desire a son' (putra).

a. Denominatives which have the causative accent (á-ya) are reckoned verbs of the tenth class by the Hindu grammarians. Such are मन्त्रय mantrá-ya, 'take counsel' (mántra), कीर्तय kīrtá-ya, 'celebrate' (kīrtí, 'fame'); वर्णय varṇá-ya, 'depict,' 'describe' (várṇa, 'colour'); कथय kathá-ya, 'tell how,' 'relate' (ka-thám, 'how?').

CHAPTER V

INDECLINABLE WORDS

Prepositions.

176. Owing to the cases having a more independent meaning than in other Āryan languages, the number of prepositions is quite small, and their use is very limited in Sanskrit. They are nearly all postpositions[1], and they do not 'govern,' but only define the general sense of, the case to which they are added.

1. In Homeric Greek the prepositions preserve their original position as well as accent in anastrophe: ἄπο (Skt. ápa), ἔπι (ápi), πάρα (párā), πέρι (pári).

Of the dozen Vedic postpositions (also employed as verbal prefixes) Sanskrit preserves only three in common use:—

1. अनु ánu, 'after,' and प्रति práti (Gk. *προτί*), 'towards,' 'about,' after the **accusative.**

2. आ ā́, 'from' or 'up to,' **before** the **ablative.**

a. The following are also occasionally met with, nearly always following their case:— अभि abhí, 'against' (acc.); पुरस् purás, 'before' (gen.); अधि ádhi, 'over' (loc.), अन्तर् antár (Lat. inter, Eng. under), 'within,' 'between' (loc., rarely gen.).

Prepositional Adverbs.

177. The loss or obsolescence of the Vedic prepositions in the true sense is compensated in Sanskrit by the increasing use of ungenuine prepositions, that is to say, those which cannot be attached to verbs and the origin of which from cases is still for the most part clear. They are employed with all the oblique cases except the locative and the dative; with the latter case no prepositional word is ever connected in Sanskrit. These adverbs are given in the following list, grouped under the cases which they accompany:—

a. **Acc.** अन्तरा antarā́ and अन्तरेण ántareṇa, 'between,' 'without'; the latter also 'regarding'; निकषा nikaṣā and समया samáyā, 'near'; अभितः abhí-taḥ, परितः parí-taḥ, सर्वतः sarvá-taḥ, समन्ततः samanta-taḥ, 'around'; उभयतः ubhayá-taḥ, 'on both sides of'; परेण páreṇa, 'beyond'; यावत् yā́vat, 'during,' 'up to,' 'till' (also abl.).

b. **Instr.** सह sahá, समम् samám, साकम् sākám, सार्धम् sārdham, '(together) with'; विना vínā, 'without,' 'except' (also acc., rarely abl.).

c. **Abl.** All the adverbs used with this case express some modification of the fundamental ablative notion of separation:–

1. 'before (of time): अर्वाक् arvấk, पुरा purá, पूर्वम् pűrvam, प्राक् prấk. 2. 'after' (of time): अनन्तरम् an-antaram, ऊर्ध्वम् ūrdhvám, परम् param, परत: para-taḥ, परेण páreṇa, प्रभृति prabhṛti (originally a fem. noun meaning 'commencement'). 3. 'outside,' 'out of': बहि: bahíḥ. 4. 'apart from': अन्यत्र anyá-tra; ऋते ṛte (also acc.).

d. **Gen.** Nearly all the adverbs used with this case express some relation in space: — 1. 'before,' 'in presence of'; अग्रे ágre, अग्रत: agra-táḥ, पुरत: pura-taḥ, पुरस्तात् purás-tāt, प्रत्यक्षम् praty-akṣam, समक्षम् sam-akṣám. 2. 'after': पश्चात् paścát. 3. 'beyond': परत: para-taḥ, परस्तात् parás-tāt. 4. 'above,' 'over,' 'upon': उपरि upári (also acc.) and उपरिष्टात् upári-ṣṭāt; the former also 'with regard to.' 5. 'below': अध: adháḥ and अधस्तात् adhás-tāt. — With the gen. is also used कृते kṛte, 'for the sake of.'

178. The case-notions of the accusative ('whither'), ablative ('whence'), and locative ('where') are often paraphrased by nouns meaning 'proximity,' such as अन्तिक antiká, उपकण्ठ upa-kaṇṭha, निकट ni-kaṭa, सकाश sa-kāśa, संनिधि saṃ-nidhi, समीप sam-īpa, पार्श्व pārśvá ('side'). In the **acc.** they mean 'towards,' 'to,' 'near'; in the **abl.**, 'from'; and in the **loc.,** 'near,' 'in the presence of': in each case governing the genitive. For example: — राज्ञोऽन्तिकं गच्छ् 'go to the king'; रघो: सकाशाद् अपासरत् 'he withdrew from Raghu'; मम पार्श्वे 'beside me,' 'near me'; तस्या: समीपे नलं प्रशशंसु: 'they praised Nala in her presence.'

Prepositional Gerunds.

179. Several indeclinable participles are used in the sense of prepositions:—

1. with **acc.** उद्दिश्य ud-diś-ya, 'pointing at' = 'towards,'

'about,' 'at,' 'for'; आदाय ā-dā-ya, गृहीत्वा gṛhī-tvā, 'taking,' नीत्वा nī-tvā, 'leading' = 'with'; अधिष्ठाय adhi-ṣṭhā-ya, अवलम्ब्य ava-lamb-ya, आश्रित्य ā-śri-tya, आस्थाय ā-sthā-ya, 'resorting to' = 'by means of'; मुक्त्वा muk-tvā, परित्यज्य pari-tyaj-ya वर्जयित्वा varjay-i-tvā, 'putting aside' = 'except'; अधिकृत्य adhi-kṛ-tya, 'putting at the head' = 'with reference to,' 'about.'

2. with **abl.** आरभ्य ā-rabh-ya, 'beginning from' = 'since.'

Conjunctive and Adverbial Particles.

180. अङ्ग aṅgá, in exhortations = 'pray': अङ्ग कुरु 'pray do it.' किमङ्ग kim aṅga: 1. 'why, pray?' 2. 'how much more?'

अथ á-tha: 1. introducing something new at the beginning of a sentence = 'now,' then,' 'afterwards.' 2. in the headings of books, chapters, sections, 'now' = 'here begins' (opposed to इति iti, 'here ends'). 3. connecting parts of a sentence = 'and,' 'also.' 4. 'if': अथ तान्नानुगच्छामि गमिष्यामि यमक्षयम् 'if I do not follow them, I shall go to Yama's abode.' — अथ किम् atha kim, 'what else?' = 'it is so,' 'certainly,' 'yes.' — अथ वा atha vā: 1. 'or else,' 'or.' 2. correcting a previous statement = 'or rather,' 'but.' 3. adding a corroborative statement, 'or so' = 'so for instance': अथवा साध्विदमुच्यते 'thus it is well said.'

अथो átho, 'then,' 'afterwards' (see उ u).

अन्यच्च anyac ca, 'and another thing' = 'and besides,' 'moreover.'

अपरम् aparam, 'further,' 'moreover,' 'besides.'

अपि ápi: 1. connecting (like च ca) parts of a sentence = 'like-wise,' 'moreover,' 'and' (अपि — अपि 'both — and'). 2. 'also,' 'on one's own part': दमनकोऽपि निर्जगाम 'Damanaka also (on his part) went away.' 3. 'even,' 'though': बालोऽपि 'even

a child; एकाक्यपि ekākī‿api, 'though alone.' 4. 'only,' 'but' (of time): मुहूर्तमपि 'but a moment.' 5. 'all' with numerals: चतुर्णामपि वर्णानाम् 'of all the four castes.' In the above five senses अपि api always follows the word to which it belongs. It is also used at the beginning of a sentence as an interrogative particle, and with the optative to express a wish or preference: अपि तपो वर्धते 'is your penance prospering? अपि स कालः स्यात् 'would that the time had come'; अपि प्राणानहं जह्यां न त्वाम् 'I would rather abandon life than thee.' — अपि नाम api nāma, 'perhaps' (see नाम nāma).

अलम् **álam,** 'enough,' construed with the instrumental, gerund or infinitive, expresses a prohibition: अलं भयेन 'away with fear'; अलमुपालभ्य 'cease reproaching me'; अलं प्रबोधयितुम् 'do not awaken.'

इति **íti,** 'thus': 1. is used after the exact words of quotations. With verbs of saying it supplies the place of inverted commas a. d of the indirect construction in English: तवाज्ञां करिष्यामीति स मामुवाच 'he said to me, I will do they bidding (tava‿ājñām),' or 'he told me that he would do my bidding.'

a. It is similarly used to quote thoughts, intensions, knowledge, though not uttered: बालोऽपि नावमन्तव्यो मनुष्य इति भूमिपः 'one should not despise a king, though a child, (thinking =) because he is a mere human being'; दातव्यमिति यद्दानं दीयते 'a gift which is presented (thinking 'it ought to be given' =) from a sense of duty'; न धर्मशास्त्रं पठतीति कारणम् '(the knowledge) that he reads the book of the law, is not a cause (of confidence in him).'

2. = 'here ends,' at the end of books, chapters, sections, acts: इति तृतीयोऽङ्कः 'here ends the third act.'

3. 'in the capacity of,' 'as regards,' 'as for': शीघ्रमिति सुकरं निभृतमिति चिन्तनीयं भवेत् 'as for (doing it) quickly, it (would

be) easy; for (doing it) secretly, it would require consideration.' (See also किम् kim and तथा tathā.)

इव iva, being enclitic, follows the word to which it belongs in sense:— 1. 'like': अयं चोर इवाभाति 'this man looks like a thief.' 2. 'as if,' 'as it were': साक्षात् पश्यामीव पिनाकिनम् 'I see, as it were, Śiva himself before me.' 3. 'somewhat': सरोषमिव 'somewhat angrily.' 4. 'almost': मुहूर्तमिव 'almost an hour.' 5. 'just,' 'quite': अकिंचिदिव 'just a little'; नचिरादिव 'quite soon.' 6. 'indeed,' 'pray' (German 'wohl'), with interrogatives: किमिव मधुराणां मण्डनं नाकृतीनाम् 'what, indeed, is not an ornament to lovely figures?'

उ u, an old particle of frequent occurrence in the Veda, meaning 'and,' is preserved in Sanskrit only in combination with किम् kim (q.v.), and in अथो átho (for átha‿u, 'and so'), 'then,' and नो nó (for ná‿u, 'and not'), 'not.'

उत utá, a common particle in the Veda, meaning 'and,' 'also,' 'or,' survives only 1. in combination with प्रति and किम्: — प्रत्युत prati‿uta, 'on the contrary'; किमुत kim uta, 'how much more,' 'how much less'; 2. in the second part of a double question:— किम् — उत (= utrum — an) 'whehter — or.' It is also frequent as an expletive at the end of a line in the Epics.

एव evá is a restrictive particle following the word which it emphasizes. It may often be rendered by 'just,' 'only,' 'exactly,' 'quite,' as well as in various other ways, sometimes merely by stress: — एक एव 'quite alone'; दर्शनमेव 'the very sight'; अहमेव 'I myself'; तदेव 'that very,' 'the same'; मृत्युरेव 'sure death'; वसुधैव 'the whole earth.' — चैव ca‿eva, 'and also.' — तथैव tathā‿eva, 'likewise,' 'also.' — नैव na‿eva, 'not at all,' 'by no means.'

एवम् evám, 'thus,' 'so': — एवमस्तु 'so be it'; मैवम् mā‿evam, 'not so!'

कच्चित् **kác-cit** (Vedic neuter of interr. कद् ká-d + चिद् cid), used in questions expecting the answer 'yes' (Lat. nonne) = 'I hope': — कच्चिद्दृष्टा त्वया राजन् दमयन्ती 'I hope you have seen Damayantī, O king?' With negative = 'I hope not' (Lat. num): — कच्चित्तु नापराधं ते कृतवानस्मि 'I have not done you any injury, I hope?'

कामम् **kāma-m** (acc. of काम 'deisre'), primarily used as an adverb meaning 'at will,' 'gladly,' is frequently employed as a concessive particle: — 1. 'indeed,' 'certainly,' 'forsooth,' 'to be sure'; 2. 'granted,' 'supposing' (generally with imperative), followed by adversative adverb: — कामम् — तु, किंतु, तथापि, or पुन: 'it is true — but,' 'although — yet'; कामम् — न तु 'certainly — but not,' 'rather — than' (cp. वरम् varam — न na).

किम् **kí-m:** 1. 'what?' 2. 'why?' 3. a simple interrogative particle not to be translated, and expecting the answer 'no' (Lat. num). 4. 'whether?' in double questions, followed by किं वा, किमुत, or simply उत, वा, or आहोस्विद् 'or.'

Combinations of किम् kim with other particles are the following :— किं च 'moreover?' — किं तु 'put,' 'however' — किमिति, किमिव 'wherefore?' — किं वा 'perchance?' — किंस्विद् 'why, pray?' 'I wonder?' — किमपि 1. 'very,' 'vehemently': किमपि रुदती 'weeping bitterly'; 2. 'nay, more.' — किमु, किमुत, किं पुन: 'how much more,' 'how much less': एकैकम् अप्यनर्थाय किमु यत्र चतुष्टयम् 'even each singly (leads) to ruin, how much more (is it so) when the four (are combined)!'

किल **kíla** (quidem): 1. 'indeed,' 'certainly,' 'to be sure' follows the word it emphasizes: अर्हति किल कितव उपद्रवम् 'to be sure the rogue deserves calamity.' Sometimes किल may be rendered by stress merely: एकस्मिन् दिने व्याघ्र आजगाम किल 'one day a tiger *did* come.' 2. 'they say,' 'we are told':

बभूव योगी किल कार्तवीर्यः 'there lived, it is said, a devotee named Kārtavīrya.'

कृतम् **kṛ-ta-m** (neut. of past part.), 'done,' is used (like अलम् álam) with the instrumental in the sense of 'have done with':— कृतं संदेहेन 'away with doubt.'

केवलम् **kevala-m,** 'only': केवलं स्वपिति 'he merely sleeps.' — न केवलम् — अपि 'not only — but.'

क्व **kva,** 'where?' if **repeated** with another question, expresses great difference, incogruity, or incompatibility: क्व सूर्यप्रभवो वंशः क्व चाल्पविषया मतिः 'where (is) the race sprung from the sun, and where (my) limited intelligence?' i.e. 'how great is the discrepancy between the glory of the solar race and my powers of description.'

खलु **khálu:** 1. 'indeed,' 'surely,' often merely emphasizing the preceding word. 2. 'pray,' 'please,' in entreaties: देहि खलु मे प्रतिवचनम् 'please give me an answer' (German 'doch'). 3. with gerund = 'enough of,' 'do not' (like अलम् álam): खलु रुदित्वा 'do not weep.' — न खलु 'not at all,' 'certainly not,' 'I hope not.'

च ca, enclitic (= τε, que), 'and,' 'also': — गोविन्दो रामश्च 'Govinda and Rāma.' In poetry the particle is occasionally misplaced: इह चामुच for इहामुच च 'in this world and in the next.' When more than two words are connected, the conjunction is commonly used with the last only, as in English. — च — च 1. 'both — and.' 2. 'on the one hand — on the other,' 'though — yet.' 3. 'no sooner — than.'

चेद् **céd** (ca + íd), 'if,' never begins a sentence or half-line (as यदि yádi, 'if,' does). — अथ चेद् 'but if.' — न चेद् or नो चेद् 'if not' (elliptically) = 'otherwise': सर्वं विमृश्य कर्तव्यं नो चेत् पश्चात्तापं व्रजिष्यसि 'everything should be done after deliberation, otherwise you will come to repentance.' — चेन्न cen na, 'if —

not' (apodosis): भावि चेन्न तदन्यथा 'if it (is) to be, it (will) not (be) otherwise.' — इति चेन्न 'if this (is objected, it is) not (so).'

जातु **jātu:** 1. 'at all,' 'ever.' 2. 'possibly,' 'perhaps.' 3. 'once,' 'one day.' न जातु 'not at all,' 'by no means'; 'never.'

ततः **tá-taḥ:** 1. 'thence.' 2. 'thereupon,' 'then.' ततस्ततः tatas tataḥ = 'what next,' 'pray go on' (with what you are saying).

तथा **tá-thā:** 1. 'thus,' 'so,' 'accordingly.' 2. 'likewise,' 'also,' 'as well as,' 'and' (= च). 3. 'that is so,' 'yes,' 'it shall be done.' — तथा च 'so also,' 'similarly.' — तथापि tathā‿api, 'nevertheless.' — तथा हि 'for so (it is),' 'so for instance,' 'that is to say,' 'namely.' — तथेति tathā‿iti, 'yes.'

तद् **tá-d** (neut. of pron. 'that'): 1. 'then,' 'in that case.' 2. 'therefore,' 'accordingly': राजपुत्रा वयं तद् विग्रहं श्रोतुं नः कुतूहलमस्ति 'we are princes; therefore we have a curiosity to hear of war.'

तावत् **tá-vat:** 1. 'so long' (correlative to यावत् 'how long,' 'while,' 'till'). 2. 'meanwhile.' 3. 'in the first place,' 'first.' 4. 'just,' 'at once' (with imperative = before doing anything else): इतस्तावदागम्यताम् 'pray come here at once.' 5. 'already,' 'even' (as opposed to 'how much more,' 'how much less'). 6. 'only,' 'merely.' 7. 'at least': न तावन्मानुषी 'she is at least not a human being.' 8. (concessively) 'indeed,' 'certainly,' 'it is true' (followed by तु 'but,' &c.). 9. emphasizes a notion (like एव): 'as for,' 'as regards,' 'only,' 'just,' 'quite,' or to be rendered by stress only.

तावत्—च 'scarcely — when.' न तावत् 'not yet.'

तु **tú** (never commences a sentence): 'but,' 'however.' It is sometimes = च or वा, or a mere expletive; it is even found combined with च or repeated in the same sentence. — अपि तु 'but rather.' न तु 'but not.' न त्वेव तु na tu‿eva tu, 'never

at all.' परं तु 'yet,' 'however.' तु — तु 'indeed — but.' च — न तु 'although — yet not.'

न ná, 'not'; with indefinite pronoun = 'no': न कोऽपि ('not any' =) 'no man'; न किंचित् 'nothing'; न क्वचित् 'nowhere': न कदाचित् 'never.' न if repeated amounts to an emphatic positive: न तत्र कश्चिन्न बभूव तर्पितः 'no one was there (who was) not satisfied,' i.e. 'every one was thoroughly satisfied.' — नापि na‿api, 'not even.' — नैव na‿eva, 'not at all.'

ननु **na-nú:** 1. 'not?' in questions expecting an affirmative answer (Lat. non-ne) = 'surely': नन्वहं ते प्रियः nanu‿ahaṃ te priyaḥ, 'surely I am thy beloved?' 2. with interrogative pronouns and imperatives = 'pray': ननु को भवान् 'pray who are you?' ननूच्यताम् nanu‿ucyatām, 'pray tell.' 3. in arguments: 'is it not the case that?' = 'it may be objected'; followed by अत्रोच्यते atra‿ucyate, 'to this the reply is.'

नाम **nā́ma,** besides its adverbial meaning 'by name' (e.g. नलो नाम 'Nala by name'), has the following senses as a particle: 1. 'indeed,' 'certainly,' 'to be sure': मया नाम जितम् 'I have indeed conquered.' 2. 'perhaps': दृष्टस्त्वया कश्चिद् धर्मज्ञो नाम 'you have perhaps seen a righteous man.' 3. ironically, with interrogatives = 'pray': को नाम राज्ञां प्रियः 'who, pray, is a favourite with kings?' 4. with imperatives = 'granted,' 'no matter if,' 'ever so much': स धनी भवतु नाम 'let him be ever so rich.' — अपि नाम 1. at the beginning of a sentence with potential = 'perhaps.' 2. emphasizes a preceding word more strongly than अपि alone. — ननु नाम 'surely': ननु नामाहमिष्टा किल तव 'surely I am dear to thee.'

नु **nú,** 'now,' with interrogatives = 'pray': को नु 'who, pray?' नु—नु, in double questions expressing uncertainty, '(either) — or': अयं भीमो नु धर्मो नु 'can this be Bhīma or Dharma?'

नूनम् **nū-ná-m,** usually the first word in a sentence: 'in all probability,' 'undoubtedly,' 'assuredly': नूनं मन्ये न दोषोऽस्ति नैषधस्य 'assuredly, I think, it is not the fault of the king of Niṣadha.'

नो **nó** (ná + u) in the Veda meant 'and not,' 'nor,' but in Sanskrit simply = 'not' (cp. चेद् céd).

परम् **pára-m:** 1. 'highly,' 'greatly,' 'entirely,' 'very': परमनुगृहीतोऽस्मि 'I am greatly obliged.' 2. 'at the most': आयुस् तत्र मर्त्यानां परं त्रिंशद् भवति 'in it the life of mortals (lasts) at most thirty (years).' 3. 'nothing but,' 'only': विषाणे स्तः परं न ते 'you only lack the horns.' 4. 'but,' 'however': सर्वशास्त्रपारगाः परं बुद्धिरहिताः 'they (are) thoroughly versed in all learning, but lack intelligence.'

पुनः **púnaḥ:** 1. 'again,' 2. 'on the other hand,' 'on the contrary,' 'but.' — पुनः पुनः, or simply पुनः, 'again and again,' 'repeatedly.'

प्रायः **prāyaḥ,** प्रायशः prāya-śaḥ, प्रायेण prāyeṇa: 1. 'for the most part,' 'generally,' 'as a rule.' 2. 'in all probability.'

बाढम् **bāḍhá-m:** 1. 'certainly,' 'assuredly,' 'indeed.' 2. expressing consent: 'very well.' 3. expressing assent: 'so it is,' 'yes.'

मा **mā́,** prohibitive particle (= Gk. μή), generally used with imperative or unaugmented aorist: मा गच्छ or मा गमः 'do not go.' मा स्म mā sma is employed in the same way. Both मा and मैवम् mā‿evam are used elliptically = 'not so!' 'don't'; similarly मा तावत् 'not for heaven's sake!' 'God forbid.' मा नाम with potential or elliptically: = 'would that not,' 'if only not': मा नाम रक्षिणः 'heaven forbid (that it should be) the warders.'

मुहुः **múhuḥ:** 1. 'every moment,' 'repeatedly,' 'incessantly'

(often repeated: मुहुर्मुहुः). 2. 'on the contrary.' मुहुः — मुहुः 'now — now,' 'at one time — at another.'

यतः **yá-taḥ:** 1. 'whence' (often = 'where,' sometimes = 'whither'; often = ablative of the relative य ya). 2. 'wherefore,' 'for which reason.' 3. 'because,' 'since,' 'for' (often introducing a verse in support of a previous statement). 4. 'that,' after questions or before *oratio recta*: किं नु दुःखमतः परम् इच्छासंपद् यतो नास्ति 'what misery is greater than this, that there is no fulfilment of desire?'

यत्र **yá-tra:** 1. 'where.' 2. 'if.' 3. 'when.' 4. 'since.'

यथा **yá-thā:** 1. 'as': यथाज्ञापयति देवः 'as your Majesty commands.' 2. 'like' (= इव): राजते भैमी सौदामिनी यथा 'the daughter of Bhīma shone like the lightning.' 3. 'as for instance.' 4. 'in order that': यथा त्वदन्यं पुरुषं न मंस्यति 'in order that she shall think of no other man than thee.' 5. 'so that': अहं तथा करिष्ये यथा स वधं करिष्यति 'I shall so contrive that he will slay him.' 6. 'that,' introducing (like यद् yád) a direct assertion, with or without इति at the end: त्वयोक्तं मे यथा 'you told me that —.' यथा यथा — तथा तथा 'in proportion as — so,' 'the more — the more.' तद्यथा tad yathā, 'that (is) as (follows),' thus for instance.'

यद् **yá-d:** 1. 'that,' introducing direct assertions (like Gk. ὅτι) with or without इति at the end: वक्तव्यं यदिह मया हता प्रियेति 'you must say, I have slain my beloved here.' 2. (so) 'that': किं यन्न वेत्सि त्वम् 'how (is it) that you do not know?' 3. 'in order that': किं शक्यं कर्तुं यन्न क्रुध्यते नृपः 'what can be done in order that the king be not angry?' 4. 'inasmuch as,' 'because,' 'since.'

यदि **yád-i,** 'if' (cp. चेद् céd). — यदि वा: 1. 'or else,' 'or rather,' 'or': अज्ञानाद्यदि वा ज्ञानात् 'unwittingly or wittingly.' 2. sometimes = 'however.' — यद्यपि yadi̯ a̯pi, 'even if,' 'although.'

यावत् **yá-vat:** 1. (with correlative तावत्) 'as long as,' 'while,' till,' 'as soon as.' 2. 'meanwhile,' 'just,' expressing intended action: यावदिमां छायामाश्रित्य प्रतिपालयामि ताम् 'having resorted to this shade, I will just wait for her.' — यावन्न yāvan na: 1. 'while not' = 'till.' 2. sometimes = 'if not.' — न यावत् — तावत् 'scarcely — when,' no sooner — than.'

येन **yéna:** 1. 'in which manner,' 'as' (corr. तेन). 2. 'whereby,' 'on what account,' 'wherefore,' 'why': शृणु येन न दृश्यन्ते महीक्षितः 'hear why the kings do not appear.' 3. 'because,' 'since' (generally with corr. तेन): दूरस्थामपि येन पश्यसि कान्तां तं योगं मम चक्षुषोऽप्युपदिश 'since thou seest my beloved even when far away, teach this spell to my eye also.' 4. (so) 'that' : उयायो दृष्टो येन दोषो न भविता 'a device has been contrived so that no blame will be incurred.' 5. 'in order that': तस्य च्छात्रतां व्रजामि येन विश्वस्तो भवति 'I will become his pupil, in order that he may be inspired with confidence.'

वत् **vat,** 'like, 'is used at the end of compounds in the sense of इव iva: मृतवत् mṛta-vat, 'like a dead man.'

वरम् **vara-m** — न **na,** lit. 'the better thing (is) — (and) not' = 'better — than' (च, तु, or पुनः being generally added to the न na): वरं प्राणत्यागो न पुनरधमानाम् उपगमः 'better death than association with the base.'

वा **vā,** enclitic (Lat. ve), following its word (but for metrical reasons sometimes preceding it): 1. 'or.' 2. 'either or not,' 'optionally': जातदन्तस्य वा कुर्युः 'for (a child) that has cut its teeth, they may optionally make (the offering).' 3. 'like,' 'as it were' (=इव): जातां मन्ये शिशिरमथितां पद्मिनीं वान्यरूपाम् 'I believe her to have become changed in apperance like a lily blighted with cold.' 4. with interrogative = 'pray': काणेन चक्षुषा किं वा 'what, pray, (with =) is the use of a blind eye?' वा — वा 'either — or.'

वै **vái,** used in the older language as a particle emphasizing the preceding word, is common in Sanskrit poetry as a mere expletive.

सत्यम् **satyá-m:** 1. 'truly,' 'certainly,' 'indeed.' 2. 'rightly,' 'justly.' 3. 'true,' 'it is so.' 4. 'very well' (in asnwers). 5. 'it is true — but' (तु, किं तु, तथापि).

ह **ha,** an enclitic particle, which in the older language slightly emphasized the preceding word, is in Sanskrit a mere expletive, mostly occurring at the end of a verse.

हि **hí,** never at the beginning of a sentence, but generally after the first word: 1. 'for,' 'because.' 2. 'to be sure,' 'indeed': त्वं हि तस्य प्रियवयस्यः 'thou art indeed his dear friend.' 3. with interrogatives or imperatives = 'pray': कथं हि देवाञ्जानीयाम् 'how, pray, shall I know the gods?' तद्धि दर्शय 'pray, show it.' 4. Often used as a mere expletive, especially in order to avoid a hiatus or to obtain a long vowel in poetry. The particle sometimes occurs twice in the same sentence.

Interjections.

181. अयि **ayi,** used with the vocative or supplying its place, = 'friend,' 'prithee': अयि मकरोद्यानं गच्छावः 'prithee, let us go to the garden of love.'

अये **aye:** 1. a particle expressive of surprise, occurring chiefly in dramas: अये वसन्तसेना प्राप्ता 'Ah, Vasantasenā has arrived!' 2. sometimes used like अयि as a vocative particle.

अरे **are,** exclamation of address: 'ho!' 'sirrah!'

अहह **ahaha,** expresses 1. joy, 'ha!' 2. sorrow, 'alas!': अहह महापङ्के पतितोऽस्मि 'alas! I have fallen into a deep quagmire.'

अहो **aho,** exclamation of surprise, joy, sorrow, anger, praise, or blame, commonly used with the nominative: अहो गीतस्य

माधुर्यम् 'Oh, the sweetness of the song!' अहो हिरण्यक श्लाघ्योऽसि 'Ah, Hiraṇyaka, you are praiseworthy!'

आ ā (cp. 24) is used especially to express sudden recollection: आ एवं किल तत् 'Ah, so indeed it was!'

आः **āḥ** (cp. 24) expresses joy or indignation, 'ah': आः अतिथिपरिभाविनि 'Ah, you who slight your guest!'

कष्टम् **kaṣṭa-m,** 'woe!' 'alas!' often combined with धिक् dhik or हा धिक् hā dhik.

दिष्ट्या **diṣṭi ā** (inst. 'by good luck' =) 'thank heaven!' often with वृध् vṛdh, 'prosper' = 'to have cause for joy or congratulation': दिष्ट्या महाराजो विजयेन वर्धते 'your Majesty is to be congratulated upon your victory!'

धिक् **dhik**, exclamation of dissatisfaction, reproach, or lamentation: 'fie!' 'woe!' It is regularly used with the accusative, but the nom. gen. voc. also occur: धिक् त्वामस्तु 'shame on you!'

बत **bata,** expresses 1. astonishment: ah!' 2. regret: 'alas!' It is also combined with other interjections in the same sense : बतारे bata are, अहो बत, अयि बत.

भोः **bhoḥ:** 1. usually an exclamation of address: 'sir!' 'ho!' 'listen!' Though a contracted form of an old masculine singular vocative (bhavas), it is used in addressing female as well as male persons, and is connected even with the plural number. It is often repeated: — भो भोः पण्डिताः 'listen, Paṇḍits!' 2. it sometimes occurs in soliloquies = 'alas!'

साधु **sādhú:** 1. 'well done!' 'bravo!' 2. with imperative = 'come': दमयन्त्याः पणः साधु वर्तताम् 'come, let Damayantī by played for as a stake.' 3. 'well' with 1. per. pres.: साधु यामि 'well, I will go.' 4. 'assuredly': यदि जीवामि साध्वेव पश्येयम् 'if I live, I shall undoubtedly see him.'

स्वस्ति **sv-astí:** 1. 'hail!' 2. 'farewell!'

हन्त **hánta:** 1. exclamation of exhortation = 'come,' 'look,' 'pray': हन्त ते कथयिष्यामि 'come, I will tell thee'; शृणु हन्त 'pray listen.' 2. expresses grief: 'alas!' 3. joy, surprise, or hurry: 'oh!' 'ah!'

हा **hā,** expresses 1. astonishment or satisfaction: 'ah!' 2. pain: 'alas!' हा हतास्मि 'alas! I am undone.' It is frequently accompanied by a vocative; and is sometimes used with a following acc. = 'alas for!' It is often combined with कष्टम्, धिक् or हन्त.

CHAPTER VI

NOMINAL STEM FORMATION AND COMPOUNDS

A. Nominal Stems.

182. Declinable stems, though they often consist of the bare root (either verbal or pronominal), are chiefly formed by means of suffixes added to roots. These **suffixes** are of two kinds: **primary**, or those added directly to roots (which may be compounded with verbal prefixes); **secondary,** or those added to stems already ending in a suffix.

1. **Primary** derivatives as a rule show the root in its strong form; — e.g. वेद véd-a, 'knowledge' (विद् 'know'). In meaning they may be divided into the two classes of abstract action nouns (cognate in sense to infinitives) and concrete agent nouns (cognate in sense to participles) used as adjectives or substantives; — e.g. मति ma-tí, f. 'thought' (मन् man, 'think'); योध yodh-á, m. 'fighter' (युध् yudh, 'fight'). Other meanings are only modifications of these two. Thus abstract substantives often acquire a concrete sense; — e.g. नयन nay-ana, n. 'leading' comes to mean 'eye' (the organ that leads).

a. When the **bare root** is used as a declinable stem, it usually remains unchanged; — e.g. द्विष् dvíṣ, m. (hater) 'enemy' (80); युध् yúdh, f. 'fight,' m. 'fighter.' Many of these stems are used only at the end of compounds; — e.g. °दुह् -duh, 'milking' (81). Roots ending in आ ā are shortened to अ a, and those in इ i, उ u, or ऋ ṛ, are always modified by adding a त् t: these stems are only used as the last members of compounds; — e.g. सुकृत् su-kṛ́-t, 'doing well' (cp. 187 *b*).

b. Several primary nominal suffixes connected with the verbal system have already been sufficiently dealt with, viz. those of the present and future participles: अत् at (85; 156), आन् āna and मान māna (158); of the perfect: वांस् vāṃs (89; 157); of the past passive participle (160): त ta and न na; of the gerundive: अनीय an-īya[1], तव्य[1] tav-ya[2], and य ya (162). The formation of stems to which the primary suffixes of the comparative and superlative, ईयांस् iyāṃs and इष्ठ iṣṭha, are added has also been explained (88; 103, 2). Of the rest, the following, in alphabetical order, are the most usual and important:—

अ **a:** substantives and adjectives; — e.g. सर्ग sárg-a, m. 'creation' (सृज् sṛj, 'emit'); मेघ megh-á, m. 'cloud' (lit. 'discharger': मिह् mih); भाग bhāg-á, m. 'share' (भज् bhaj, 'divide'); प्रिय priy-á, 'pleasing,' 'dear' (प्री prī, 'please'). The substantives are almost exclusively masc.; but युग yug-á, n. 'yoke' (Gk. *ζυγ-ό-ν*, Lat. yug-u-m).

अन् **an:** masc. agent nouns and a few defective neuter stems; — e.g. राजन् rā́j-an, m. 'ruler,' 'king' (90, 1); अहन् áh-an, n. 'day' (91, 2).

---

1. The latter part, ईय īya and य ya, of these two suffixes is secondary (182, 2), but the whole is employed as a primary suffix (162, 3).
2. The first part of तव्य tav-ya is probably derived from the old infinitive ending तवे tave (App. III, 13 *b*).

अन **ana:** neut. action nouns; — e.g. दर्शन dárś-ana, n. 'sight' (दृश् dṛś, 'see'), भोजन bhój-ana, n. 'enjoyment' (भुज् bhuj, 'enjoy'); also agent nouns; — e.g. वाहन vā́h-ana. 'conveying,' n. 'vehicle'; very rarely with weak vowel: कृपण kṛp-aṇá ('lamenting'), 'miserable.'

अस् **as,** इस् **is,** उस् **us:** neuter action nouns, often with concrete meaning (cp. 83); — e.g. वचस् vác-as, 'speech'; ज्योतिस् jyót-is, 'light'; धनुस् dhán-us, 'bow.'

इ **i:** fem. action nouns, also agent nouns (adj. and subst.), and a few neuters of obscure origin; — e.g. कृषि kṛṣ-í, f. 'tillage'; शुचि śúc-i, 'bright'; पाणि pāṇ-í, m. 'hand'; अक्षि ákṣ-i, n. 'eye,' अस्थि ásth-i, n. 'bone,' दधि dádh-i, n. 'sour milk' (cp. 99, 3).

उ **u:** agent nouns, adj. and subst., the latter being mostly masc., but including several fem. and neut.; — e.g तनु tan-ú, 'thin' (Lat. ten-u-i-s); बाहु bāh-ú, m. 'arm' (Gk. *πῆχ-υ-s*); हनु han-u, f. 'jaw'; जानु jā́n-u, n. 'knee' (Gk. *γόν-υ*).

उन **una:** adj. and masc. neut. subst.; — e.g. तरुण tár-uṇa, 'young'; मिथुन mith-uná (m.), n. 'pair,' शकुन śak-uná, m. 'bird.'

ऊ **ū:** fem., mostly corresponding to m. and f. in उ u; — e.g. तनू tan-ū́, 'body'; independently formed: चमू cam-ū́, 'army,' वधू vadh-ū́, 'bride.'

त **ta:** besides ordinarily forming past passive participles appears, in a more general sense, as the suffix of a few adjectives and substantives; — e.g. शीत śī-tá, 'cold,' असित ás-i-ta, 'black'; दूत dū-tá, m. 'messenger,' हस्त hás-ta, m. 'hand.'

ति **ti:** fem. action nouns; — e.g. भूति bhū-tí, 'well-being' (Gk. *φύ-σι-s*); जाति jā-ti, 'birth'; ज्ञाति jñā-tí, 'kinsman,' is, however, **masc.** (owing to its concrete sense designating a male being).

M

तु **tu:** chiefly forms the stem of infinitives in °तुम् -tum; — e.g. गन्तुम् gan-tum, 'to go'; also a few masc. and neut. substantives:— तन्तु tán-tu, m. 'thread,' हेतु he-tú, m. 'cause' (हि hi, 'impel'); वास्तु vā́s-tu, n. 'dwelling' (Gk. *ἄσ-τυ*).

तृ **tṛ:** masc. agent nouns; — e.g. कर्तृ kar-tṛ́, 'doer'; also names of relationship, fem. as well as masc.; — e.g. मातृ mā-tṛ́, f. 'mother,' पितृ pi-tṛ́, m. 'father' (101).

त्र **tra,** m. n., त्रा **trā,** f.: expressive of the instrument or means; — e.g. पात्र pā́-tra, n. 'cup' (पा pā, 'drink'); दंष्ट्र dáṃṣ-ṭra, m. 'tusk' ('biter': दंश् daṃś), मन्त्र mán-tra, m. 'prayer' (मन् man, 'think'); मात्रा mā́-trā, f. 'measure' (Gk. *μέ-τρο-ν*).

थ **tha,** m. n., था **thā,** f.; — e.g. अर्थ ár-tha, m. 'aim,' 'object'; तीर्थ tīr-thá, n. 'ford'; गाथा gā́-thā, f. 'song.'

न **na,** m.n., ना **nā,** f.: besides ordinarily forming past pass. participles (160, 1), also adjectives and substantives; — e.g. कृष्ण kṛṣ-ṇá, 'black'; वर्ण vár-ṇa, m. 'colour'; पर्ण par-ṇá, n. 'wing'; तृष्णा tṛ́ṣ-ṇā, f. 'thirst.'

नि **ni,** m. f.; — e.g. अग्नि ag-ní, m. 'fire' (Lat. ig-ni-s); श्रेणि śré-ṇi, f. 'line.'

नु **nu,** m. f.; — e.g. भानु bhā-nú, m. 'light,' सूनु sū-nú, m. 'son'; धेनु dhe-nú, f. 'cow.'

म **ma,** adj.; m. subst.; — e.g. भीम bhī-má, 'terrible'; धूम dhū-má, m. 'smoke.'

मन् **man,** m. n.: chiefly neut. action nouns; — e.g. कर्मन् kár-man, n. 'action,' ब्रह्मन् bráh-man, n. 'prayer'; अश्मन् áś-man, m. 'stone' (Gk. *ἄκ -μων*), ब्रह्मन् brah-mán, m. 'one who prays' (90, 3).

मि **mi**, m.f., मी **mī,** f.; — e.g. रश्मि raś-mí, m. 'ray;' भूमि bhū́-mi, f. 'earth'; भूमी bhū́-mī, f. id.; लक्ष्मी lakṣ-mī́, f. 'prosperity.'

यु **yu**, m.; — e.g. मन्यु man-yú, 'anger'; मृत्यु mṛt-yú, 'death.'

र **ra**, adj.; m. n. subst.; — e.g. उग्र ug-rá, 'terrible'; रुद्र rud-rá, m. name of a god; अभ्र abh-rá, n. 'cloud.'

रु **ru**, adj.; n. subst.; — e.g. भीरु bhī-rú, 'timid'; अश्रु aś-ru, n. 'tear.'

व **va**, adj.; m. subst.; —e.g. सर्व sár-va, 'all' (Lat. sal-vo-s); अश्व áś-va, m. 'horse' (Lat. eq-uo-s).

वन् **van**, adj.; m.n. subst.; — e.g. पीवन् pī́-van, 'fat'; ग्रावन् grā́-van, m. 'stone' (90, 4); पर्वन् pár-van, n. 'joint.'

2. **Secondary nominal Suffixes:—**

अ **a**, adj.; m. n. subst.: forms adjectives, chiefly with initial Vṛddhi, expressing the sense of relation to or connexion with the primitive word; — e.g. मानव mānav-á, 'belonging to man' (मनु manu). Many of these have become substantive in the masc. and, as abstracts, in the neuter; — e.g. मानव mānav-ā́, m. 'human being'; वैश्वामित्र vaiśvāmitra, m. 'descendant of Viśvāmitra'; पौरुष pauruṣ-á, 'manly,' n. 'manliness.' When formed with Vṛddhi, these derivatives always take ई ī in the feminine.

आ **ā:** forms the fem. of adjectives which in the masc. and neut. end in अ a; — e.g. कान्ता kānt-ā, 'beloved' (97).

आनी **ānī:** forms the fem. of the names of deities ending in अ a; — e.g. इन्द्राणी indr-āṇī́, 'wife of Indra.'

आयन **āyana**, m.: forms patronymics with initial Vṛddhi;— e.g. आश्वलायन āśval-āyana, 'descendant of Aśvala.'

इ **i**, m.: forms patronymics with initial Vṛddhi; — e.g. मारुति mārut-i, 'descendant of the Maruts.' Similarly formed is सारथि sārath-i, 'charioteer' (सरथ sa-rátha, 'driving on the same car').

इन **in:** forms, in the sense of 'possessing,' adjectives from stems ending in अ a; — e.g. बलिन् bal-in, 'strong,' from बल bala, n. 'strength' (87).

ई **ī:** forms the fem. of masc. stems made with suffixes ending in consonants (95), or with तृ tṛ (101 *e*), often to those in उ u

(98 *c*), or in अ a (always when formed with Vṛddhi); — e.g. देवी dev-ī́, 'goddess' (देव dev-á, 'god'). Cp. 107.

ईन **īna:** forms adjectives, chiefly expressive of direction and made from words in अञ्च् añc; — e.g. प्राचीन prāc-ī́na, 'eastern' (प्राञ्च् prāñc, 'eastward').

ईय **īya:** forms general adjectives; — e.g. पर्वतीय parvat-ī́ya, 'mountainous'; तदीय tad-īya, 'belonging to him,' 'his.'

क **ka:** forms adjectives and diminutives; — e.g. अन्तक ánta-ka, 'ending'; with Vṛddhi, वार्षिक vārṣ-i-ka, 'belonging to the rains' (varṣāḥ); राजक rāja-ka, m. 'petty king,' पुत्रक putra-ka, 'little son.' The fem. of such derivatives (in a-ka) is often formed with इका **ikā**; — e.g. पुत्रिका putr-ikā, 'little daughter.'

तन **tana:** foms adjectives with a temporal meaning; — e.g. नूतन nū́-tana, 'present,' पुरातन purā-tana (f. ī), 'ancient.'

तम **tama:** forms superlatives and ordinals; — e.g. ut-tamá, 'highest'; śata-tamá, 'hundredth.'

तर **tara:** forms comparatives; — e.g. उत्तर út-tara, 'higher.'

ता **tā**, f., त्व **tva**, n.: form abstract substantives with the sense conveyed by the English suffix '-ness'; — e.g. देवता devá-tā, 'divinity'; अमृतत्व amṛta-tvá, n. 'immortality'; पञ्चत्व pañca-tva, 'five-ness' (i.e. dissolution into the five elements), 'death.'

त्य **tya**, adj.; m. n.; forms nouns from prepositions and adverbs; — e.g. नित्य ní-tya, 'constant'; अपत्य ápa-tya, n. 'offspring'; अमात्य amā́-tya, m. 'companion' (अमा amā́, 'at home').

थ **tha**, adj.: forms some ordinals from cardinals; — e.g. चतुर्थ catur-thá, 'fourth.'

भ **bha**, m.: forms the names of animals; — e.g. गर्दभ garda-bhá, 'ass,' वृषभ vṛṣa-bhá, 'bull.'

म **ma**, adj.: forms some superlatives, partly from prepositions, and some ordinals; — e.g. अवम ava-má, 'lowest,' मध्यम madhya-má, 'middlemost'; पञ्चम pañca-má, 'fifth.'

मत् **mat**, adj.: forms, in the sense of 'possessing,' derivatives from substantives (except such as end in अ a); — e.g. अग्निमत् agni-mát, 'maintaining the (sacred) fire'; 'fiery.'

मय **maya**, adj. (**f.** ई **ī**), 'consisting of'; — e.g. मनोमय mano-máya, 'consisting of mind,' 'spiritual.'

य **ya**, adj.; m. n. subst.: forms adjectives in the sense of 'relating to,' masc. patronymics and neuter abstracts with Vṛddhi, as well as ordinary adjectives without Vṛddhi; — e.g. ग्रैव्य gráiv-ya, 'relating to the neck' (ग्रीवा grīvā́); आदित्य ādit-yá, m. 'son of Aditi'; सौभाग्य saubhāg-ya, n. 'good fortune' (from सुभग su-bhága, 'fortunate'); पित्र्य pítr-ya, 'paternal' (पितृ pitṛ́, 'father').

र **ra**, adj.: forms comparatives from prepositions and ordinary adjectives; — e.g. अवर áva-ra, 'lower'; धूम्र dhūm-rá, 'grey' (from धूम dhūma, 'smoke').

ल **la**, adj.; m. subst.: forms adjectives and a few diminutives; — e.g. कपिल kapi-lá ('monkey-coloured'), 'brown,' बहुल bahu-lá, 'abundant'; वृषल vṛṣa-lá, m. 'little man,' 'man of low caste,' 'Śūdra.'

वत् **vat**, adj. 'possessing'; — e.g. प्रजावत् prajā́-vat, 'having offspring'; नभस्वत् nábhas-vat, 'cloudy,' m. 'wind.'

वन् **van:** forms in the sense of 'possessing' adjectives and masc. substantives; — e.g. मघवन् maghá-van, 'bountiful,' m. au epithet of Indra; अथर्वन् áthar-van, m. 'fire-priest.'

विन् **vin:** forms adjectives meaning 'possessing'; — e.g. यशस्विन् yaśas-vin, 'glorious.'

183. The above lists practically supply the rules of **gender** for the Sanskrit noun. These may be summarized as follows.

Speaking generally, all stems ending in the long vowels आ ā, ई ī, ऊ ū, are feminine; stems ending in अ a, त् t, न् n, may be

masculine or neuter; stems ending in इ i or उ u may be of any gender.

***a.* Feminine** are all stems formed with the suffixes आ ā, ई ī, ऊ ū, ता tā, त्रा trā, ति ti.

***b.* Neuter** are all stems formed with the suffixes त्व tva, रु ru, इस् is, उस् us, and (unless the name of a living being) अस् as, and (unless meaning an agent) अन ana.

***c.* Masculine** are (insofar as they are not used adjectivally) all stems formed with the suffixes त ta, व va, यु yu; आयन āyana, इ i (patronymic), क ka, भ bha, ल la.

***d.* Masc. of fem.** are stems formed with the suffixes नि ni, नु nu, मि mi, तृ tṛ; also stems formed with the bare root (neuter also if adjectives).

***e.* Masc. of neut.** are stems formed with the suffixes अ a, थ tha, न na, उन una, म ma, य ya, र ra, त्य tya, त्र tra, तु tu, अन् an, मन् man, वन् van; also the adjectives formed with इन् in, विन् vin, ईन īna, ईय īya, तन tana, तम tama, तर tara, मय maya, मत् mat, वत् vat.

***f.* Masc., fem., or neut.** are stems formed with इ i or उ u.

B. Compounds.

184. 1. Verbal Compounds are formed by combining roots with some twenty prepositions and a few adverbs. The compound verb is conjugated like the simple verb. Thus गम् gam, 'to go,' combines with सम् sam, 'together,' to संगम् saṃ-gam, 'to go together,' 'unite'; 3. sing. pres. संगच्छति saṃ-gacchati. The compound root can be used to form nominal stems by means of the primary suffixes enumerated above (182, 1); — e.g. संगम sam-gam-á, m. 'union.'

a. The prepositions which are compounded with roots are the following:— अति áti, 'beyond'; अधि ádhi, 'upon'; अनु ánu,

'after'; अन्तर् antár, 'between'; अप ápa, 'away'; अपि ápi, 'on'; अभि abhí, 'against'; अव áva, 'down'; आ ā́[1], 'near'; उद् úd, 'up'; उप úpa, 'up to'; नि ní, 'down'; निस् nís, 'out'; परा párā, 'away'; परि pári, 'around'; प्र prá, 'forth'; प्रति práti, 'towards'; वि ví, 'asunder'; सम् sám, together.'

b. A few adverbs are also compounded with a limited number of verbs: तिरस् tirás, 'across,' 'aside,' with कृ kṛ, 'make,' धा dhā, 'put,' भू bhū, 'be'; — e.g. तिरस्कुर्वन्ति tiras-kurvanti, 'they abuse'; तिरोधा tiro-dhā, 'put aside,' 'conceal'; तिरोऽभवन् tiro-'bhavan, 'they disappeared'; पुरस् purás with कृ kṛ, and धा dhā, 'put in front,' 'honour'; — e.g. पुरस्क्रियन्ताम् puras-kriyantām, 'let them be honoured'; आविस् āvís, 'openly,' with कृ kṛ, 'to manifest,' with अस् as and भू bhū, 'to appear'; — e.g. आविष्करोति āviṣ-karoti, 'he shows'; आविरासीत् āvir-āsīt, 'he appeared'; अलम् álam, 'enough,' with कृ kṛ, 'to adorn.' श्रद् śrád, an old word meaning 'heart' (Lat. cord-), having acquired the character of an adverb, is compounded with धा dhā, 'put'; and similarly नमस् námas, 'obeisance,' अस्तम् ásta-m, acc. of अस्त ásta, 'home,' are compounded with participles of कृ kṛ, 'do,' and इ i, 'go,' respectively; — e.g. श्रद्दधामि śrad-dadhāmi, 'I put faith,' 'credit' (Lat. crēdo); नमस्कृत्य namas-kṛ́tya, 'having adored'; अस्तमित ástam-ita, 'set' (of the sun).

Note. Adjectives or substantives may be compounded with कृ kṛ and भू bhū, before which final अ a, आ ā, or इ i becomes ई ī, final उ u becomes ऊ ū; — e.g. वश vaśa, m. 'control': वशीकृ vaśī-kṛ, 'reduce to subjection,' वशीभू vaśī-bhū, 'become subject'; परिखीकृत parikhī-kṛta, 'turned into a moat' (परिखा parikhā). The sense of these verbal compounds implies a transformation;

---

1. The preposition आ ā reverses the sense of verbs of going or giving; — e.g. आगम् ā-gam, 'come'; आदा ā-dā, 'take.'

thus रत्नीभूत ratnī-bhūta would mean 'turned into a jewel,' but रत्नभूत ratna-bhūta, 'being a jewel,' as a nominal compound (188, 1 *c*).

II. Nominal Compounds.

185. The power of combining two or more words into one, which belongs to all the Indo-European languages, has been more largely developed in Sanskrit than in any of the others. Not only are long and complex compounds here in constant use, but they also take the place of the analytical modes of expression which prevail in the other cognate tongues. Thus Kālidāsa describes a river as 'wave-agitation-loquacious-bird-row-girdle-string-ed,' while we should say: 'her girdle-string is a row of birds loquacious because of the agitation of the waves.' Compounds being therefore of great syntactical importance in Sanskrit, it is necessary to distinguish and classify the various kinds, in order that the meaning of a Sanskrit sentence may be clearly understood. The most convenient division is into the three classes of Co-ordinatives, Determinatives, and Possessives. The Determinatives, so called because the former member determines (or qualifies) the latter, are of two kinds, Dependent and Descriptive. Possessives are secondary compounds, consisting chiefly of Determinatives turned into adjectives.

a. All words making up a compound except the last, ordinarily appear in the form of their uninflected stem; those with two stems using the weak, and those with three, the middle stem (73 *a*). The last word in the case of Co-ordinatives and Determinatives, retains, as a rule, its usual form and inflexion, as well as, if a substantive, its gender; while, in Possessives, it is variable like an adjective.

E.g. देवदासः deva-dāsaḥ, m. 'servant of a god, or of the gods';

स्वामिसेवा svāmi-sevā, f. 'serving a master'; राजकर्म rāja-karma, n. 'duty of a king'; सनामन् sa-nāman, 'homonymous': nom. m. सनामा, f. सनाम्नी, n.सनाम.

1. Co-ordinative (Dvandva) Compounds.

186. These consist of two (or more) nouns, far less commonly adjectives, very rarely adverbs, connected in sense by the copula 'and.' Dvandva, the name applied to Co-ordinatives by the Hindu grammarians, means 'pair' or 'couple.'

1. Compound substantives are inflected in the dual or plural according as two or more objects are denoted, the gender being that of the last member; — e.g. हस्त्यश्वौ hasty-aśvau, 'an elephant and a horse'; हस्त्यश्वाः hasty-asvāḥ[1], 'elephants and horses.' When, however, the parts of the compound express not individuals but categories, the Dvandva is inflected in the neuter singular as a collective; — e.g. गवाश्वम् gava‿aśvam, 'kine and horses.' Names of objects associated in pairs by way of contrast are often combined in Dvandvas; — e.g. सिंहगजाः siṃha-gajāḥ, 'lions and elephants'; सारमेयमार्जाराः sārameya-mārjārāḥ, 'dogs and cats'; अहोरात्र aho-rātra, m.n. 'day and night[2].' The number of members in the compound is not limited and is often considerable; — e.g. देवगन्धर्वमानुषोरगराक्षसाः deva-gandharva-mānuṣa‿uraga-rākṣasāḥ, 'gods, heavenly musicians, men, serpents, and demons.'

2. Adjectives (including past participles) are comparatively seldom compounded as Dvandvas; — e.g. उत्तरदक्षिण uttara-dakṣiṇa, 'north and south'; शीतोष्ण śita‿uṣṇa, 'cold and hot'; सितासित sita‿asita, 'white and black'[3]; घनायत ghana‿āyata,

---

1. Cp. Lat. su-ove-taurilia.
2. Cp. Gk. *νυχθήμερον*
3. Cp. *λευκο-μέλας.*

'dense and extensive' (forest); कृताकृत kṛta‿akṛta, 'done and undone'; मृताजात mṛta‿ajāta, 'dead and unborn.'

a. Two past participles are sometimes compounded to express immediate sequence, the relation of the second to the first being often translatable by 'as soon as'; — e.g. दृष्टनष्ट dṛṣṭa-naṣṭa, 'seen and vanished' = 'vanished as soon as seen'; जातप्रेत jāta-preta, 'died as soon as born'; उत्खातप्रतिरोपित ut-khāta + prati-ropita, 'uprooted and replanted'; सुप्तोत्थित supta‿utthita, 'having slept and arisen,' i.e. 'having just arisen from sleep.'

3. Examples of the rare Dvandvas composed of adverbs are सायंप्रातर् sāyám-prātar, 'in the evening and morning'; दिवानक्तम् divā-naktam, 'by day and night.'

a. Occasionally complex Dvandvas, made up of compounds of another class, are met with; — e.g. व्याकीर्णकेसरकरालमुख vyākīrṇa-kesara + karāla-mukha, 'having a dishevelled mane and terrific jaws,' consists of two possessives (189).

b. Of the numerous Vedic Dvandvas consisting of the names of deities, each member being in the dual and separately accented, only very few survive in Sanskrit: मित्रावरुणौ mitrā́[1]-váruṇau, 'Mitra and Varuṇa'; द्यावापृथिव्यौ dyā́vā[1]-pṛthivyaú, 'Heaven and Earth.' In cases other than nom. voc. acc. the final member only is inflected: मित्रावरुणयोः mitrā-varuṇayoḥ and द्यावापृथिव्योः dyāvā-pṛthivyoḥ.

c. मातृ mātṛ, 'mother,' and पितृ pitṛ, 'father,' as the first member of a Dvandva of relationship, assume the form of the nom. sing.: मातापितरौ mātā-pitarau, 'mother and father'; पितापुत्रौ pitā-putrau, 'father and son.'

---

1. Mitrā́ and Dyā́vā are Vedic duals. This type of compound was perhaps originally due to the juxtaposition of elliptic duals (*c*); — e.g. Mitrā́, 'the two Mitras' being = 'Mitra and Varuṇa.' द्वादश dvā́-daśa is a numeral Dvandva ('two and ten') in which the first number is an old dual.

The masc. of co-ordinate pairs of relations can be used alone in the dual so as to include the female; — e.g. पितरौ pitarau = 'parents'; श्वशुरौ śvaśurau[1] = 'parents-in-law'; पुत्रौ putrau = 'son and daughter' (as well as 'two sons'); भ्रातरौ bhrātarau = 'brother and sister[2].'

2a. Dependent (Tatpuruṣa) Determinatives.

187. A dependent determinative is one in which the first member depends on the last, the syntactical relation of the former to the latter being that of an attribute (noun or pronoun) in an oblique case. The compound may be a substantive or an adjective, according as the last member is one or the other.

E.g. तत्पुरुष tat-puruṣa, m. 'the man of him,' 'his man' (an example used by the Hindu grammarians to designate the class); शूरमानिन् śūra-mānin, adj. 'thinking oneself a hero'; गुणोपेत guṇa͜upeta, adj. 'endowed with virtues' (upa͜ita is a past part.).

In dependent compounds the first member may have the sense of any oblique case, but that of the gen. is by far the commonest.

1. Acc. The last member is naturally always an adjective of a verbal nature;[3] — जयप्रेप्सु jaya-prepśu, adj. 'desiring victory' (pra͜īpsu is a desid. adj., cp. 170, 2); वर्षभोग्य varṣa-bhogya, adj. 'to be enjoyed for a year' (bhogya is a fut. part. pass.); गृहागत gṛha͜āgata, adj. 'come to the house' (āgata is a past part.); ग्रामप्राप्त grāma-prāpta, 'arrived at the village.[4]' (A past part. is more commonly placed at the beginning, when the compound

1. Cp. Lat. soceri = socer et socrus.
2. Cp. Gk. ἀδελφοί and Lt. fraters = 'brother and sister.'
3. Cp. Gk. ἱππό-δαμο-ς, 'horse-taming,' Lat. jū-dex, 'pointing out the law,' 'judge.'
4. The past part. गत gata, 'gone to,' is often used at the end of Tatpuruṣas in the sense of 'relating to,' 'existing in'; — e.g. हस्तगत hasta-gata, 'held in the hand'.

becomes a possessive; — e.g. प्राप्तग्राम prāpta-grāma, lit. 'having a reached village.')

2. **Instr.** मासपूर्व māsa-pūrva, 'earlier by a month'; स्वामिसदृश svāmi-sadṛśa, 'like (his) master' (cp. 199, 2 *c*); अल्पोन alpa͜ūna, 'deficient by a little' = 'almost finished'; अहिहत ahi-hata, 'killed by a snake'; देवदत्त deva-datta, 'given by the gods' (cp. *θεό-δοτος*), commonly used as a proper name with an auspicious sense (Dieu-donné) and often denoting an indefinite person = 'so-and-so.'

3. **Dat.** यूपदारु yūpa-dāru, n. 'wood for a sacrificial post'; विष्णुबलि viṣṇu-bali, m. 'offering to Viṣṇu'; प्रभुहित prabhu-hita, adj. 'advantageous to the king.'

4. **Abl.** स्वर्गपतित svarga-patita, adj. 'fallen from heaven'; भवदन्य bhavad-anya, adj. 'different from you.'

5. **Gem.** राजपुरुष rāja-puruṣa, m. 'king's man'; व्याघ्रबुद्धि vyāghra-buddhi, f. 'thought of (its being) a tiger.'

6. **Loc.** उरोज uro-ja, adj. 'produced on the breast'; अश्वकोविद aśva-kovida, adj. 'skilled in houses'; गृहजात gṛha-jāta, adj. 'born in the house'; पूर्वाह्णकृत pūrvāhṇa-kṛta, adj. 'done in the fore-noon.'

a. Some dependent compounds retain the case termination in the governed noun; — e.g. धनंजय dhanaṃ-jaya, adj. 'winning booty,' m. as a proper name; परस्मैपद para**smai**-pada, n. 'word for another'; वाचस्पति vāc**as**-pati, m. 'lord of speech'; युधिष्ठिर yudhi-ṣṭhira, adj. 'firm in battle,' m. as a proper name.

b. If a root forms the last member of a Tatpuruṣa it undergoes no change except that आ ā is shortened to अ a, while इ i, उ u, ऋ ṛ add त् t (cp. 182, 1 *a*); — e.g. वरद vara-da, adj. 'granting boons' (दा dā, 'give'); विश्वजित् viśva-ji-t, adj. 'all-conquering'; कर्मकृत् karma-kṛ-t, adj. 'doing work,' 'laborious.'

c. At the end of a dependent, विशेष viśeṣa, m. means 'special kind of,' i.e. 'choice,' 'pre-eminent'; similarly अन्तर antara, n.

'difference,' generally means 'other,' sometimes 'special,' 'particular'; — e.g. तेजोविशेष tejo-viśeṣa, m. 'extraordinary splendour'; देशान्तर deśa‿antara, n. 'another country'; उपायान्तर upāya‿antara, n. 'a special means'; भाष्यान्तर bhāṣya‿antara, n. 'particular conversation.'

d. अर्थ artha, m. 'object,' 'purpose,' is often used adverbially at the end of dependents in the acc. and less commonly in the dat. and loc.; — e.g. दमयन्त्यर्थम् damayanty-artham, 'for the sake of Damayantī.'

2b. Descriptive (Karmadhāraya) Determinatives.

188. A descriptive determinative is one in which the first member describes the last, the syntactical relation of the former to the latter being that of a predicate. This relation may be expressed in three ways:—

1. By a **Noun** (in apposition); — e.g. राजर्षि rāja‿ṛṣi, m. 'king sage,' i.e. 'royal sage'; स्त्रीजन strī-jana, m. 'women-folk.'

a. A title is thus sometimes compounded with a proper name; — e.g. अमात्यराक्षस amātya-Rākṣasa, 'Minister Rākṣasa.' Occasionally the proper name comes first; — e.g. शाण्डिलीमातृ Śāṇḍilī-mātṛ, 'Mother Śāṇḍilī.'

b. The apposition often expresses a comparison; — e.g. जलदश्याम jalada-śyāma, adj. 'dark as a cloud'; हिमशिशिर hima-śiśira, adj. 'cold as ice'; जलान्तश्चन्द्रचपल jala‿antaś-candra-capala, adj. 'fickle as the moon reflected in the water.' When both members are substantives the object with which a comparison is made is placed not at the beginning of the compound, but at the end; — e.g. पुरुषव्याघ्र puruṣa-vyāghra, m. 'man-tiger,' i.e. 'tiger-like man,' 'human tiger'; वाङ्मधु vāṅ-madhu, n. 'speech-honey,' i.e. 'honied speech; पादपद्म pāda-padma, n. 'foot-lotus,' i.e. 'lotus-like foot.'

c. The past part. भूत bhūta, 'become,' 'existent,' is often added, in the sense of 'being,' to an appositional substantive (which is thus turned into an adj.); — e.g. तमोभूत tamo-bhūta, 'existing in a state of darkness'; रत्नभूत ratna-bhūta, 'being a jewel' (cp. 184 *b*, note).

2. By an **Adjective**; — e.g. कृष्णसर्प kṛṣṇa-sarpa, m. 'black snake'; नीलोत्पल nīla‿utpala, n. 'blue lotus'; मध्याह्न madhya‿ahna, m. 'midday'; अर्धमार्ग ardha-mārga, m. 'half way'; वर्तमानकवि vartamāna-kavi, m. 'living poet.'

a. Those compounds in which the adjective is a **numeral** are by the Hindu grammarians treated as a special class, called **Dvigu** ('two-cow'). They are generally neuters or feminines (in ई ī) expressing aggregates; — e.g. त्रिलोक tri-loka, n. or त्रिलोकी tri-lokī, f. 'the three worlds.' They may also become adjectives by being turned into possessives (189); — e.g. त्रिगुण tri-guṇa, n. 'the three qualities'; adj. 'possessing the three qualities.'

b. पूर्व pūrva, 'previous,' is put at the end, instead of adverbially at the beginning, in the sense of 'before,' after past participles; — e.g. दृष्टपूर्व adj. 'seen before.'

c. At the beginning of a descriptive compound महत् mahat becomes महा mahā, while at the end राजन् rājan, अहन् ahan, सखि sakhi, रात्रि rātri, become राज, अह, सख, रात्र (m. n.) respectively; — e.g. महाराजः 'great king'; पुण्याहम् puṇya‿aham, 'auspicious day'; प्रियसखः 'dear friend'; अर्धरात्र ardha-rātra, m. 'midnight.'

d. अन्योन्य anyo-(a)nya and परस्पर para-s-para, 'one another,' are a kind of irregular compound in which the nom. masc. form, due to frequent syntactical juxtaposition, became generalized; thus अन्योन्याम् acc. sing. fem. = अन्या-अन्याम् anyā-anyām.

3. By an **Adverb** (inclusive of particles and prepositions);—

e.g. सुजन su-jana, m. 'honest man'; अधिलोक adhi-loka, m. 'highest world'; अज्ञात a-jñāta, adj. 'unknown'; यथोक्त yathā‿ukta, adj. 'as stated'; एवंगत evaṃ-gata, adj. 'thus faring.'

a. Compounds of this kind, when used in the acc. neuter as adverbs, are treated by the Hindu grammarians as a special class called **Avyayī-bhāva** ('indeclinable state'). Such are अनुरूपम् anu-rūpam, 'conformably'; यथाशक्ति yathā-śakti, 'according to ability'; सविनयम् sa-vinayam, 'politely'; यावज्जीवम् yāvaj-jīvam, 'for life.'

3. Possessive (Bahuvrīhi) Compounds.

189. These compounds are essentially adjectives agreeing with a substantive expressed or understood. They are determinatives (generally of the adjectivally descriptive class) ending in substantives, which are made to agree in gender, number, and case with another substantive. Thus बहुव्रीहि bahu-vrīhi, m. 'much rice,' becomes an adjective in the sense of 'having much rice' (an example used by the Hindu grammarians to designate the class).

Every kind of determinative can be turned into a possessive;— e.g. इन्द्रशत्रु indra-śatru, m. 'foe of Indra': adj. 'having Indra as a foe'; भीमपराक्रम bhīma-parākrama, m. 'terrible prowess': adj. 'of terrible prowess'; त्रिपद् tri-pád, adj. 'three-footed' (Gk. τρί-ποδ-, Lat. tri-ped-); अधोमुख adho-mukha, adj. 'downcast' (mukha, n. 'face'); अपुत्र a-putra, adj. 'sonless'; सभार्य sa-bhārya, adj. 'accompanied by his wife' (bhāryā); तथाविध tathā-vidha, adj. 'of such a kind' (vidhi, m.); दुर्मनास् dur-manās, adj. nom. m.f. (δυσ-μενής), 'ill-minded,' 'dejected.'

a. In the Vedic language possessives were distinguished from determinatives by accent; — e.g. rāja-putrá, 'king's son'; rājá-putra, adj. 'having kings as sons.'

b. Possessives often come to be used as substantives or pro-

per names; — e.g. सुहृद् su-hṛd, 'good-hearted,' becomes masc. 'friend'; सत्यश्रवास् satyá-śravās, adj. nom. m. 'of true fame,' becomes the name of a man (cp. 'Ετεο-κλέης).

c. Possessives are often very intricate, containing several other compounds. Thus [(vīci-kṣobha)-stanita-(vihaga-śreṇi)]-(kāñcī-guṇā) is based on an appositional descriptive consisting of two main parts. The second, 'kāñcī-guṇa,' m. 'girdle-string,' is a Tatpuruṣa. The first is an adjectival descriptive in which the Tatpuruṣa 'vihaga-śreṇi,' 'row of birds,' is described by 'vīci-kṣobha-stanita,' 'loquacious through wave-agitation.' The latter is a compound Tatpuruṣa, in which 'stanita' is qualified by the simple Tatpuruṣa 'vīci-kṣobha,' 'agitation of the waves.' शीतोष्णकिरणौ śīta‿uṣṇa-kiraṇau, 'moon and sun,' is an example of a Bahuvrīhi which is used as a substantive and contains a Dvandva. It is in reality a kind of contracted Dvandva ('the cool and the hot-rayed' for 'the cool-rayed and the hot-rayed').

b. Bahuvrīhis with a past participle at the beginning are syntatically often equivalent to a gerund or loc. absolute; — e.g. त्यक्तनगर tyakta-nagara, 'having the city left' = नगरं त्यक्त्वा nagaraṃ tyaktvā, 'having left the city,' or नगरे त्यक्ते nagare tyakte, 'the city being left.'

e. Bahuvrīhis based on appositional descriptives often imply a comparison; — e.g. चन्द्रानन candra‿ānana, 'moon-faced'; पद्माक्ष padma‿akṣa (f. ī), 'lotus-eyed.' Inversion of the natural order does not take place here as in descriptives (cp. 188, 1 *b*).

f. कल्प kalpa, m. 'manner,' and प्राय prāya, m. 'chief part,' are used at the end of Bahuvrīhis in the sense of 'like,' 'almost'; e.g. अमृतकल्प amṛta-kalpa, adj. 'ambrosia-like'; प्रभातप्राय prabhāta-prāya, adj. 'almost dawning.' In the same position पर para and परम parama, adjectives meaning 'highest,' 'chief,' used as substantives, signify 'engrossed in,' 'intent on' (lit. 'having

as the chief thing'); — e.g. चिन्तापर cintā-para, 'immersed in thought.'

g. मात्रा mātrā, f. 'measure,' is used at the end of Bahuvrīhis in the sense of 'only'; — e.g. नाममात्रा नराः nāmamātrā narāḥ, 'men bearing the name only.' At the end of past participles it means 'as soon as'; — e.g. जातमात्रः शत्रुः jāta-mātraḥ śatruḥ, 'an enemy as soon as (he has) come into being.' It is, however, generally employed as a neuter substantive in this way; — e.g. जलमात्रम् jala-mātram, 'water alone' (lit. 'that which has water for its measure').

h. आदि ādi, m. and प्रभृति prabhṛti, f. 'beginning,' आद्य ādya, 'first' (used as a substantive), are employed at the end of Bahuvrihis in the sense of 'and the rest,' 'and so forth,' 'etcetera,' primarily as adjectives and secondarily as substantives; — e.g. (देवा) इन्द्रादयः (devā) Indra‿ādayaḥ, '(the gods) Indra and the rest' (lit. 'having Indra as their beginning'); इत्यादि iti‿ādi, n. 'beginning thus' (i.e. with these words) = 'and so on.'

पुरोगम puro-gama, पूर्व pūrva, पुरःसर puraḥ-sara, 'preceding' = 'leader,' are similarly employed in the sense of 'preceded, led, or accompanied by'; — e.g. देवा इन्द्रपुरोगमाः 'the gods led by Indra.' पूर्व and पुरःसर are also used adverbially at the end of Bahuvrībhis; — e.g. स्मितपूर्वम् 'with the accompaniment of a smile,' 'smilingly'; बहुमानपुरःसरम् bahumāna-puraḥsaram, 'with respect,' 'respectfully.'

i. Words meaning 'hand' are placed at the end of possessives;— e.g. शस्त्रपाणि śastra-pāṇi, 'weapon-handed,' 'having a weapon in one's hand'; कुशहस्त kuśa-hasta, 'with kuśa-grass in (his) hand.'

j. The suffix इन् in is pleonastically added to धर्म dharma, 'duty,' शील śila, 'character,' माला mālā, 'garland,' शाला śālā, 'house,' शोभा śobhā, 'beauty,' वर्ण varṇa, 'colour'; — e.g.

वरवर्णिन् vara-varṇ-in, of excellent colour.' The adjectival suffix क ka is similarly often added, especially to unusual finals, as to words in ऋ ṛ, to feminines in ई ī (like नदी nadī), and in the feminine to words in इन् in; — e.g. मृतभर्तृका mṛta-bhartṛ-kā, 'whose husband is dead'; सपत्नीक sa-patnī-ka, 'accompanied by his wife.'

CHAPTER VII

OUTLINES OF SYNTAX

190. As the great bulk of the literature consists of poetry, the syntactical arrangement of the Sanskrit sentence is primitive and undeveloped, as compared with Latin and Greek. Its main characteristic is the predominance of co-ordination, long compounds and gerunds constantly taking the place of relative and other subordinate clauses, while the *oratio obliqua* is entirely absent. Another feature is the comparatively rare use of the finite verb (frequent enough in the Vedic language), for which past participles or verbal nouns are very often substituted. There is also a marked fondness for passive constructions. A special feature of Sanskrit syntax is the employment of the **locative absolute.**

The Order of Words.

191. The usual arrangement of words in a Sanskrit sentence is: — first, the subject with its attributes (a genitive preceding its nominative); second, the object with its adjuncts (which precede it); and lastly, the verb.

Adverbs or extensions of the predicate are commonly placed near the beginning, and unemphatic connective particles

follow the first word; — e.g. जनकस्तु सत्वरं स्वीयं नगरं जगाम 'but Janaka went in haste to his own city.'

When there is a vocative, it generally comes first. Instead of the subject any other word requiring emphasis may be placed at the head of the sentence; — e.g. रात्रौ त्वया मठमध्ये न प्रवेष्टव्यम् 'at night you must not enter the monastery.'

a. The subject, if a personal pronoun, is not expressed unless emphatic, being inherent in finite verbal forms. Even the general subject 'one' or 'they' is often indicated by the verb alone; — e.g. ब्रूयात् 'one should say'; आहुः 'they say' = 'it is said.'

b. The copula अस्ति 'is,' unless the tense or mood has to be expressed, is generally omitted. In that case the predicate precedes its noun; — e.g. शीतला रात्रिः 'the night (is) cold.' If the predicate bears any emphasis, भवति is used, not अस्ति; — e.g. यो विद्यया तपसा जन्मना वा वृद्धः स पूज्यो भवति द्विजानाम् 'he who is distinguished by knowledge, penance, or birth, is (certainly) to be respected by the twice-born.'

c. Just as attributes precede their nouns and the qualifying word comes first in compounds, so a relative or other subordinate clause precedes the principal clause, which regularly begins with a correlative word; — e.g. यस्य धनं तस्य बलम् lit. 'of whom wealth, of him power,' i.e. 'he who has wealth has power.' Similarly यदा — तदा, यावत् — तावत् & c.

The Article.

192. There is properly neither an indefinite nor a definite article in Sanskrit. But एक 'one' and कश्चिद् 'some' (119), being frequently used to express 'a certain,' may sometimes be translated by 'a.' Similarly स 'that' (110) may, when referring to persons or things just mentioned, be rendered by 'the'; — e.g. स राजा 'the king' (of whom we are speaking).

Number.

193. 1. Singular collective words are sometimes used at the end of compounds to form a plural; — e.g. स्त्रीजन stri-jana, m. 'womenfolk' = 'women.' Such collectives are sometimes themselves used in the plural; — e.g. लोक: or लोका: 'the world,' 'people.'

2. The dual number is in regular use and of strict application, the plural practically never referring to two objects. It is therefore invariably employed with the names of things occurring in pairs, such as parts of the body; — e.g. हस्तौ पादौ च 'the hands and the feet.' A masc. dual is sometimes used to express a male and female of the same class; — e.g. जगत: पितरौ 'the parents of the universe' (see 186, 3*c*, p. 171).

3. ***a.*** The plural is sometimes applied to others by the speaker or writer as a mark of great respect, यूयम् and भवन्त: taking the place of त्वम् and भवान्; — e.g. श्रुतं भवद्भि: 'has your Majesty heard?' In this sense the plur. पादा: 'feet' is employed instead of the dual (cp. 193, 2); — e.g. एष देवपादान् अधिक्षिपति 'he insults your Majesty('s feet).' Proper names are occasionally used in the same way; — e.g. इति श्रीशंकराचार्या: 'thus (says) the revered teacher Śaṃkara.'

b. The 1. pres. pl. is sometimes used by the speaker referring to himself (like our editorial 'we') instead of the singular or dual (cp. 193, *2*); — e.g. वयमपि किंचित्पृच्छाम: 'we (= I) too ask something'; किं कुर्म: साम्प्रतम् 'what shall we (= you and I) do now?'

c. The names of countries are plural, being really the names of the peoples (like 'Sweden' in English and 'Sachsen' in German);— e.g. विदर्भेषु 'in Vidarbha' (Berar). In the singular the name of the people often denotes the king of the country.

d. Some nouns are used in the plural only: — आपः f. 'water' (96, 1); प्राणाः m. 'life'; वर्षाः f. 'the rains' = 'the rainy season'; दाराः m. 'wife.'

Concord.

194. The rules of concord in case, person, gender, and number are in general the same as in other inflexional languages, but the following special points may be noted:—

1. The nominative with इति may take the place of a predicative acc. governed by verbs of calling, considering, knowing, &c.; — e.g. ब्राह्मण इति मां विद्धि 'know me to be a Brahmin' (instead of ब्राह्मणं मां विद्धि).

2. When a dual or plural verb refers to two or more subjects the first person is preferred to the second or third, and the second person to the third; — e.g. त्वमहं च गच्छावः 'you and I go.'

3. *a.* A dual or plural adjective agreeing with masc. and fem. substantives is put in the masc., but when neuters are associated with masculines and feminines, in the **neuter** (sometimes singular); — e.g. मृगयाक्षास्तथा पानं गर्हितानि महीभुजाम् 'the chase, dice (akṣāḥ), and drinking are reprehensible in kings'; पक्षविकलश्च पक्षी शुष्कश्च तरुः सरश्च जलहीनं सर्पश्चोद्धृतदंष्ट्रस् तुल्यं लोके दरिद्रश्च 'a bird with clipped wings, a withered tree, a dried-up pond, a toothless serpent and a poor man are of equal account (neut. sing.) in (the eyes of) the world.'

b. Occasionally an attribute or predicate takes the natural instead of the grammatical gender; — e.g. त्वां चिन्तयन्तो निराहाराः कृताः प्रजाः 'thinking (masc.) of thee the subjects (fem.) have been reduced to taking no food.'

c. As in Greek and Latin, a demonstrative pronoun agrees with its predicate in gender; — e.g. असौ परमो मन्त्रः 'this (masc.) is the best counsel' (masc.).

A participle used in place of a finite verb, which should

agree with the subject, may be attracted in gender by a substantive predicate if in close proximity with it; — e.g. त्वं मे मित्रं जातम् 'thou (masc.) hast become (neut.) my friend' (neut.).

4. A singular collective noun is necessarily followed by a singular verb. Two singular subjects require a predicate in the dual, three or more require it in the plural. Occasionally, however, the predicate agrees in number with the nearest subject, being mentally supplied with the rest; — e.g. कान्तिमती राज्यमिदं मम च जीवितमपि त्वदधीनम् 'Kāntimatī, this kingdom, and my very life (are) at your mercy' (sing.).

a. Similarly, the verb which should agree with a single plural subject may be attracted in number by a noun predicate in its immediate proximity; — e.g. सप्तप्रकृतयो ह्येताः समस्तं राज्यमुच्यते 'these seven constituent parts are said (sing.) to form the entire kingdom.'

Pronouns.

195. 1. **Personal. *a.*** Owing to its highly inflexional character Sanskrit uses the nominatives of personal pronouns far less frequently than modern European languages do (cp. 191*a*).

b. The unaccented forms of अहम् and त्वम् (109 *a*) being enclitic, can be used neither at the beginning of a sentence or metrical line (Pāda), nor after vocatives, nor before the particles च, वा, एव, ह;— e.g. मम मित्रम् 'my friend' (not मे); देवास्मान् पाहि 'O God, protect us' (अस्मान्, not नः); तस्य मम वा गृहम् 'his house or mine.'

c. भवान् 'your Honour' (f. भवती), the polite form of त्वम् 'thou' (with which it often alternates even in the same sentence), takes the verb in the 3. person; — e.g. किमाह भवान् 'what does your Honour say?' The plural भवन्तः (f. भवत्यः) is construed in the same way; it frequently has a singular sense (193, 3 *a*). Two compounds of भवान् are often used in the drama:— अत्रभवान्

atra-bhavān refers to someone present, either the person addressed or some third person = 'your Honour here' or 'his Honour here'; तत्रभवान् tatra-bhavān, 'his Honour there,' 'referring to someone off the stage, can only be used of a third person. Both take the verb in the 3. sing.

2. **Demonstrative.** ***a.*** एष and अयम् refer to what is near or present = 'this.' The former is the more emphatic of the two. Both are often employed agreeing with a subject in the 1. or 3. pers. sing. in the sense of 'here'; — e.g. एष तपस्वी तिष्ठति 'here a devotee stands'; अयमस्मि 'here am I'; अयम् आगतस्तव पुत्रः 'here comes your son.' अयं जनः 'this person' is frequently used as an equivalent of 'I.'

b. स and असौ refer to what is absent or remote = 'that.' स is the more definitely demonstrative of the two, being, for instance, the regular correlative to an antecedent relative. It has the following special uses. It has often (like Lat. ille) the sense of 'well-knwon,' 'calebrated'; — e.g. सा रम्या नगरी 'that well-known charming city.' It is frequently also the equivalent of 'the aforesaid'; — e.g. सोऽहम् 'I (being) such' (as just described). In this sense it may often be translated simply by the definite article 'the' (cp. 192). When unaccompanied by a noun स supplies the place of a personal pronoun of the third person = 'he, she, it, they,' but with a certain amount of emphasis when used in the nominative (अयम् and असौ are employed in the same way as personal pronouns of the third person). Finally स when repeated means 'various,' 'several,' 'all sorts of'; — e.g. तानि तानि शास्त्राण्यध्यैत 'he read various treatises.'

3. **Possessive.** These pronouns (116) are comparatively little used, as the genitive of the personal pronouns is generally employed. In accordance with the sense of भवत् (195, 1 *c*), its derivatives भवदीय bhavad-īya and भावत्क bhāvat-ka are used as possessive pronouns of the second person in respectful address.

THE CASES

Nominative.

196. The nominative is far less frequently used in Sanskrit as the subject of a sentence than in other Indo-European languages. Its place is very commonly supplied by the instrumental of the agent with a passive verb; — e.g. केनापि सस्यरक्षकेणैकान्ते स्थितम् 'a certain field-watcher was standing aside' (lit. 'by a certain field-watcher it was stood aside').

a. The nominative is used predicatively with verbs meaning 'to be, become, seem, appear,' as well as with the passive of verbs of calling, considering, sending, appointing, making, &c.; — e.g. तेन मुनिना कुक्कुरो व्याघ्रः कृतः 'the dog was turned into a tiger by the sage.'

b. The nominative followed by इति may in certain circumstances take the place of the accusative (see 194, 1).

Accusative.

197. Besides its ordinary use of denoting the object of transitive verbs, the accusative is employed to express —

1. the goal with verbs of motion; — e.g. स विदर्भान् अगमत् 'he went to Vidarbha.'

a. verbs of going, like गम् and या, are very commonly joined with an abstract substantive where either the corresponding adjective with 'to become,' or merely an intransitive verb would be used in English; — e.g. स कीर्तिं याति 'he becomes famous' (lit. 'goes to fame'); पञ्चत्वं गच्छति 'he dies' (lit. 'goes to death').

2. duration of time and extension of space; — e.g. मासमधीते 'he learns for a month'; योजनं गच्छति 'he goes (the distance of) a Yojana' (nine miles).

3. the object of desiderative adjectives in उ (cp. 169) and of some compound adjectives beginning with prepositions; — e.g.

तितीर्षुर् अस्मि सागरम् 'I am desirous of crossing the ocean'; दमयन्तीम् अनुव्रत: 'devoted to Damayantī.'

4. the cognate object of intransitive verbs in the case of substantives and the analogous adverbial sense in the case of adjectives; — e.g. कामान् सर्वान् वर्षतु 'may he rain (i.e. grant) all desires'; शीघ्रं गच्छाम 'let us go quickly' (originally, 'go a quick gait').

Double Accusative.

198. Two accusatives are governed by—

1. verbs of calling, considering, knowing, making, appointing, choosing; — e.g. जानामि त्वां प्रकृतिपुरुषम् 'I know thee (to be) the chief person.'

2. verbs of speaking (ब्रू, वच, अह्), asking (प्रछ्), begging (याच्, प्रार्थय), instructing (अनु-शास्), fining (दण्डय), winning (जि), milking (दुह्); — e.g. अन्तरिक्षगो वाचं व्याजहार नलम् 'the bird addressed a speech to Nala'; साक्ष्यं पृच्छेदृतं द्विजान् 'he should ask true evidence from the twice-born'; बलिं याचते वसुधाम् 'he asks Bali for the earth'; यदनुशास्ति माम् 'what she commands me'; तान् सहस्रं दण्डयेत् 'he should fine them a thousand (paṇas)'; जित्वा राज्यं नलम् 'having won the kingdom from Nala'; रत्नानि दुदुहुर्धरित्रीम् 'they milked (i.e. extracted) gems from the earth.'

a. कथय 'tell,' वेदय 'make known,' and आ-दिश् 'enjoin,' never take the accusative of the person addressed, but the dative (or gen.).

3. verbs of bringing, conveying, leading, dispatching; — e.g. ग्रामम् अजां नयति 'he brings the goat to the village'; शकुन्तलां पतिकुलं विसृज्य 'having sent Śakuntalā away to her husband's house.'

4. causative verbs; — e.g. रामं वेदमध्यापयति 'he causes Rāma to learn the Veda'; if stress is laid on the agent (the direct acc.), it may be put in the instrumental: तां श्वभिः खादयेत् 'he should cause her to be devoured by dogs.'

a. When the causative meaning has faded, the dat. or gen. of the person is used instead of all acc.; this is generally the case with दर्शय 'show' ('cause to see'), and श्रावय 'tell' ('cause to hear'), and always with वेदय 'make known,' 'tell' ('cause to know').

b. In the passive construction the direct acc. (the person or agent) becomes the nom., the indirect acc. (the object or thing) remains; — e.g. रामो वेदम् अध्याप्यते 'Rāma is caused to learn the Veda'; तां श्वानः खाद्यन्ते 'dogs are caused to devour her'; बलिर्याच्यते वसुधाम् 'Bali is asked for the earth.'

Instrumental.

199. The fundamental notion of the instrumental, which may be rendered by 'by' or 'with,' expresses the **agent,** the **instrument** (means), or **concomitant** by or with which an action is performed; — e.g. तेनोक्तम् 'it was said by him' = 'he said'; स खड्गेन व्यापादितः 'he was killed with a sword'; यस्य मित्रेण संलापस् ततो नास्तीह पुण्यवान् 'there is no one happier (201, 2*a*) in this world than he who has converse with a friend.'

1. The following are modifications of the **instrumental sense** expressing—

a. the **reason:** 'by,' 'through,' 'by reason of,' 'because of,' 'on account of'; — e.g. भवतोऽनुग्रहेण 'through your favour'; तेनापराधेन त्वां दण्डयामि 'I punish you for that fault'; व्याघ्रबुद्ध्या 'by the thought of a tiger' = 'because he thought it was a tiger.' (cp. p. 172, 5); सुखभ्रान्त्या 'under the delusion of (the existence of) pleasure.'

b. **accordance**: 'by,' 'in comformity with'; — e.g. प्रकृत्या 'by nature'; जात्या 'by birth'; स मम मतेन वर्तते 'he goes by (acts in accordance with) my opinion.'

c. the **price**: ('with,' 'by means of'=) 'for,' 'at the price of'; — e.g. रूपकशतेन विक्रीयमाणं पुस्तकम् 'a book sold for a hundred rupees'; आत्मानं सततं रक्षेद् दारैरपि धनैरपि 'a man should always save himself even at the cost of his wife or of his wealth.'

d. **time within which** anything is done: ('by the lapse of' =) 'in'; — e.g. द्वादशभिर् वर्षैर् व्याकरणं श्रूयते 'grammar is learnt in twelve years.'

e. the **way, vehicle** or part of the body **by which** motion is effected; — e.g. कतमेन मार्गेण प्रनष्टाः काकाः 'in what direction (lit. 'by what road') have the crows disappeared?' वाजिना चरति 'he goes on horseback' (lit. 'by means of a horse'); स श्वानं स्कन्धेनोवाह 'he carried (uvāha) the dog on his shoulder.'

f. **'in respect of':** with words implying superiority, inferiority or defectiveness; — e.g. एताभ्यां शौर्येण हीनः 'inferior to these two (abl.) in valour'; पूर्वान् महाभाग तयातिशेषे 'O fortunate man, you excel your ancestors in that (devotion)'; अक्ष्णा काणः 'blind of an eye.'

g. **'of,' 'with':** with words meaning **need** or **use,** अर्थः, प्रयोजनम् (used interrogatively or with a negative), or किम् 'what?' (with or without कृ 'do'); — e.g. को मे जीवितेनार्थः 'what is the use of life to me' (gen.); देवपादानां सेवकैर्न प्रयोजनम् 'your Majesty's feet have no need of servants'; किं तया क्रियते धेन्वा 'what is to be done with that cow?' किं न एतेन 'what have we (to do) with this?' Similar is the use of कृतम् 'done with' = 'away with' and अलम् 'enough of' (cf. 180): कृतमभ्युत्थानेन 'away with rising' = 'pray do not rise.'

***h.* 'with,' 'at':** with verbs of rejoicing, laughing, being pleased, satisfied, astonished, ashamed, disgusted; — e.g. कापुरुषः स्वल्पेनापि तुष्यति 'a low person is satisfied even with very little'; जहास तेन 'he laughted at it.'

***i.* 'of,' 'by':** with verbs of boasting or swearing; — e.g. भरतेनात्मना चाहं शपे 'I swear by Bharata and myself.'

j. the object (victim) with यज् 'sacrifice'; — e.g. पशुना रुद्रं यजते 'he sacrifices a bull to Rudra.' Here we have the real inst. sense surviving from the time when यज् meant 'worship' a god (acc.) with (inst.).

2. The **concomitant** or sociative **sense** is generally supplemented by the prepositional adverbs सह, साकम्, सार्धम् and समम् 'with,' which are used (like 'with' in English) even when separation or antagonism is implied; — e.g. पुत्रेण सह पिता गतः 'the father went with his son'; मित्रेण सह चित्तविश्लेषः 'disagreement with a friend'; स तेन विदधे समं युद्धम् 'he engaged in a fight with him.' This sense is also applied —

a. to express the accompanying **circumstances** or the **manner** in which an action is performed; — e.g. तौ दंपती महता स्नेहेन वसतः 'that pair lives in great affection'; महता सुखेन 'with great pleasure.'

b. with the passive of verbs which have the sense of accompanying, joining, endowing, possessing, and the opposite; — e.g. त्वया सहितः 'accompanied by you;' धनेन संपन्नो विहीनो वा 'possessed or destitute of wealth'; प्राणैर् वियुक्तः 'benefit of life.'

c. with adjectives expressive of **identity, equality,** or **likeness:** सम, समान, सदृश, तुल्यः— e.g. शक्रेण समः 'equal to Indra'; अनेन सदृशः 'like him'; अयं न मे पादरजसापि तुल्यः 'he is not even equal to the dust of my feet.' The genitive is also used with these adjectives (cp. 202, 2 *d*).

Dative.

200. The dative case expresses either the **indirect object,** generally a person, or the **purpose** of an action.

A. The dative of the **indirect object** is used—

1. with **transitive** verbs, with or without a direct object:—

a. of giving (दा, अर्पय), telling (चक्ष्, शंस्, कथय, ख्यापय, निवेदय), promising (प्रति° or आ-श्रु, प्रति-ज्ञा), showing (दर्शय); — e.g. विप्राय गां ददाति 'he gives a cow to the Brahmin'; कथयामि ते भूतार्थम् 'I tell you the truth.'

b. of sending, casting; — e.g. भोजेन दूतो रघवे विसृष्टः 'a messenger was sent by Bhoja to Raghu'; शूलांश्चिक्षिपू रामाय 'they cast (47) darts at Rāma.'

2. with intransitive verbs meaning to please (रुच्), desire (लुभ्, स्पृह्), be angry with (असूय, कुप्, क्रुध्), injure (द्रुह्);— e.g. रोचते मह्यम् 'it pleases me'; न राज्याय स्पृहये 'I do not long for the kingdom'; किंकराय कुप्यति 'he is angry with his servant.' (क्रुध् and द्रुह् when compounded with prepositions govern the acc.).

3. with words of salutation; — e.g. गणेशाय नमः 'salutation to Gaṇeśa'; कुशलं ते 'health to thee'; रामाय स्वस्ति 'hail to Rāma'; स्वागतं देव्यै 'welcome to her Majesty.'

B. The dative of **purpose** expresses the end for which an action is done, and is very often equivalent to an infinitive; — e.g. मुक्तये हरिं भजति 'he worships Hari for (= to obtain) salvation'; फलेभ्यो याति 'he goes for (= to obtain) fruit'; अस्मत्पुत्राणां नीतिशास्त्रोपदेशाय भवन्तः प्रमाणम् 'your Honour (has) full authority for the instruction of (= to instruct) my sons in the principles of morality'; युद्धाय प्रस्थितः 'he started for a fight' (= 'to fight'); पुनर्दर्शनाय 'au revoir.'

This dative is specially taken by verbs meaning—

1. 'be fit for,' 'tend or conduce to' (क्लृप्, सं-पद्, प्र-भू); — e.g. भक्तिर्ज्ञानाय कल्पते 'piety conduces to knowledge.'

a. अस् and भू are used in the same way, but are often omitted;— e.g. लघूनामपि संश्रयो रक्षायै भवति 'the combination even of the weak leads to safety'; आर्तत्राणाय वः शस्त्रम् 'your weapon (serves) for the protection of (= to protect) the distressed.'

2. 'be able,' 'begin,' 'strive,' 'resolve,' 'order,' 'appoint';— e.g. इयं कथा क्षत्रियस्याकर्षणायाशकत् 'this story was able to win over (ākarṣaṇāya) the warrior'; प्रावर्तत शपथाय 'he began to (take) an oath'; तदन्वेषणाय यतिष्ये 'I will try to find her'; तेन जीवोत्सर्गाय व्यवसितम् 'he has resolved on abandoning his life'; दुहितरम् अतिथिसत्कारायादिश्य 'having charged (ā-diśya) his daughter with the reception of the guests'; रावणोच्छित्तये देवैर्नियोजितः 'he was appointed by the gods for the destruction of (= to destroy) Rāvaṇa.'

a. The adverb अलम् 'sufficient' is used in the sense of 'be able to cope with,' 'be a match for'; — e.g. दैत्येभ्यो हरिरलम् 'Hari (is) a match for the demons.'

Ablative.

201. The ablative primarily expresses the starting-point or source from which anything proceeds. It thus answers to the question 'whence?' and may in general be translated by 'from.'

E.g. अहम् अस्माद् वनाद् गन्तुमिच्छामि 'I wish to depart from this forest'; पापान्नाश उद्भवति 'ruin results from sin' (pāpād); निश्चयान्न चचाल सः 'he did not swerve from his purpose' (niścayād); स्वजनेभ्यः सुतविनाशं शुश्राव 'he heard of the death of his son from his relations'; तां बन्धनाद्विमुच्य 'releasing her from her bonds'; विरम कर्मणोऽस्मात् 'desist from this act'; पाहि मां नरकात् 'protect me from hell.'

a. The source of apprehension is put in the ablative with **verbs of fearing** (भी, उद्विज् ud-vij); — e.g. लुब्धकाद् बिभेषि 'you are afraid of the hunter'; संमानाद् ब्राह्मणो नित्यमुद्विजेत 'a Brahmin should always shrink from marks of honour.'

b. Verbs expressing separation 'from' naturally take the ablative; — e.g. भवद्भ्यो वियोजित: 'parted from you'; सा पतिलोकाच्च हीयते 'and she is deprived of her husband's place' (such words also take the instr.: cp. 199, 2 *b*). Allied to this use is that of वञ्चय 'to cheat of' (= so as to separate from); — e.g. वञ्चयितुं ब्राह्मणं छागलात् 'to cheat a Brahmin of his he-goat.'

c. As the abl. expresses the *terminus a quo*, it is employed with all words meaning 'far,' or designating the cardinal points; —e.g. दूरं ग्रामात् 'far from the village'; ग्रामात् पूर्वो गिरि: 'the mountain (is) to the east of the village.'

d. Similarly the abl. also expresses the **time after which** anything takes place; — e.g. बहोर्दृष्टं कालात् 'seen after a long time'; सप्ताहात् 'after a week.'

The abl. also expresses the following senses connected with its original meaning:—

1. the **cause, reason,** or **motive** = 'on account of,' 'because of,' 'through,' 'from'; — e.g. लौल्याद् मांसं भक्षयति 'he eats the flesh through greed.' This use of the abl. is especially common, in commentaries, with abstract nouns in त्व tva; — e.g. पर्वतोऽग्निमान् धूमत्वात् 'the mountain is fiery because of its smokiness.' (The instr. is also employed in this sense: 199, 1 *a*.)

2. **Comparison:—**

a. with comparatives (= 'than') or words with a comparative meaning; — e.g. गोविन्दाद् रामो विद्वत्तर: 'Rāma is more learned than Govinda'; कर्मणो ज्ञानम् अतिरिच्यते 'knowledge is superior to action.' In this sense it is used even with positives (= 'in comparison with'); — e.g. भार्या सर्वलोकादपि वल्लभा भवति 'a

wife is dear even in comparison with (i.e. dearer than) the whole world'; वज्रादपि कठोराणि मृदूनि कुसुमादपि चेतांसि 'hearts harder even than adamant, more tender even than a flower.'

b. with words meaning 'other' or 'different' (अन्य, इतर, अपर, भिन्न); — e.g. कृष्णादन्यो गोविन्दः 'Govinda is different from Kṛṣṇa.'

c. Allied to the comparative abl. is that used with multiplicative words like 'double,' 'treble,' &c.; — e.g. मूल्यात् पञ्चगुणो दण्डः 'a fine five times (in comparison with) the value.'

Genitive.

202. The primary sense of the genitive is quasi-adjectival, since its qualification of another substantive means 'belonging to' or 'connected with.' It may generally be expressed in English by the preposition 'of.' With substantives the gen. is used in a possessive, subjective, objective, or partitive sense; — e.g. राज्ञः पुरुषः 'the king's man'; राक्षसकलत्रप्रच्छादनं भवतः 'your concealment of Rākṣasa's wife' (i.e. 'by you'); शङ्कया तस्याः 'by the supposition of her' (i.e. 'supposing it was she'); धुर्यो धनवताम् 'the foremost of the wealthy.'

1. The **gen.** is used **with** a number of **verbs:—**

a. in the possessive sense with ईश् iś, प्र-भू 'be master of,' 'have power over,' and with अस्, भू 'be,' विद्यते 'exists'; — e.g. आत्मनः प्रभविष्यामि 'I shall be master of myself'; मम पुस्तकं विद्यते 'I have a book.'

b. in the objective sense (concurrently with the acc.) with दय् 'have mercy,' स्मृ 'remember,' अनु-कृ 'imitate'; — e.g. एते तव दयन्ताम् 'may these men have mercy on you'; स्मरति ते प्रसादानाम् 'he remembers your favours'; भीमस्यानुकरिष्यामि 'I will imitate Bhīma.'

c. in the objective sense (concurrently with the loc.) with verbs meaning 'do good or harm to' (उप-कृ, प्र-सद्, अप-कृ, अप-राध्), 'trust in' (वि-श्वस्), 'forbear with' (क्षम्); — e.g. मित्राणाम् उपकुर्वाणः 'benefiting his friends'; किं मया तस्या अपकृतम् 'how have I done her an injury?' क्षमस्व मे 'forbear with me.'

d. with verbs meaning 'speak of' or 'expect of'; — e.g. ममादोषस्याप्येवं वदति 'he speaks thus of me though I am guiltless'; सर्वमस्य मूर्खस्य संभाव्यते 'anything may be expected of that fool.'

e. frequently (instead of the dat. of the indirect object) with verbs of giving, telling, promising, showing, sending, bowing, pleasing, being angry; — e.g. मया तस्याभयं प्रदत्तम् 'I have granted safety to him' (tasya); किं तव रोचत एषः 'does he please you?' ममानतिक्रुद्धो मुनिः 'the sage (is) not very angry with me' (mama).

f. sometimes (instead of the instr.) with verbs meaning 'be filled or satisfied'; — e.g. नाग्निस्तृप्यति काष्ठानाम् 'fire is not satiated with logs.' So also the past part. पूर्ण 'full of' (gen.), or 'filled with' (instr.).

2. The **gen.** is frequently used **with adjectives:—**

a. allied to transitive verbs: — e.g. जरा विनाशिनी रूपस्य 'old age is destructive of beauty.'

b. meaning 'dependent on,' 'belonging or attached to,' 'dear to'; — e.g. तवायत्तः स प्रतीकारः 'that remedy depends on you' (tava); यत् त्वयास्य सक्तं किंचिद् गृहीतमस्ति तत् समर्पय 'give up whatever you have taken belonging to him' (asya); को नाम राज्ञां प्रियः 'who, pray, is dear to kings?'

c. meaning 'acquainted with,' 'versed or skilled in,' 'accustomed to' (concurrently with the loc.: 203 *f*); — e.g. अभिज्ञः खल्वसि लोकव्यवहाराणाम् 'you are, indeed, conversant with the ways of the world'; संग्रामाणाम् अकोविदः 'unskilled

in battle'; उचितो जनः क्लेशानाम् 'people accustomed to hardships.'

d. meaning 'like' or 'equal to' (concurrently with the instr.: 199, 2*c*); — e.g. रामः कृष्णस्य तुल्यः 'Rāma is equal to Kṛṣṇa.'

3. The **gen.** expresses the agent **with passive participles:—**

a. past participles having a pres. sense, formed from roots meaning 'think,' 'know,' 'worship'; — e.g. राज्ञां मतः ('well thought of' =) 'approved of kings'; विदितो भवान् आश्रमसदाम् इहस्थः 'you are known to the hermits to be staying here.'

b. future participles (which also take the instr.: 199); — e.g. मम (मया) सेव्यो हरिः 'Hari should be worshipped by me.'

4. The **gen.** is used **with adverbs** of direction in °तस् -tas (cp. 177*d*); — e.g. ग्रामस्य दक्षिणतः 'to the south of the village'; sometimes also with those in °एन -ena (concurrently with the acc.); — e.g. उत्तरेणास्य 'to the north of this' (asya) place.

5. The **gen. of time** is used in the following ways:—

a. with multiplicative (108) or other numerals similarly used it expresses how often anything is repeated within a stated period; — e.g. श्राद्धं त्रिरब्दस्य निर्वपेत् 'he should offer the funeral sacrifice three times a year'; संवत्सरस्यैकमपि चरेत् कृच्छ्रं द्विजोत्तमः 'a Brahmin should perform at least one severe penance a year.'

b. Words denoting time are put in the gen. (like the abl.) in the sense of 'after'; — e.g. कतिपयाहस्य (kati-paya ahasya), 'after some days'; चिरस्य कालस्य 'after a long time': चिरस्य is also used alone in this sense.

c. A noun and past part. in the gen., accompanying an expression of time, have the sense of 'since';— e.g. अद्य दशमो मासस् तातस्योपरतस्य 'to-day (is) the tenth month since our father died' (uparatasya). This construction is akin to the gen. absolute (205, 2).

6. Two genitives are employed to express an option or a difference between two things; — e.g. व्यसनस्य च मृत्योश्च व्यसनं कष्टमुच्यते 'of vice and death, the former is called the worse'; एतावानेवायुष्मतः शतक्रतोश्च विशेषः 'this is the only difference between you (the long-lived) and Indra.'

Locative.

203. The locative denotes either the place where an action occurs, or, with verbs of motion, the place whither an action is directed. The former sense may variously be translated by 'in, at, on, among, by, with, near,' the latter by 'into, upon'; corresponding to Lat. *in* with abl. and acc. respectively.

The following are examples of the ordinary use of the loc. in the sense of **'where?'** पक्षिगणस्तस्मिन् वृक्षे निवसन्ति 'birds live in that tree'; विदर्भेषु 'in Vidarbha' (193, 3c); आत्मानं तव द्वारि व्यापादयिष्यामि 'I will kill myself at your door'; काश्याम् 'at Kāśī' (Benares); फलं दृष्टं द्रुमेषु 'fruit (is) seen on the trees'; आसेदुर्गङ्गायाम् 'they encamped on (= close to) the Ganges'; न देवेषु न यक्षेषु तादृग्रूपवती क्वचिद् मानुषेष्वपि चान्येषु दृष्टपूर्वा 'neither, among gods, nor Yakṣas, or among men either, had such a beauty anywhere been seen before'; मम पार्श्वे 'by my side.'

a. When the loc. means 'among' it is often equivalent to a partitive gen. (202); — e.g. सर्वेषु पुत्रेषु रामो मम प्रियतमः 'among (= of) all the sons Rāma is dearest to me.'

b. The person 'with' whom one dwells or stays is put in the loc.; — e.g. गुरौ वसति 'he lives with his teacher.'

c. The loc. with the verbs तिष्ठति 'stands' and वर्तते 'goes on' (= Lat. versatur) expresses 'abides by,' 'complies with'; — e.g. नमे शासने तिष्ठसि 'you do not (stand by =) obey my command'; मातुर्मते वर्तस्व 'comply with your mother's desire.'

d. The loc. is used to express the effect 'of' a cause; — e.g. दैवमेव नृणां वृद्धौ क्षये कारणम् 'fate alone (is) the cause of the prosperity or decline of men.'

e. The loc. expresses contact with verbs of seizing by (ग्रह्), fastening to (बन्ध्), clinging or adhering to (लग्, श्लिष्, सञ्ज्), leaning on, relying on or trusting to; — e.g. केशेषु गृहीत्वा 'seizing by the hair'; पाणौ संगृह्य 'taking by the hand'; वृक्षे पाशं बबन्ध 'he fastened a noose to the tree'; व्यसनेष्वसक्तः शूरः 'a hero not addicted to vices'; वृक्षमूलेषु संश्रिताः 'reclining on the roots of trees'; विश्वसिति शत्रुषु 'he trusts in his enemies'; आशंसन्ते सुरा अस्याधिज्ये धनुषि विजयम् 'the gods fix their hopes of victory on his bent bow.'

f. The loc. is used (concurrently with the gen.: 202, 2 *c*) with adjectives meaning 'acquainted with,' 'versed or skilled in'; — e.g. रामोऽक्षद्यूते निपुणः 'Rāma (is) skilled in the game of dice'; नाट्ये दक्षा वयम् 'we (are) expert in acting.'

g. The loc. is used figuratively to express the person or thing in which some quality or state is to be found; — e.g. सर्वं संभावयाम्यस्मिन् 'I look for everything in him' (cp. 202, 1*d*); दृष्टदोषा मृगया स्वामिनि 'hunting (is) recognized as sinful in a prince'; आर्तानामुपदेशे न दोषः 'there is no harm in (giving) advice to the afflicted.' Similarly, when the meaning of a word is explained, the loc. expresses 'in the sense of'; — e.g. कलापो बर्हे 'kalāpa (is used) in the sense of peacock's tail.'

h. The circumstances in which an action takes place are expressed by the loc.; — e.g. आपदि 'in case of distress'; भाग्येषु 'in fortune'; छिद्रेष्वनर्था बहुलीभवन्ति ('in the presence of' =) 'there being openings, misfortunes multiply.' In the last example the loc. expresses the reason; if it were accompanied by a predicative participle, it would be a loc. absolute (cp. 205, 1 *a*).

i. The **loc. of time,** expressing when an action takes place, is only a special application of the preceding sense; — e.g. वर्षासु 'in the rainy season'; निशायाम् 'at night'; दिने दिने 'every day.'

j. The loc. expresses the distance at which anything takes place; — e.g. इतो वसति... अध्यर्धयोजने महर्षिः 'the great sage lives at (a distance of) a yojana and a half from here.'

204. The loc. answering to the question **'whither?'** is always used with verbs of falling and placing; concurrently with the dat., with those of throwing and sending (200 A 1*b*); and, concurrently with the acc., with those of going, entering, ascending, striking, bringing, sending; — e.g. भूमौ पपात 'he fell on the ground'; तत्रैव भिक्षापात्रे निधाय 'having put (it) in that same begging bowl'; हस्तमुरसि कृत्वा 'placing his hand on his breast' (कृ 'do,' is frequently used in the sense of putting); अरौ बाणान् क्षिपति 'he darts arrows at his enemy'; मत्स्यो नद्यां प्रविवेश 'the fish entered the river'; समीपवर्तिनि नगरे प्रस्थितः 'he set out for a neighbouring town'; तं शिरस्यताडयत् 'he struck him on the head.'

Secondary applications of this loc. are the following:—

a. It expresses the person or object towards which an action is directed or to which it refers = 'towards,' 'about,' 'with regard to'; — e.g. प्राणिषु दयां कुर्वन्ति साधवः 'the good show compassion towards animate beings'; भव दक्षिणा परिजने 'be courteous to your attendants'; क्षेत्रे विवदन्ते 'they are disputing about a field.'

b. Concurrently with the dat. (and gen.), it expresses the indirect object with verbs of giving, telling, promising, buying, selling (cp. 200 A 1*a*; 202, 1*e*); — e.g. सहस्राक्षे प्रतिज्ञाय 'having promised (it) to Indra'; शरीरं विक्रीय धनवति 'having sold himself to a rich man'; वितरति गुरुः प्राज्ञे विद्याम् 'a teacher imparts knowledge to an intelligent pupil.'

c. Concurrently with the dat. (200 B 1, 2), it may express the aim of an action with words expressive of striving after, resolving on, wishing for, of appointing, choosing, enjoining, permitting, of being able or fit for; — e.g. सर्वस्वहरणे युक्तः शत्रुः 'an enemy prepared for the appropriation of all property'; कर्मणि न्ययुङ्क्त 'he appointed (him) to a task'; पतित्वे वरयामास तम् 'she chose him for her husband'; असमर्थोऽयमुदरपूरणेऽस्माकम् 'he is incapable of supplying food for us'; त्रैलोक्यस्यापि प्रभुत्वं तस्मिन् युज्यते 'the sovereignty even of the three worlds is fitting for him.' A predicative loc. alone is capable of expressing fitness; — e.g. नयत्यागशौर्यसंपन्ने पुरुषे राज्यम् 'sovereignty befits a man who is endowed with worldly wisdom, liberality, and heroism.' The loc. is sometimes used with verbs which do not in themselves imply an aim, to express the object gained as the result of an action;— e.g. चर्मणि हन्ति द्वीपिनम् 'he kills the panther for the sake of (obtaining) his skin.'

d. Nouns expressive of desire, devotion, regard, friendship, confidence, compassion, contempt, neglect, are often connected with the loc. (as is also the gen.) of the object to which those sentiments are directed; — e.g. न खलु शकुन्तलायां ममाभिलाषः 'my love is, indeed, not towards Śakuntalā'; न मे त्वयि विश्वासः 'I have no faith in you'; न लघुष्वपि कर्तव्येष्वनादरः कार्यः 'neglect of duties, however small, should not be indulged in.'

e. The loc. is similarly used with adjectives or past participles meaning 'fond of,' 'devoted to,' 'intent on,' and their opposites;— e.g. नार्यः केवलं स्वसुखे रताः 'women (are) intent on their own pleasure only.'

Locative and Genitive Absolute.

205. 1. The **locative** is the usual **absolute** case in Sanskrit, and has much the same general application as the Greek geni-

tive and the Lat. ablative absolute; — e.g. गच्छत्सु दिनेषु 'as the days went by'; गोषु दुग्धासु स गतः 'the cows having been milked, he departed'; कर्णं ददाति मयि भाषमाणे 'she gives ear when I speak.'

a. The predicate of the absolute loc. is practically always a participle; the only exception being that the part. सत् 'being,' is frequently omitted; — e.g. कथं धर्मक्रियाविघ्नः सतां रक्षितरि त्वयि 'how (can there be any) interference with the good in the performance of their duties, when you (are) their protector?'

b. The part. सत् 'being' (or its equivalents वर्तमान and स्थित) is often pleonastically added to another absolute part.; — e.g. सूर्योदयेऽन्धता प्राप्तेषूलूकेषु सत्सु 'at sunrise, when the owls had become blind.'

c. The subject is of course always omitted when a past pass. part. is used impersonally; it is also omitted when the part. is accompanied by indeclinable words like एवम्, तथा, इत्थम्, इति; — e.g. तेनाभ्युपगते 'when consent had been given by him'; एवं गते 'this being the case' (lit. 'it having gone thus'); तथा कृते सति or तथानुष्ठिते 'this being done.'

d. The particle एव and the noun मात्र (as latter member of a compound) may be used after an absolute participle to express 'no sooner — than,' 'scarcely — when'; — e.g. प्रभातायामेव रजन्याम् 'scarcely had it dawned, when'; प्रविष्टमात्र एव तत्रभवति 'no sooner had his Honour entered, than.'

2. The **gen. absolute** is much less common than the loc. and more limited in its application. It is restricted to contemporaneous actions, the subject being a person and, the predicate a present participle in form or sense. Its meaning may be rendered by 'while,' 'as,' or 'though'; — e.g. पश्यतो मे परिभ्रमन् 'wandering about, though I was looking on'; एवं वदतस्तस्य स लुब्धको निभृतः स्थितः 'while he was speaking thus, the hunter

remained concealed'; इति चिन्तयतस्तस्य तत्र तोयार्थमाययुः स्त्रियः 'while he was thus reflecting women came there to fetch water.'

Participles.

206. Participles are constantly used in Sanskrit to qualify the main action, supplying the place of subordinate clauses. They may, as in Latin and Greek, express a relative, temporal, causal, concessive, or hypothetical sense. A final sense is also expressed by the future participle. All these meanings are inherent in the participle, without the aid of particles, except that अपि is usually added when the sense is concessive.

E.g. सृगालः कोपाविष्टम् तम् उवाच 'the jackal, being filled with anger, said to him'; निषिद्धस्त्वं मयानेकशो न शृणोषि 'though you have been frequently dissuaded by me, you do not listen to me'; अजल्पतो जानतस्ते शिरो यास्यति खण्डशः 'if you do not tell, though knowing it, your head will be shattered to pieces'; ताडयिष्यन् भीमं पुनरभ्यद्रवत् 'he ran again at Bhīma in order to strike him.'

a. Bahuvrīhi compounds are very frequently employed in a participial sense, the part. सत् being omitted; — e.g. अथ शङ्कितमना व्यचिन्तयत् 'then being anxious he reflected.'

207. Present Participle. This participle (as well as a past with a present sense) is used with अस्ति or भवति 'is,' आस्ते 'sits,' तिष्ठति 'stands,' वर्तते 'goes on,' to express continuous action, like the English 'is doing'; — e.g. एतदेव वनं यस्मिन्नभूम चिरमेव पुरा वसन्तः 'this is the very forest in which we formerly dwelt for a long time'; भक्षयन्नास्ते 'he keeps eating'; सा यत्नेन रक्ष्यमाणा तिष्ठति 'she is being carefully guarded'; परिपूर्णोऽयं घटः सक्तुभिर्वर्तते 'this pot is filled with porridge.'

a. The negative of verbs meaning 'to cease' is similarly construed with a present participle; — e.g. सिंहो मृगान् व्यापादयन्नोपरराम 'the lion did not cease (= kept) slaying the animals.'

b. Verbs expressing an emotion such as 'to be ashamed,' 'to endure,' may be accompanied by a pres. part. indicating the cause of the emotion; — e.g. किं न लज्जस एवं ब्रुवाणः 'are you not ashamed of speaking thus?'

c. A predicative present (or past) part. accompanies the acc., or the nom. in the passive construction, with verbs of seeing, hearing, knowing, thinking, wishing (cp. 198, 1); — e.g. प्रविशन्तं न मां कश्चिदपश्यत् 'no one saw me entering'; स भूपतिरेकदा केनापि पठ्यमानं श्लोकद्वयं शुश्राव 'the king one day heard someone repeating a couple of ślokas'; गान्धर्वेण विवाहेन बह्व्यो राजर्षिकन्यकाः श्रूयन्ते परिणीताः 'many daughters of royal sages are recorded to have been wedded according to the marriage of the Gandharvas.'

208. Past Participles. The passive part. in त and its active form (161; 89, n.[3]) in वत् (but hardly ever the perf. act. part. in वस्: 89) are very frequently used as finite verbs (the copula being omitted); — e.g. तेनेदम् उक्तम् 'this was said by him'; स इदमुक्तवान् 'he said this.'

a. The passive of intransitive verbs is used impersonally; otherwise its past participle has an active sense; — e.g. मयात्र चिरं स्थितम् 'I stood there for a long time'; स गङ्गां गतः 'he went to the Ganges'; स पथि मृतः 'he died on the way.'

b. Some past participles in त have both a passive and a transitive active sense; — e.g. प्राप्त 'obtained' and 'having reached'; प्रविष्ट 'entered (by)' and 'having entered'; पीत 'imbibed' and 'having drunk'; विस्मृत 'forgotten' and 'having forgotten';

विभक्त 'divided' and 'having divided'; प्रसूत 'begotten' and 'having borne' (f.); आरूढ 'ridden,' &c., and 'riding,' &c.

c. The past participles in न never seem to occur with a transitive active meaning.

209. Future Participles Passive. These (162) express necessity, obligation, fitness, probability. The construction is the same as with the past pass. part.; — e.g मयावश्यं देशान्तरं गन्तव्यम् 'I must needs go to another country'; हन्तव्योऽस्मि न ते राजन् 'you must not (= do not) kill me, O king'; ततस्तेनापि शब्दः कर्तव्यः 'then he too will surely make a noise.'

a. Occasionally the fut. pass. part. has a purely future sense;— e.g. युवयोः पक्षबलेन मयापि सुखेन गन्तव्यम् 'I too shall go with ease by the strength of your wings.'

b. भवितव्यम् and भाव्यम् (from भू 'be') are used impersonally to express necessity or high probability. The adjective or substantive of the predicate agrees with the subject in the instr.;— e.g. तया संनिहितया भवितव्यम् 'she must be (= is most probably) near'; तस्य प्रारिगनो बलेन सुमहता भवितव्यम् 'the strength of that animal must be very great.'

210. The **Indeclinable Participle (Gerund)** nearly always expresses that an action is completed before another begins (rarely that it is simultaneous). Referring to the grammatical or the virtual subject of the main action, it generally agrees with the nom., or, in the passive construction, with the instr., but occasionally with other cases also; — e.g. तं प्रणम्य स गतः 'having bowed down to him, he departed'; अथ तेनात्मानं तस्योपरि प्रक्षिप्य प्राणाः परित्यक्ताः 'then he throwing himself upon him lost his life' (प्रक्षिप्य agrees with तेन); तस्य दृष्ट्वैव ववृधे कामस्तां चारुहासिनीम् 'his love increased as soon as he had seen the sweetly smiling maiden' (दृष्ट्वा agrees with तस्य).

a. It may frequently be translated by 'in' or 'by' with a verbal

noun; — e.g. मां निर्धनं हत्वा किं लभेध्वम् 'what would you gain by killing a poor man like me?' This use represents the original sense of the form as an old instrumental of a verbal noun.

b. Having the full value of inflected participles, it may express the various logical relations of the latter, and may even be accompanied, like them, by आस्ते, तिष्ठति, वर्तते to express continuous action; — e.g. सर्वपौरान् अतीत्य वर्तते 'he is the foremost of all the townsmen.'

c. A number of gerunds are equivalent in sense to prepositions (179).

d. The original instr. nature of the gerund is preserved in its employment with किम् or अलम् or with a general subject expressed by the impersonal passive construction; — e.g. किं तव गोपायित्वा 'what (gain accrues) to you by concealing?' अलं ते वनं गत्वा 'have done with going to the forest'; पशून् हत्वा यदि स्वर्गे गम्यते 'if one goes to heaven by killing animals.'

Infinitive.

211. This frequent form expresses the aim of an action and may in general be used wherever the dative of purpose is employed (200 B). It differs from the dative of an ordinary verbal noun solely in governing its object in the acc. instead of the gen.; — e.g. तं जेतुं यतते 'he strives to conquer him' = तस्य जयाय यतते 'he strives for the conquering of him.' It preserves its original acc. sense inasmuch as it is used as the direct object of verbs (e.g. स्नातुं लभते 'he obtain a bathe'), and cannot be employed as the subject of a sentence. Verbal nouns usually supply its place as the subject; — e.g. वरं दानं न तु प्रतिग्रहः 'giving (= to give) is better than receiving' (= to receive). The construction of the acc. with the infinitive is unknown to Sanskrit, its place being supplied, with verbs of saying, &c., by *oratio recta* with इति (180), or otherwise by the use of a predicative acc. (198, 1 and 207 *c*).

The infinitive may be used with substantives (e.g. 'time,' 'opportunity'), adjectives ('fit,' 'capable'), as well as verbs (e.g. 'be able,' 'wish,' 'begin'); — e.g. नायं कालो विलम्बितुम् 'this is not the time to delay'; अवसरोऽयम् आत्मानं प्रकाशयितुम् 'this is an opportunity to show yourself'; लिखितमपि ललाटे प्रोज्झितुं कः समर्थः 'who (is) able to escape from what is written on his forehead (by fate)?' अहं त्वां प्रष्टुम् आगतः 'I have come (in order) to ask you'; कथयितुं शक्नोति 'he is able to tell'; इयेष सा कर्तुम् 'she wished to make.'

a. The 2. and 3. sing. ind. of अर्ह् 'deserve' are used with an infinitive in the sense of a polite imperative = 'please,' 'deign to'; — e.g. भवान् मां श्रोतुमर्हति 'will your Honour please to hear me?'

b. The infinitive, after dropping its final म्, may be formed into a Bahuvrīhi compound (189) with काम 'desire,' or मनस् 'mind,' in the sense of wishing or having mind to do what the verb expresses; — e.g. द्रष्टुकामः 'desirous of seeing'; किं वक्तुमना भवान् 'what do you intend to say?'

c. There being **no passive** form of the **infinitive** in Sanskrit, verbs governing the infin. are put in the passive in order to give it a passive meaning; — e.g. कर्तुं न युज्यते 'it is not fit to be done'; मया नीतिं ग्राहयितुं शक्यन्ते 'they can be taught morality by me'; तेन मण्डपः कारयितुम् आरब्धः 'a hut (was) begun to be erected by him.'

d. The fut. part. pass. शक्य śak-ya may either agree with the subject or put in the neut. sing.; — e.g. न शक्यास्ते (दोषाः) समाधातुम् 'those (mischiefs) cannot be repaired'; सा न शक्यम् उपेक्षितुं कुपिता 'she cannot be ignored (lit. 'she is not a possible thing to ignore') when angry.' युक्त 'fitting' and न्याय्य 'suitable' may be construed in the same way; — e.g. सेयं न्याय्या मया मोचयितुं भवत्तः 'she should rightly be released by me from you.'

TENSES AND MOODS

Present.

212. The use of this tense is much the same as in English. But the following differences should be noted:—

1. In narration the **historical** present is more commonly used than in English, especially to express the durative sense (which the Sanskrit imperfect lacks); — e.g. दमनकः पृच्छति कथमेतत् 'Damanaka asked, "How was it?"' हिरण्यको भोजनं कृत्वा बिले स्वपिति 'Hiraṇyaka, having taken his food, used to sleep in his hole.'

a. पुरा 'formerly,' is sometimes added to this present; — e.g. कस्मिंश्चिद् वृक्षे पुराहं वसामि 'I formerly used to live in a certain tree.' The particle स्म (which in the older language frequently accompanied पुरा, and thus acquired its meaning when alone) is much more frequently used thus; — e.g. कस्मिंश्चिद् अधिष्ठाने सोमिलको नाम कौलिको वसति स्म 'in a certain place a weaver named Somilaka used to live.'

b. The present is used to express the immediate past; — e.g. अयम् आगच्छामि 'here I come,' i.e. 'I have just come.'

2. The present also expresses the near future, पुरा 'soon' and यावत् 'just' (180) being sometimes added; — e.g. तर्हि मुक्त्वा धनुर्गच्छामि 'then leaving the bow, I am off'; तद् यावच्छत्रुघ्नं प्रेषयामि 'therefore I will just send Śatrughna.'

a. With interrogatives it implies a doubt as to future action; — e.g. किं करोमि 'what shall I do?'

b. It may express an exhortation to perform an action at once; — e.g. तर्हि गृहमेव प्रविशामः 'then we (will) enter (= let us enter) the house.'

Past Tenses.

213. All the three past tenses, imperfect, perfect, and aorist, besides the past participles in त ta and तवत् ta-vat (and the historical present), are used promiscuously to express the

historical or remote past, applying equally to facts which happened only once, or were repeated or continuous.

a. The **perfect** is properly restricted to the statement of facts of the remote past, not coming within the experience of the speaker. The 1. and 2. sing. are therefore very rare.

b. The **imperfect**, in addition to describing the historical past, states past facts of which the speaker himself has been a witness.

c. The **aorist** has (along with the participles in त and तवत्) the special sense of the present perfect, being therefore appropriate in dialogues; — e.g. अभूत्संपादितस्वादुफलो मे मनोरथः 'my desire has obtained sweet fulfilment'; तुभ्यं मया राज्यम् अदायि 'I have bestowed the sovereignty on you'; तं दृष्टवानस्मि 'I have seen him.'

d. The aorist (very rarely the imperfect) without the augment is used imperatively with मा (215 *e* and 180).

e. As there is no pluperfect in Sanskrit, its sense (to be inferred from the context) has to be expressed by the other past tenses or the gerund, or occasionally by a past participle with an auxiliary verb.

Future.

214. The simple future is a general tense, referring to any future action, while the periphrastic future, which is much less frequently employed, is restricted to the remote future. Both can therefore often be employed in describing the same action, and they frequently interchange.

a. The future is sometimes used in an imperative sense, when accompanying an imperative; — e.g. भद्रे यास्यसि मम तावद् अर्थित्व श्रूयताम् 'go, my dear, but first hear my request.'

Imperative.

215. Besides the ordinary injunctive or exhortative sense, this mood has some special uses.

a. The first persons, which are survivals of old subjunctive forms, may be translated by 'will' or 'let'; — e.g. दीव्यावेत्यब्रवीद् भ्राता 'his brother said, "Let us play" '; अहं करवाणि 'I will make.'

b. The 3. sing. pass. is commonly used as a polite imperative instead of the 2. pers. act.; — e.g. देव श्रूयताम् 'Sire, pray listen!' (cp. 211 *a*).

c. The imperative may be used, instead of an optative or benedictive, to express a wish or blessing; — e.g. चिरं जीव 'may you live long'; शिवास् ते पन्थानः सन्तु 'may your paths be auspicious' = 'Godspeed.'

d. It may express possibility or doubt, especially with interrogatives; — e.g. विषं भवतु मा वास्तु फटाटोपो भयंकरः 'whether there be poison or not, the swelling of a serpent's hood is terrifying'; प्रत्येतु कस्तद् भुवि 'who on earth would believe it?' किमधुना करवाम 'what should we do now?'

e. The imperative with the prohibitive particle मा is somewhat rare, its place being commonly supplied by the unaugmented aor. (213 *d*), by the opt. with न, or अलम् and कृतम् with the instr. (180).

Optative or Potential.

216. Besides its proper function this mood also expresses the various shades of meaning appropriate to the subjunctive (which has become obsolete in Sanskrit).

1. **In principal sentences** it expresses the following meanings:—

a. a wish (often with the particle अपि added); — e.g. अपि पश्येयमिह राघवम् 'O that I could see Rāma here!'

b. possibility or doubt; — e.g. कदाचिद् गोशब्देन बुध्येत 'perhaps he may be awakened by the lowing of the cows'; पश्येयुः क्षितिपतयश् चारदृष्ट्या 'kings can see through the eye of their

spies'; एकं हन्यान्न वा हन्यादिषुर् मुक्तो धनुष्मता 'the arrow shot by an archer may hit an individual, or may not hit him.'

c. probability, being often equivalent to a future; — e.g. इयं कन्या नात्र तिष्ठेत् 'this girl (is not likely to =) will not stay here.'

d. exhortation or precept; — e.g. त्वमेवं कुर्याः 'do you act thus'; आपदर्थं धनं रक्षेत् 'one should save wealth against calamity.'

2. The optative is used in the following kinds of **subordinate clauses** :—

a. in general relative clauses; — e.g. कालातिक्रमणं वृत्तेर् यो न कुर्वीत भूपतिः 'the king who (= every king who) does not neglect the time for the payment of salaries.'

b. in final clauses ('in order that'); — e.g. आदिश मे देशं यत्र वसेयम् 'indicate to me the place where I am to live' (= that I may live there).

c. in consequential clauses ('so that'); — e.g. स भारो भर्तव्यो यो नर नावसादयेत् '(only) such a burden should be borne as may not weigh a man down.'

d. in the protasis (as well as the apodosis) of hypothetical clauses, with the sense of the Lat. present (possible condition) or imperfect (impossible condition) subjunctive (cp. 218);— e.g. यदि न स्यान् नरपतिर् विप्लवेत नौरिव प्रजा 'if there were not a king, the state would founder like a ship.'

Benedictive or Precative.

217. This rare form (150), a kind of aorist optative, is properly restricted to the expression of blessings, or, in the first person, of the speaker's wish; — e.g. वीरप्रसवा भूयाः 'mayst thou give birth to a warrior'; कृतार्थो भूयासम् 'may I become successful.' The imperative is also employed in this sense (215 *c*). In a few

rare cases the benedictive is indistinguishable in meaning from an imperative or an ordinary optative; — e.g. इदं वचो ब्रूयास्त 'do ye proclaim this speech'; न हि प्रपश्यामि ममापनुद्याद् यच्छोकम् 'for I do not perceive what should drive away my sorrow.'

Conditional.

218. The conditional, as its form (an indicative past of the future) well indicates, is properly used to express a past condition, the unreality of which is implied, and is equivalent to the pluperfect (conditional) subjunctive in Latin or English, or the aorist indicative, used conditionally, in Greek. It is employed in both protasis and apodosis; — e.g. सुवृष्टिश्चेदभविष्यद् दुर्भिक्षं नाभविष्यत् 'if there had been abundant rain, there would have been no famine.' If a potential is used in the protasis, a conditional in the apodosis may acquire the sense of a hypothetical present (= imperf. subjunctive); — e.g. यदि न प्रणयेद्राजा दण्डं शूले मत्स्यानिवापक्ष्यम् दुर्बलान् बलवत्तराः 'if the king did not inflict punishment, the strong would roast the weak like fish on a spit.'

APPENDIX I

LIST OF VERBS

The order of the parts of the verb, when all are given, is: Present (PR.) Imperfect (IMP.), Imperative (IPV.), Optative (OP.); Perfect (PF.), Aorist (AO.); Future (FT.); Passive (PS.), present, aorist, participle (PP.); Gerund (GD.); Infinitive (INF.); Causative (CS.), aorist; Desiderative (DS.); Intensive (INT.).

The Roman numerals signify the conjugational class of the verb; P. indicates that the verb is conjugated in the Parasmaipada only, A. that it is conjugated in the Ātmanepada only.

अञ्च् añc, 'bend,' I. P. अञ्चति ॥ PS. अच्यते । PP. अञ्चित । CS. अञ्चयति ॥

अञ्ज् añj, 'anoint,' VII, P. अनक्ति । IMP. आनक् । IPV. अनक्तु । OP. अञ्ज्यात् ॥ PS. अज्यते । PP. अक्त । CS. अञ्जयति ॥

अद् ad, 'eat,' II, P. अद्मि, अत्सि; अदन्ति । IMP. आदम्, आदः, आदत्; आदन् । IPV. अदानि, अद्धि, अत्तु; अदन्तु । OP. अद्यात् ॥ FT. अत्स्यति । PS. अद्यते । PP. जग्ध (अन्न n. 'food') । GD. जग्ध्वा । INF. अत्तुम् । CS. आदयति ॥

अन् an, 'breathe,' II, P. अनिति । IMP. आनम्, आनीः or आनः, आनीत् or आनत् । IPV. अनानि, अनिहि । OP. अन्यात् ॥ CS. आनयति ॥

अश् aś, 'attain,' V. अश्नोति, अश्नुते । A. IMP. आश्नुवि, आश्नुथाः, आश्नुत । IPV. अश्नवै, अश्नुष्व, अश्नुताम् । OP. अश्नुवीत ॥ PF. आनश, आनशे ॥

अश् aś, 'eat,' IX, P. अश्नाति। IPV. अश्नानि, अशान, अश्नातु। OP. अश्नीयात्॥ PF. आश। AO. आशीत्। FT. अशिष्यति। PS. अश्यते। PP. अशित। GD. अशित्वा। INF. अशितुम्। CS. आशयति। DS. अशिशिषति॥

अस् as, 'be,' II, P. अस्मि, असि, अस्ति; स्वः; स्थः, स्तः, स्मः, स्थ, सन्ति। IMP. आसम्, आसीः, आसीत्; आस्व, आस्तम्, आस्ताम्; आस्म, आस्त, आसन्। IPV. असानि, एधि, अस्तु; असाव, स्तम्, स्ताम्; असाम, स्त, सन्तु। OP. स्याम्, स्याः, स्यात्; स्याव, स्यातम्, स्याताम्; स्याम, स्यात, स्युः॥ PF. आस, आसिथ, आस; आसिव, आसथुः, आसतुः; आसिम, आस, आसुः॥

अस् as, 'throw,' IV, P. अस्यति॥ PF. आस, आसिथ, &c., like अस् 'be'। AO. आस्थत्। FT. असिष्यति। PS. अस्यते। AO. आसि। अस्त। CS. आसयति॥

आप् āp, 'obtain,' V, P. आप्नोति। IMP. आप्नोत्। IPV. आप्नवानि, आप्नुहि, आप्नोतु। OP. आप्नुयात्॥ PF. आप। AO. आपत्। आप्स्यति। PS. आप्यते। आप्त। GD. आप्त्वा, °आप्य। आप्तुम्। CS. आपयति। PS. ईप्सति॥

आस् ās, 'sit,' II, A. आस्ते। IMP. आस्त। IPV. आस्ताम्। OP. आसीत॥ PF. आसांचक्रे। FT. आसिष्यते। PS. आस्यते। PP. आसित। आसीन irreg. pres. part. A.। INF. आसितुम्॥

इ i, 'go,' II, P. एमि, एषि, एति; इवः; यन्ति। IMP. आयम्, ऐः, ऐत्; ऐव; आयन्। IPV. अयानि, इहि, एतु; अयाव; यन्तु। OP. इयात्॥ PF. इयाय, इयेथ, इयाय; ईयिव; ईयुः। FT. एष्यति; एता। PS. ईयते। PP. इत। इत्वा, °इत्य। एतुम्। CS. आययति॥

अधी adhi‿i, 'read,' II, A. अधीते। IMP. अध्यैत; 3. du. अध्यैयाताम्; 3. pl. अध्यैयत। IPV. अध्ययै, अधीष्व, अधीताम्;

अध्ययावहै, अधीयाथाम्, अधीयाताम्; अध्ययामहै, अधीध्वम्, अधीयताम्। OP. अधीयीत ॥ AO. अध्यैष्ट; 3. du. अध्यैषाताम्; 3. pl. अध्यैषत्। FT. अध्येष्यते। PS. अधीयते। PP. अधीत। CS. अध्यापयति ॥

इध् idh or इन्ध् indh, 'kindle,' VII, A. इन्द्धे; इन्धते। IMP. ऐन्द्ध। IPV. इनधै, इन्त्स्व, इन्द्धाम्। OP. इन्धीत ॥ FT. इन्धिष्यते। PS. इध्यते। PP. इद्ध ॥

इष् iṣ, 'wish,' VI, P. इच्छति। IMP. ऐच्छत् ॥ PF. इयेष, इयेषिथ, इयेष; ईषिव; ईषुः। AO. ऐषीत्। FT. एषिष्यति। PS. इष्यते। PP. इष्ट। INF. एष्टुम्। CS. एषयति ॥

ईक्ष् īkṣ, 'see,' I, A. ईक्षते। IMP. ऐक्षत ॥ PF. ईक्षांचक्रे। AO. ऐक्षिष्ट। FT. ईक्षिष्यते। PS. ईक्ष्यते। AO. ऐक्षि। PP. ईक्षित। ईक्षितुम्। CS. ईक्षयति ॥

उष् uṣ, 'born,' I, P. ओषति। IMP. औषत् ॥ AO. औषीत्। PS. उष्यते। PP. उष्ट ॥

ऋ ṛ, 'go,' VI, P. ऋच्छति। IMP. आर्छत् ॥ PF. आर, आरिथ, आर; आरिव, &c.। PP. ऋत। CS. अर्पयति ॥

एध् edh, 'grow,' I, A. एधते। IMP. ऐधत। IPV. एधताम्। एधेत ॥ PF. एधामास। एधित। एधितुम्। एधयति। DS. एदिधिषते ॥

कम् kam, 'love,' A. (no present) ॥ PF. चकमे or कामयांचक्रे। FT. कामयिष्यते। PP. कान्त। CS. कामयते ॥

काश् kāś, 'shine,' I, A. काशते ॥ चकाशे। काशित। काशयति ॥

कृ kṛ, 'do,' VIII, करोमि, करोषि, करोति; कुर्वः, कुरुथः, कुरुतः; कुर्मः, कुरुथ, कुर्वन्ति। अकरवम्, अकरोः, अकरोत्; अकुर्व; अकुर्वन्। करवाणि, कुरु, करोतु; करवाव; कुर्वन्तु। OP. कुर्यात् ॥ PF. चकार (138)। AO. अकार्षम्, अकार्षीः, अकार्षीत्; अकार्ष्व, अकार्ष्टम्, अकार्ष्टाम्; अकार्ष्म, अकार्ष्ट, अकार्षुः। FT. करिष्यति; कर्ता ॥

A. कुर्वे, कुरुषे, कुरुते; कुर्वहे; कुर्वते। अकुर्वि, अकुरुथाः, अकुरुत; अकुर्वहि; अकुर्वत। करवै, कुरुष्व, कुरुताम्; करवामहै; कुर्वताम्। OP. कुर्वीत॥ PF. चक्रे (138)। AO. अकृषि, अकृथाः, अकृत; अकृष्वहि; अकृषत। FT. करिष्यते। PS. क्रियते। AO. अकारि। PP. कृत। GD. कृत्वा, °कृत्य। INF. कर्तुम्। CS. कारयति। AO. अचीकरत्। DS. चिकीर्षति॥

कृत् kṛt, 'cut,' VI, P. कृन्तति॥ PF. चकर्त। कर्तिष्यति। PS. कृत्यते। PP. कृत्त। CS. कर्तयति। DS. चिकर्तिषति॥

कृष् kṛṣ, 'draw,' I, P. कर्षति; 'plough,' VI, P. कृषति॥ PF. चकर्ष, चकर्षिथ, चकर्ष; चकृषिव। FT. क्रक्ष्यति। PS. कृष्यते। कृष्ट। कृष्ट्वा, °कृष्य। INF. क्रष्टुम्। CS. कर्षयति॥

कॄ kṝ, 'scatter,' VI, P. किरति॥ PF. चकार। FT. करिष्यति। PS. कीर्यते। कीर्ण। GD. °कीर्य॥

क्लृप् kḷp, 'be able,' I, A. कल्पते॥ PF. चक्लृपे। FT. कल्पिष्यते। PP. क्लृप्त। CS. कल्पयति। AO. अचीक्लृपत्॥

क्रम् kram, 'stride,' I, क्रामति, क्रमते॥ PF. चक्राम, चक्रमे। AO. अक्रमीत्। FT. क्रमिष्यति, °ते। PS. क्रम्यते। क्रान्त। क्रान्त्वा, °क्रम्य। CS. क्रमयति or क्रामयति। DS. चिक्रमिषति। INT. चङ्क्रमीति, चङ्क्रम्यते॥

क्री krī, 'buy,' IX, क्रीणाति, क्रीणीते (p. 102)॥ PF. चिक्राय। FT. क्रेष्यति, °ते। PS. क्रीयते। क्रीत। क्रीत्वा, °क्रीय। INF. क्रेतुम्। DS. चिक्रीषते॥

क्षन् kṣan, 'kill,' VIII, क्षणोति, क्षणुते॥ PP. क्षत॥

क्षि kṣi, 'destory,' V, P. क्षिणोति॥ PS. क्षीयते। PP. क्षित। CS. क्षययति or क्षपयति॥

क्षिप् kṣip, 'throw,' VI, क्षिपति, °ते। IPV. क्षिपाणि, क्षिपै॥

PF. चिक्षेप, चिक्षिपे। FT. क्षेप्स्यति, °ते। PS. क्षिप्यते। क्षिप्त। GD. क्षिप्त्वा, °क्षिप्य। INF. क्षेप्तुम्। CS. क्षेपयति। DS. चिक्षिप्सति॥

क्षुभ् kṣubh, 'quake,' IV, क्षुभ्यति, °ते॥ PF. चुक्षोभ, चुक्षुभे। PP. क्षुब्ध or क्षुभित। CS. क्षोभयति, °ते॥

खन् khan, 'dig,' I, खनति, °ते॥ PF. चखान; चख्नुः। FT. खनिष्यति। PS. खन्यते or खायते। PP. खात। खात्वा or खनित्वा, °खाय। खनितुम्। CS. खानयति॥

खाद् khād, 'eat,' I, P. खादति॥ PF. चखाद्। FT. खादिष्यते। PS. खाद्यते। PP. खादित। CS. खादयति। CS. चिखादिषति॥

ख्या khyā, 'tell,' II, P. ख्याति। IPV. SING. 2. ख्याहि, ख्यातु॥ PF. चख्यौ; चख्युः। AO. अख्यत्। FT. ख्यास्यति। PS. ख्यायते। ख्यात। °ख्याय। ख्यातुम्। CS. ख्यापयति, °ते। DS. चिख्यासति॥

गद् gad, 'speak,' I, P. गदति॥ PF. जगाद। गदिष्यति। गद्यते। गदित। गदितुम्। CS. गादयति। DS. जिगदिषति। INT. जागद्यते॥

गम् gam, 'go,' I, P. गच्छति॥ जगाम (138, 7)। AO. अगमत्। FT. गमिष्यति; गन्ता। PS. गम्यते। गत। गत्वा, °गम्य or °गत्य। गन्तुम्। CS. गमयति। DS. जिगमिषति। INT. जङ्गन्ति; जङ्गम्यते॥

गाह् gāh, 'plunge,' I, A. गाहते॥ PF. जगाहे। FT. गाहिष्यते। PS. गाह्यते। PP. गाढ or गाहित। GD. °गाह्य। CS. गाहयति॥

गुह् guh, 'hide,' I, गूहति, °ते॥ PF. जुगूह। AO. अघुक्षत्। PS. गुह्यते। PP. गूढ। GD. °गुह्य। INF. गूहितुम्। CS. गूहयति॥

गै gai, 'sing,' I, गायति, °ते॥ PF. जगौ, जगे। AO, अगासीत्। FT. गास्यति। PS. गीयते। गीत। GD. गीत्वा, °गीय। INF. गातुम्। CS. गापयति॥

ग्रथ् grath or ग्रन्थ् granth, 'tie,' IX, P. ग्रथ्नाति॥ PS. ग्रथ्यते। ग्रथित। GD. °ग्रथ्य। CS. ग्रथयति or ग्रन्थयति॥

ग्रह् grah, 'take,' IX, गृह्णाति, गृह्णीते। IPV. गृहाण, गृह्णातु॥

PF. जग्राह, जगृहे। AO. अग्रहीत्, अग्रहीष्ट। FT. ग्रहीष्यति, °ते; ग्रहीता। PS. गृह्यते। गृहीत। GD. गृहीत्वा, °गृह्य। INF. ग्रहीतुम्। CS. ग्राहयति, °ते। AO. अजिग्रहत्। DS. जिघृक्षति, °ते॥

ग्लै glai, 'droop,' I, P. ग्लायति॥ PP. ग्लान। CS. ग्लापयति or ग्लपयति॥

घुष् ghuṣ, 'sound,' I, घोषति, °ते॥ PS. घुष्यते। घुष्ट। GD. °घुष्य। CS. घोषयति॥

घ्रा ghrā, 'smell,' I, P. जिघ्रति॥ PF. जघ्रौ। PS. घ्रायते। घ्रात। CS. घ्रापयति॥

चक्ष् cakṣ, 'speak,' II, A. चक्षे, चक्षे, चष्टे; PL. चक्ष्महे, चड्ढ्वे, चक्षते॥ PF. चचक्षे। FT. चक्ष्यते। GD. °चक्ष्य। चष्टुम्। CS. चक्षयति॥

चर् car, 'move,' I, P. चरति॥ PF. चचार, चचर्थ; 3. PL. चेरुः। FT. चरिष्यति। PS. चर्यते। चरित। GD. चरित्वा, °चर्य। INF. चरितुम्। CS. चारयति। AO. अचीचरत्॥

चल् cal, 'move,' I, P. चलति॥ PF. चचाल; 3. PL. चेलुः। FT. चलिष्यति। PP. चलित। चलितुम्। CS. चलयति or चालयति। DS. चिचलिषति॥

चि ci, 'collect,' V, चिनोति, चिनुते॥ PF. चिकाय, चिक्ये। FT. चेष्यति, °ते; चेता। PS. चीयते। चित। GD. चित्वा, °चित्य। INF. चेतुम्। CS. चाययते। DS. चिकीषते or चिचीषति॥

चिन्त् cint, 'think,' X, P. चिन्तयति॥ PER. PF. चिन्तयामास। PS. चिन्त्यते। चिन्तित। GD. चिन्तयित्वा, °चिन्त्य॥

चुर् cur, 'steal,' X, P. चोरयति॥ PER. PF. चोरयांचकार। AO, अचूचुरत्। PS. चोर्यते। चोरित॥

छिद् chid, 'cut,' VII, छिनत्ति; छिन्दन्ति॥ PF. चिच्छेद, चिच्छिदे। AO. अच्छिदत् or अच्छैत्सीत्। FT. छेत्स्यति, °ते। PS. छिद्यते। छिन्न। GD. छित्त्वा, °छिद्य। INF. छेत्तुम्। CS. छेदयति॥

जन् jan, 'be born,' IV, A. जायते॥ PF. जज्ञे। AO. अजनिष्ट। FT. जनिष्यते; जनिता। PP. जात। CS. जनयति, °ते। AO. अजीजनत्। DS. जिजनिषते॥

जागृ jāgṛ, 'awake,' II, P. (134 A4) जागर्ति; जागृतः; जाग्रति। IMP. अजागरम्, अजागः, अजागः; अजागृताम्; अजागरुः। IPV. जागराणि, जागृहि, जागर्तु॥ PF. जजागार or जागरामास। FT. जागरिष्यति। PP. जागरित। CS. जागरयति॥

जि ji, 'conquer,' I, P. (A. with परा and वि) जयति॥ PF. जिगाय; जिग्यिव; जिग्युः। AO. अजैषीत्। FT. जेष्यति। PS. जीयते। जित। GD. जित्वा, °जित्य। INF. जेतुम्। CS. जापयति। DS. जिगीषति॥

जीव् jīv, 'live,' I, P. जीवति॥ PF. जिजीव; जिजीवुः। AO. अजीवीत्। FT. जीविष्यति। PS. जीव्यते। जीवित। GD. °जीव्य। INF. जीवितुम्। CS. जीवयति। DS. जिजीविषति॥

जॄ jṝ, 'grow old,' IV, P. जीर्यति॥ PF. जजार। PS. जीर्यते। PP. जीर्ण। CS. जरयति॥

ज्ञा jñā, 'know,' IX, जानाति, जानीते॥ PF. जज्ञौ, जज्ञे। AO. अज्ञासीत्। FT. ज्ञास्यति; ज्ञाता। PS. ज्ञायते। AO. अज्ञायि। PP. ज्ञात। GD. ज्ञात्वा, °ज्ञाय। INF. ज्ञातुम्। CS. ज्ञापयति, °ते or ज्ञपयति, °ते, PP. ज्ञापित and ज्ञप्त। DS. जिज्ञासते॥

तन् tan, 'stretch,' VIII, तनोति, तनुते॥ PF. ततान, तेने। PS. तन्यते or तायते। तत। GD. तत्वा, °तत्य or °ताय। CS. तानयति॥

तप् tap, 'burn,' I, तपति, °ते or IV, तप्यति, °ते॥ PF. तताप, तेपे। FT. तप्स्यति। PS. तप्यते। तप्त। GD. तप्त्वा, °तप्य। INF. तप्तुम्। CS. तापयति॥

तुद् tud, 'strike,' VI, तुदति, °ते॥ PF. तुतोद। PS. तुद्यते। PP. तुन्न। CS. तोदयति॥

तृप् tṛp, 'be pleased,' IV, P. तृप्यति ॥ PF. ततर्प; ततृपिव । PP. तृप्त । CS. तर्पयति । AO. अतीतृपत् ॥

तॄ tṝ 'cross,' I, P. or VI, A. तरति or तिरते ॥ PF. ततार; तेरुः । AO. अतार्षीत् or अतारीत् । FT. तरिष्यति, °ते । PP. तीर्ण । GD. तीर्त्वा, °तीर्य । INF. तर्तुम्, तरितुम्, तरीतुम् । CS. तारयति, °ते । DS. तितीर्षति ॥

त्यज् tyaj, 'abandon,' I, त्यजति, °ते ॥ PF. तत्याज, तत्यजे । AO. अत्याक्षीत् । FT. त्यक्ष्यति, °ते or त्यजिष्यति, °ते । PS. त्यज्यते । त्यक्त । GD. त्यक्त्वा, °त्यज्य । CS. त्याजयति । DS. तित्यक्षति ॥

त्रस् tras, 'tremble,' I, P. or IV, P.A. त्रसति or त्रस्यति, °ते ॥ PF. तत्रास; तत्रसुः or त्रेसुः । FT. त्रसिष्यति । PP. त्रस्त । CS. त्रासयति ॥

त्वर् tvar, 'hasten,' I, A. त्वरते ॥ PF. तत्वरे । PP. त्वरित । CS. त्वरयति ॥

दंश् daṃś, 'bite,' I, P. दशति ॥ PF. ददंश । FT. दशिष्यति । PS. दश्यते । PP. दष्ट । GD. दंष्ट्वा, °दश्य । CS. दंशयति ॥

दह् dah, 'burn,' I, P. दहति ॥ PF. SING. 2. देहिथ or ददग्ध, ददाह । AO. अधाक्षीत् । F.T. धक्ष्यति । PS. दह्यते । PP. दग्ध । GD. दग्ध्वा, °दह्य । INF. दग्धुम् । CS. दाहयति । DS. दिधक्षति ॥

दा dā, 'give,' III, ददाति, दत्ते ॥ PF. ददौ, ददे । AO. अदात्; अदित, 3. PL. अदिषत् । FT. दास्यति, °ते; दाता । दीयते । दत्त । GD. दत्त्वा, °दाय । CS. दापयति । DS. दित्सति ॥

दिव् div, 'play,' IV, P. दीव्यति ॥ AO. अदेवीत् । FT. देविष्यति । PP. द्यूत् । INF. देवितुम् । CS. देवयति ॥

दिश् diś, 'point,' VI, दिशति, °ते ॥ PF. दिदेश, दिदिशे । AO. अदिक्षत् । FT. देक्ष्यति, °ते । PS. दिश्यते । PP. दिष्ट । GD. °दिश्य । INF. देष्टुम् । CS. देशयति । DS. दिदिक्षति ॥

दिह् dih, 'anoint,' II, देह्मि, धेक्षि, देग्धि; दिह्वः, दिग्धः, दिग्धः; दिह्मः, दिग्ध, दिहन्ति। A. दिहे, धिक्षे, दिग्धे; दिह्वहे, दिहाथे, दिहाते; दिह्महे, धिग्ध्वे, दिहते। IMP. अदेहम्, अधेक्, अधेक्; अदिह्व, अदिग्धम्, अदिग्धाम्; अदिह्म, अदिग्ध, अदिहन्। A. अदिहि, अदिग्धाः, अदिग्ध; अदिह्वहि, अदिहाथाम्, अदिहाताम्; अदिह्महि, अधिग्ध्वम्, अदिहत। IPV. देहानि, दिग्धि, देग्धु; देहाव, दिग्धम्, दिग्धाम्; देहाम्, दिग्ध, दिहन्तु। A. देहै, धिक्ष्व, दिग्धाम्; देहावहै, दिहाथाम् दिहाताम्; देहामहै, धिग्ध्वम्, दिहताम्। OP. दिह्यात्, A. दिहीत॥ PF. दिदेह, A. दिदिहे। PS. दिह्यते॥ PP. दिग्ध। GD. °दिह्य। CS. देहयति॥

दुह् duh, 'milk,' II, (like दिह्) SING. 3. दोग्धि। IMP. अधोक्। IPV. दोग्धु। OP. दुह्यात्॥ PF. दुदोह, दुदुहे। AO. अधुक्षत्, अधुक्षत। FT. धोक्ष्यते। PS. दुह्यते। PP. दुग्ध। GD. दुग्ध्वा। INF. दोग्धुम्। CS. दोहयति। AO. अदूदुहत्। DS. दुधुक्षति॥

दृश् dṛś, 'see,' I, P. पश्यति॥ PF. ददर्श; ददृशुः। AO. अद्राक्षीत् or अदर्शत्। FT. द्रक्ष्यति; द्रष्टा। PS. दृश्यते। दृष्ट। GD. दृष्ट्वा, °दृश्य। द्रष्टुम्। CS दर्शयति। AO. अदीदृशत्। DS. दिदृक्षते॥

द्युत् dyut, 'shine,' I, A. द्योतते॥ PF. दिद्युते। AO. अद्युतत्। CS. द्योतयति॥

द्रु dru, 'run,' I, P. द्रवति॥ PF. दुद्राव, दुद्रोथ; I. DU. दुद्रुव। AO. अदुद्रुवत्। PP. द्रुत। °द्रुत्य। द्रोतुम्। CS. द्रावयति॥

द्रुह् druh, 'hurt,' IV, P. द्रुह्यति॥ PF. SING. I. 3. दुद्रोह, 2. दुद्रोहिथ; 1. DU. दुद्रुहिव। AO. अद्रुहत्। PP. द्रुग्ध॥

द्विष् dviṣ, 'hate,' II, द्वेष्टि (p. 94)॥ PP. द्विष्ट। द्वेष्टुम्। द्वेषयति॥

धा dhā, 'place,' III; दधाति; धत्तः; दधति। A. धत्ते; दधाते; दधते। IMP. अदधात्; अधत्ताम्; अदधुः। A. अधत्त; अदधाताम्

अदधत। IPV. दधानि, धेहि, दधातु; धत्ताम्; दधतु। A. दधै, धत्स्व, धत्ताम्; दधाताम्; दधताम्। OP. दध्यात्, A. दधीत॥ PF. दधौ, दधे। AO. अधात्, अधित्। FT. धास्यति, °ते। PS. धीयते। AO. अधायि। PP. हित। GD. °धाय। धातुम्। CS. धापयति। DS. धित्सति॥

धाव् dhāv, 'run,' and 'wash,' I. धावति, °ते॥ PF. दधाव। PS. धाव्यते। धावित 'running': धौत 'washed'। CS. धावयति॥

धू dhū, 'shake,' V or IX, धुनोति, धुनुते or धुनाति, धुनीते॥ PF. दुधाव। FT. धविष्यति। PS. धूयते। PP. धूत। CS. धूनयति। INT. दोधवीति; दोधूयते॥

धृ dhṛ, 'bear' (no present)॥ दधार, दध्रे। धरिष्यति, °ते। ध्रियते। धृत। धृत्वा। धर्तुम्। CS. धारयति, °ते। AO. अदीधरत्॥

ध्मा dhmā, 'blow,' I, P. धमति॥ PF. दध्मौ। AO. अध्मासीत्। PS. धम्यते or ध्मायते। PP. ध्मात। GD. °ध्माय। CS. ध्मापयति॥

नद् nad, 'hum,' I, P. नदति॥ PF. ननाद, नेदिथ; नेदुः। PP. नदित। CS. नदयति or नादयति। INT. नानद्यते॥

नम् nam, 'bend,' I, P. नमति॥ PF. ननामः नेमुः। AO. अनंसीत्। नंस्यति। PS. नम्यते। नत। नत्वा, °नम्य। नमितुम् or नन्तुम्। CS. नमयति or नामयति। AO. अनीनमत्। DS. निनंसति॥

नश् naś, 'perish,' IV, P. नश्यति॥ PF. ननाश; नेशुः। AO. अनशत्। FT. नशिष्यति or नङ्क्ष्यति। PP. नष्ट। CS. नाशयति। AO. अनीनशत्॥

नह् nah, 'bind,' IV, नह्यति, °ते॥ PS. नह्यते। PP. नद्ध। GD. °नह्य। CS. नाहयति॥

नी nī, 'lead,' I, नयति, °ते॥ PF. निनाय (p. 113)। AO. अनैषीत्। FT. नेष्यति; नेता। PS. नीयते। नीत। GD. नीत्वा, °नीय। नेतुम्। CS. नाययति। DS. निनीषति, °ते। INT. नेनीयते॥

नृत् nṛt, 'dance,' IV, P. नृत्यति ॥ PF. ननर्त; ननृतुः । FT. नर्तिष्यति । PS. नृत्यते । PP. नृत्त । CS. नर्तयति । DS. निनर्तिषति । INT. नरीनर्त्ति; नरीनृत्यते ॥

पच् pac, 'cook,' I, पचति, °ते ॥ PF. पपाच, पेचे । FT. पक्ष्यति । PS. पच्यते । पक्व ADJ. = PP. । पक्त्वा CS. पाचयति । INT. पापच्यते ॥

पत् pat, 'fall,' I, P. पतति ॥ PF. पपात; पेतुः । AO. अपप्तत् । FT. पतिष्यति । PP. पतित । पतितुम् । पतित्वा, °पत्य । CS. पातयति । DS. पित्सति ॥

पद् pad, 'go,' IV, A. पद्यते ॥ PF. पेदे । अपादि AO. Ātm. । FT. पत्स्यते । PP. पन्न । °पद्य । पत्तुम् । CS. पादयते । DS. पित्सते । INT. पनीपद्यते ॥

पा pā, 'drink,' I, P. पिबति ॥ PF. पपौ, पपिथ or पपाथ; पपुः । AO. अपात् । पास्यति । PS. पीयते । AO. अपायि । PP. पीत । पीत्वा, °पाय । पातुम् । CS. पाययति । DS. पिपासति । INT. पेपीयते ॥

पा pā, 'protect,' II, P. पाति ॥ AO. अपासीत् । INF. पातुम् ॥

पुष् puṣ, 'thrive,' IV or IX, P. पुष्यति or पुष्णाति ॥ PF. पुपोष । PS. पुष्यते । PP. पुष्ट । CS. पोषयति ॥

पू pū, 'purify,' IX, पुनाति, पुनीते ॥ PF. पुपाव, पुपुवे । PS. पूयते । PP. पूत । GD. °पूय । CS. पावयति ॥

पृ pṛ (पूर् pūr), 'fill,' III, P. पिपर्ति; पिप्रति ॥ PF. (पपार), पुपूरे । PS. पूर्यते । PP. पूर्त or पूर्ण । GD. °पूर्य । CS. पूरयति ॥

प्रछ् prach, 'ask,' VI, P. पृच्छति ॥ PF. पप्रच्छ; पप्रच्छुः । AO. अप्राक्षीत्, अप्रष्ट । FT. प्रक्ष्यति । PS. पृच्छ्यते । PP. पृष्ट । GD. पृष्ट्वा, °पृच्छ्य । INF. प्रष्टुम् । DS. पिपृच्छिषति ॥

प्री prī, 'please,' IX, प्रीणाति, प्रीणीते ॥ AO. अप्रैषीत् । PP. प्रीत । CS. प्रीणयति ॥

फल् phal, 'burst,' I, P. फलति ॥ PF. पफाल । PP. फलित or फुल्ल । CS. फालयति ॥

बन्ध् bandh, 'bind,' IX, P. बध्नाति ॥ PF. बबन्ध, बबन्धिथ or बबन्द्ध, बबन्ध । FT. भन्त्स्यति । PS. बध्यते । PP. बद्ध । GD. बद्ध्वा, °बध्य । INF. बन्द्धुम् । CS. बन्धयति ॥

बुध् budh, 'perceive,' I, P.A. or IV, A. बोधति, °ते or बुध्यते ॥ PF. बुबुधे । AO. अभुत्सि, अबुद्धाः, अबुद्ध; or अबोधिषम् &c. (p. 122) । FT. भोत्स्यते । PS. बुध्यते । PP. बुद्ध । GD. बुद्ध्वा, °बुध्य । INF. बोद्धुम् । CS. बोधयति । DS. बुभुत्सते ॥

ब्रू brū, 'speak,' II, ब्रवीमि, ब्रवीषि, ब्रवीति; ब्रूवः, ब्रूथः, ब्रूतः; ब्रूमः, ब्रूथ, ब्रुवन्ति । A. ब्रूते; ब्रुवते । IMP. अब्रवम्, अब्रवीः, अब्रवीत्; अब्रूताम्; अब्रुवन् । IPV. ब्रवाणि, ब्रूहि, ब्रवीतु; ब्रवाव, ब्रूतम्, ब्रूताम्; ब्रवाम, ब्रूत, ब्रुवन्तु । OP. ब्रूयात् ॥ वच् vac is used in the other forms.

भक्ष् bhakṣ, 'eat,' I, P. भक्षति ॥ PS. भक्ष्यते । PS. AO. अभक्षि । PP. भक्षित । INF. भक्षितुम् । CS. भक्षयति ॥

भज् bhaj, 'divide,' I, भजति, °ते ॥ PF. बभाज, बभक्थ; भेजुः; भेजे । AO. अभाक्षीत्, अभक्त । FT. भजिष्यति, °ते । PS. भज्यते । भक्त । भक्त्वा, °भज्य । भक्तुम् । CS. भाजयति, °ते । DS. भिक्षति, °ते ॥

भञ्ज् bhañj, 'break,' VII, P. भनक्ति । अभनक् । भनक्तु । भञ्ज्यात् ॥ PF. बभञ्ज । AO. अभाङ्क्षीत् । FT. भङ्क्ष्यति; भङ्क्ता । PS. भज्यते । AO. अभाजि । PP. भग्न । GD. भङ्क्त्वा, °भज्य ॥

भा bhā, 'shine,' II, P. भाति; भान्ति । IMP. अभात्; अभान् or अभुः ॥ PF. बभौ । FT. भास्यति । PP. भात ॥

भाष् bhāṣ, 'speak,' I, A. भाषते ॥ PF. बभाषे । AO. अभाषिष्ट । FT. भाषिष्यते । PS. भाष्यते । PP. भाषित । GD. भाषित्वा, °भाष्य । INF. भाषितुम् । CS. भाषयति, °ते ॥

भिद् bhid, 'cleave.' VII, भिनत्ति, भिनत्ते ॥ PF. बिभेद, बिभिदे। FT. भेत्स्यति, °ते। PS. भिद्यते। भिन्न। GD. भित्त्वा, °भिद्य। INF. भेत्तुम्। CS. भेदयति ॥

भी bhī, 'fear,' III, P. बिभेति; बिभ्यति। IMP. अबिभेत्; अबिभयुः ॥ PF. बिभाय। AO. अभैषीत्। PS. भीयते। भीत। भेतुम्। CS. भाययति or भीषयते। INT. बेभीयते ॥

भुज् bhuj, 'enjoy,' VII, भुनक्ति, भुङ्क्ते ॥ PF. बुभुजे। FT. भोक्ष्यति, °ते। PS. भुज्यते। PP. भुक्त। GD. भुक्त्वा। INF. भोक्तुम्। CS. भोजयति, °ते। DS. बुभुक्षते। INT. बोभुजीति; बोभुज्यते ॥

भू bhū, 'become,' 'be,' I, भवति, °ते (p. 92) ॥ बभूव (139, 7)। अभूत् (148)। भविष्यति; भविता (152)। भूयते (154)। AO. PS. अभावि। भूत। भूत्वा, °भूय। भवितुम्। CS. भावयति, °ते। DS. बुभूषति, °ते। INT. बोभवीति ॥

भृ bhṛ, 'carry,' III, P. (also I, भरति, °ते) बिभर्ति; बिभ्रति। IPV. बिभराणि, बिभृहि, बिभर्तु ॥ PF. बभार, बभर्थ; बभृव; or बिभरांबभूव। FT. भरिष्यति। PS. भ्रियते। PP. भृत। GD. °भृत्य। INF. भर्तुम्। CS. भारयति। DS. बुभूर्षति। INT. बरीभर्ति ॥

भ्रज्ज् bhrajj, 'fry,' VI, P. भृज्जति ॥ PS. भृज्ज्यते। PP. भृष्ट। GD. भृष्ट्वा। CS. भर्ज्जयति ॥

भ्रम् bhram, 'wander,' IV, P. or I, P.A. भ्राम्यति or भ्रमति, °ते ॥ PF. बभ्राम; बभ्रमुः or भ्रेमुः (139)। FT. भ्रमिष्यति। PP. भ्रान्त। GD. भ्रान्त्वा, °भ्रम्य or °भ्राम्य। INF. भ्रान्तुम् or भ्रमितुम्। CS. भ्रामयति or भ्रमयति। INT. बम्भ्रमीति; बम्भ्रम्यते ॥

मज्ज् majj, 'sink,' I, P. मज्जति ॥ PF. ममज्ज। AO. अमाङ्क्षीत्। FT. मङ्क्ष्यति। PP. मग्न। °मज्ज्य। मज्जितुम्। मज्जयति। DS. मिमङ्क्षति ॥

मद् mad, 'rejoice,' IV, P. माद्यति ॥ AO. अमादीत् । PP. मत्त । CS. मादयति or मदयति ॥

मन् man, 'think,' IV or VIII, A. मन्यते or मनुते ॥ PF. मेने । AO. अमंस्त । FT. मंस्यते । PS. मन्यते । PP. मत । GD. मत्वा, °मन्य or °मत्य । INF. मन्तुम् । CS. मानयते । DS. मीमांसते ॥

मन्थ् manth, 'shake,' I or IX, P. मथति (or मन्थति) or मथ्नाति ॥ PF. ममन्थ, ममन्थिथ । FT. मन्थिष्यति । PS. मथ्यते । PP. मथित । GD. °मथ्य । CS. मन्थयति ॥

मा mā, 'measure,' II, P. or III, A. माति or मिमीते ॥ PF. ममौ or ममे । PS. मीयते । AO. अमायि । PP. मित । GD. मित्वा, °माय । INF. मातुम् । CS. मापयति । DS. मित्सति ॥

मुच् muc, 'loosen,' VI, मुञ्चति, °ते ॥ PF. मुमोच, मुमुचे । AO. अमुचत्, अमुक्त । FT. मोक्ष्यति, °ते । PS. मुच्यते । मुक्त । मुक्त्वा, °मुच्य । मोक्तुम् । CS. मोचयति, °ते । AO. अमूमुचत् । DS. मुमुक्षति or मोक्षते ॥

मुह् muh, 'be bewildered,' IV, P. मुह्यति ॥ PF. मुमोह, मुमोहिथ or मुमोग्ध or मुमोढ । PP. मुग्ध or मूढ । CS. मोहयति । INT. मोमुह्यते ॥

मृ mṛ, 'die,' P. (no present) ॥ PP. ममार, ममर्थ; मम्रिव । FT. मरिष्यति । PS. म्रियते । PP. मृत । GD. मृत्वा । INF. मर्तुम् । CS. मारयति । AO. अमीमरत् । DS. मुमूर्षति । INT. मरीमर्ति ॥

मृज् mṛj, 'wipe,' II, P. मार्ष्टि; मृष्टः; मृजन्ति । IMP. अमार्ट्; अमृष्टाम्; अमृजन् । IPV. मार्जानि, मृड्ढि, मार्ष्टु; मृष्टाम्; मृजन्तु । OP. मृज्यात् ॥ PF. ममार्ज; ममृजुः । AO. अमार्जीत् or अमार्क्षीत् or अमृक्षत् । FT. मार्क्ष्यते । PS. मृज्यते । PP. मृष्ट । GD. °मार्ज्य, °मृज्य । INF. मर्ष्टुम्, मार्ष्टुम्, मार्जितुम् । CS. मार्जयति । INT. मर्मृज्यते ॥

म्ना mnā, 'mention,' I, P. मनित ॥ AO. अम्नासीत् । PS. म्नायते । PP. म्नात ॥

म्लै mlai, 'fade,' I, P. म्लायति ॥ PF. मम्लौ । AO. अम्लासीत । PP. म्लान । CS. म्लापयति or म्लपयति ॥

यज् yaj, 'worship,' I, यजति, °ते ॥ PF. इयाज, ईजे । AO. अयाक्षीत्, अयष्ट । FT. यक्ष्यति । PS. इज्यते । PP. इष्ट । GD. इष्ट्वा । INF. यष्टुम् । CS. याजयति । DS. यियक्षति ॥

यम् yam, 'stop,' I, P. यच्छति ॥ PF. ययाम, ययन्थ; येमुः । FT. यमिष्यति । PS. यम्यते । PP. यत । GD. यत्वा, °यम्य । INF. यन्तुम् or यमितुम् । CS. यमयति or यामयति ॥

या yā, 'go,' II, P. याति । IMP. अयात्; अयान् or अयुः । IPV. यातु । OP. यायात् ॥ PF. ययौ । AO. अयासीत् । FT. यास्यति; याता । PS. यायते । PP. यात । GD. यात्वा, °याय । INF. यातुम् । CS. यापयति । DS. यियासति ॥

यु yu, 'join,' II, P. यौति; युवन्ति । IMP. अयौत्; अयुवन् । IPV. यौतु; युवन्तु । OP. युयात् ॥ PP. युत ॥

युज् yuj, 'join,' VII, युनक्ति, युङ्क्ते ॥ PF. युयोज, युयुजे । AO. अयुजत्, अयुक्त । FT. योक्ष्यति, °ते । PS. युज्यते । युक्त । युक्त्वा, °युज्य । योक्तुम् । CS. योजयति, °ते । AO. अयूयुजत् । DS. युयुक्षति ॥

रक्ष् rakṣ, 'protect,' I, रक्षति, °ते ॥ PF. ररक्ष । AO. अरक्षीत् । FT. रक्षिष्यति; रक्षिता । PS. रक्ष्यते । PP. रक्षित । GD. °रक्ष्य । INF. रक्षितुम् । CS. रक्षयति ॥

रञ्ज् rañj, 'tinge,' IV, P. रज्यति ॥ PS. रज्यते । PP. रक्त । GD. °रज्य । CS. रञ्जयति ॥

रभ् rabh, 'grasp' (आरभ् ā-rabh, 'begin'), I, A. रभते ॥ PF. रेभे । FT. रप्स्यते । PS. रभ्यते । AO. अरम्भि । PP. रब्ध । GD. °रभ्य । INF. रब्धुम् । CS. रम्भयति । DS. रिप्सते ॥

रम् ram, 'sport,' I, A. (P. only when transitive) रमते ॥ PF. रेमे । AO. अरंसीत् । FT. रंस्यते । INF. रन्तुम् । PF. रत । GD. रत्वा, °रम्य । PS. रम्यते । CS. रमयति । DS. रिरंसते ॥

राज् rāj, 'shine,' I, राजति, °ते ॥ रराज, रेजे । राजयति ॥

रु ru, 'cry,' II, P. रौति; रुतः; रुवन्ति ॥ PF. रुराव; रुरुवुः । PP. रुत । INF. रोतुम् । CS. रावयति । AO. अरूरुवत् । INF. रोरवीति; रोरूयते ॥

रुद् rud, 'weep,' II, P. रोदिति; रुदन्ति । IMP. अरोदम्, अरोदः or अरोदीः, अरोदत् or अरोदीत्; अरुदिव; अरुदन् । IPV. रोदानि, रुदिहि, रोदितु; रोदाव; रुदन्तु । OP. रुद्यात् ॥ PF. रुरोद । AO. अरुदत् । FT. रोदिष्यति । PS. रुद्यते । रुदित । रुदित्वा, °रुद्य । रोदितुम् । रोदयति । रुरुदिषति । रोरुद्यते ॥

रुध् rudh, 'shut out,' VII, रुणद्धि, रुन्द्धे (p. 100) ॥ PF. रुरोध, रुरुधे । AO. अरुधत् or अरौत्सीत्; अरुद्ध । FT. रोत्स्यति । PS. रुध्यते । रुद्ध । रुद्धवा, °रुध्य । रोद्धुम् । रोधयति । रुरुत्सति ॥

रुह् ruh, 'grow,' I, P. रोहति ॥ PF. रुरोह । AO. अरुक्षत् or अरुहत् । FT. रोक्ष्यति । PS. रुह्यते । PP. रूढ । GD. °रुह्य । INF. रोढुम् । CS. रोहयति or रोपयति । DS. रुरुक्षति ॥

लभ् labh, 'grasp,' I, A. लभते ॥ PF. लेभे । FT. लप्स्यते । PS. लभ्यते । PP. लब्ध । GD. लब्ध्वा, °लभ्य । CS. लम्भयति । DS. लिप्सते ॥

लिख् likh, 'scratch,' VI, P. लिखति ॥ PF. लिलेख । PS. लिख्यते । PP. लिखित । GD. लिखित्वा, °लिख्य । CS. लेखयति ॥

लू lū, 'cut,' IX, लुनाति, लुनीते ॥ PF. लुलाव, लुलुवे । PP. लून ॥

वच् vac, 'speak,' II, P. वच्मि, वक्षि, वक्ति; वच्वः, वक्थः, वक्तः; वच्मः, वक्थ, (वदन्ति) । IMP. अवचम्, अवक्, अवक्; अवच्व, अवक्तम्, अवक्ताम्; अवच्म, अवक्त, (अवदन्) । IPV. वचानि, वग्धि, वक्तु; वचाव । OP. वच्यात् ॥ PF. उवाच; ऊचुः ।

AO. अवोचत् । FT. वक्ष्यति; वक्ता । PS. उच्यते । AO. अवाचि । उक्त । उक्त्वा, °उच्य । वक्तुम् । CS. वाचयति । DS. विवक्षति ॥

वद् vad, 'speak,' I, P. वदति ॥ PF. उवाद; ऊदुः । AO. अवादीत् । FT. वदिष्यति । PS. उद्यते । PP. उदित । उदित्वा, °उद्य । INF. वदितुम् । CS. वादयति । DS. विवदिषति ॥

वप् vap, 'sow,' 1, वपति ॥ PF. उवाप, उवपिथ or उवप्थ; ऊपुः । AO. अवाप्सीत् । FT. वप्स्यति or वपिष्यति । PS. उप्यते । PP. उप्त । CS. वापयति ॥

वश् vaś, 'desire,' II, P. वश्मि, वक्षि, वष्टि; उश्वः; उशन्ति । IMP. अवशम्, अवट्, अवट्; औश्व । IPV. वशानि, उड्ढि, वष्टु । OP. उश्यात् ॥ CS. वशयति ॥

वस् vas, 'dwell,' I, P. वसति ॥ PF. उवास; ऊषुः । AO. अवात्सीत् । FT. वत्स्यति । PS. उष्यते । PP. उषित । GD. उषित्वा, °उष्य । INF. वस्तुम् । CS. वासयति ॥

वस् vas, 'wear,' II, A. वस्ते ॥ PF. ववसे । PP. वसित । GD. वसित्वा, °वस्य । INF. वसितुम् । CS. वासयति ॥

वह् vah, 'carry,' I, वहति, °ते ॥ PF. उवाह; ऊहुः । AO. अवाक्षीत् । FT. वक्ष्यति । PS. उह्यते । AO. अवाहि । PP. ऊढ । GD. °उह्य । INF. वोढुम् । CS. वाहयति । INT. वावहीति ॥

विद् vid, 'know,' II, P. वेद्मि, वेत्सि, वेत्ति; विद्वः, वित्थः, वित्तः; विद्मः, वित्थ, विदन्ति । IMP. अवेदम्, अवेः or अवेत्, अवेत्; अविद्व, अवित्तम्, अवित्ताम्; अविद्म, अवित्त, अविदन् or अविदुः । IPV. वेदानि, विद्धि, वेत्तु; वेदाव, वित्तम्, वित्ताम्; वेदाम, वित्त, विदन्तु । OP. विद्यात् ॥ PF. विवेद or विदांचकार । AO. अवेदीत् । FT. वेदिष्यति । PS. विद्यते । विदित । विदित्वा । वेदितुम् । वेदयति । विविदिषति ॥ PR. PF. वेद, °वेत्थ, वेद; विद्व, विदथुः, विदतुः; विद्म, विद, विदुः (139, 3) ॥

विद् vid, find,' VI, विन्दति, °ते ॥ विवेद, विविदे । AO. अविदत्, अविदत । वेत्स्यति, °ते । PS. विद्यते ('there exists') । PP. वित्त or विन्न । वित्त्वा, °विद्य । वेत्तुम् । CS. वेदयति । DS. विवित्सति ॥

विश् viś, 'enter,' VI, P. विशति ॥ PF. विवेश । AO. अविक्षत् । FT. वेक्ष्यति । PS. विश्यते । AO. अवेशि । PP. विष्ट । °विश्य । वेष्टुम् । CS. वेशयति । AO. अवीविशत् । DS. विविक्षति ॥

वृ vṛ, 'cover,' V, वृणोति, वृणुते ॥ PF. ववार, ववर्थ; ववृव; वव्रुः; वव्रे । PS. व्रियते । वृत । °वृत्य । INF. वरितुम् or वरीतुम् । CS. वारयति ॥

वृ vṛ, 'choose,' IX, A. वृणीते ॥ PF. वव्रे । AO. अवृत । PS. व्रियते । PP. वृत । INF. वरीतुम् । CS. वरयति ॥

वृत् vṛt, 'exist,' I, A. (P. also in AO., FT.) वर्तते ॥ PF. ववृते । AO. अवृतत् । FT. वर्तिष्यते or वर्त्स्यते । PP. वृत्त । GD. °वृत्य । INF. वर्तितुम् । CS. वर्तयति ॥

वृध् vṛdh, 'increase,' I, A. (P. also in AO., FT.) वर्धते ॥ PF. ववृधे । AO. अवृधत्, अवर्धिष्ट । FT. वर्त्स्यति । PP. वृद्ध । INF. वर्धितुम् । CS. वर्धयति, °ते । AO. अवीवृधत् ॥

व्यध् vyadh, 'pierce,' IV, P. विध्यति ॥ PF. विव्याध; विविधुः । PS. विध्यते । PP. विद्ध । GD. विद्ध्वा, °विध्य । CS. व्यधयति ॥

व्रज् vraj, 'go,' I, P. व्रजति ॥ PP. वव्राज, वव्रजिथ । AO. अव्राजीत् । FT. व्रजिष्यति । PS. व्रज्यते । PP. व्रजित । GD. व्रजित्वा, °व्रज्य । INF. व्रजितुम् । CS. व्राजयति ॥

व्रश्च् vraśc, 'cut,' VI, P. वृश्चति ॥ PS. वृश्च्यते । PP. वृक्ण । GD. वृष्ट्वा, °वृश्च्य ॥

शंस् śaṃs, 'praise,' I, P. शंसति ॥ शशंस । AO. अशंसीत् । शंसिष्यति । PS. शस्यते । शस्त । शस्त्वा, °शस्य । शंसितुम् । CS. शंसयति ॥

शक् śak, 'be able,' V.P. शक्नोति ॥ PF. शशाक; शेकुः । AO. अशकत् । FT. शक्ष्यति । PS. शक्यते । PP. शक्त and शकित । DS. शिक्षति ॥

शप् śap. 'curse,' I, शपति, °ते ॥ PP. शापित, शेपे । FT. शपिष्यते । PS. शप्यते । PP. शप्त । CS. शापयति ॥

शम् śam, 'cease,' IV, P. शाम्यति ॥ PF. शशाम; शेमुः । PF. शान्त । CS. शमयति or शामयति । AO. अशीशमत् ॥

शास् śās, 'order,' II, P. शास्ति; 1. DU. शिष्वः; 3. PL. शासति । IMP. अशासम्, अशाः or अशात्, अशात्; अशिष्व; अशासुः । IPV. शासनि, शाधि, शास्तु; शासाव, शिष्टम्, शिष्टाम्; शासाम, शिष्ट, शासतु । OP. शिष्यात् ॥ PF. शशास । AO. अशिषत् । FT. शासिष्यति । PS. शास्यते or शिष्यते । PP. शासित or शिष्ट । GD. शासित्वा । INF. शास्तुम् ॥

शिष् śiṣ, 'leave,' VII, P. शिनष्टि; शिंष्वः; शिंषन्ति । IPV. शिनषाणि, शिंड्ढि, शिनष्टु ॥ PS. शिष्यते । शिष्ट । शिष्ट्वा, °शिष्य । CS. शेषयति ॥

शी śī, 'lie,' II, A. शये, शेषे, शेते; शेवहे, शयाथे, शयाते; शेमहे, शेध्वे, शेरते । IMP. अशयि, अशेथाः, अशेत; अशेवहि, अशयाथाम्, अशयाताम्; अशेमहि, अशेध्वम्, अशेरत । IPV. शयै, शेष्व, शेताम्; शयावहै, शयाथाम्, शयाताम्; शयामहै, शेध्वम्, शेरताम् । OP. शयीत ॥ PF. शिश्ये । AO. अशयिष्ट । FT. शयिष्यते । PP. शयित । CS. शाययति । DS. शिशयिषते ॥

शुच् śuc, 'grieve,' I, P. शोचति ॥ PF. शुशोच । AO. अशुचत् । FT. शोचिष्यति । GD. शोचित्वा । INF. शोचितुम् । CS. शोचयति ॥

श्रि śri, 'go,' I, श्रयति, °ते ॥ PF. शिश्राय, शिश्रिये । AO. अशिश्रियत् । FT. श्रयिष्यति, °ते । PS. श्रीयते । PP. श्रित । GD. श्रयित्वा, °श्रित्य । INF. श्रयितुम् ॥

श्रु śru, 'hear,' V, P. शृणोति; शृणुतः; शृण्वन्ति ॥ शुश्राव, शुश्रोथ, शुश्राव; 1. DU., 2. PL. शुश्रुव; शुश्रुवुः । AO. अश्रौषीत् । PT. श्रोष्यति; श्रोता । PS. श्रूयते । AO. अश्रावि । PP. श्रुत । GD. श्रुत्वा, °श्रुत्य । INF. श्रोतुम् । CS. श्रावयति । DS. शुश्रूषते ॥

श्वस् śvas, 'breathe,' II, P. श्वसिति ॥ PF. शश्वास । FT. श्वसिष्यति । PP. श्वस्त or श्वसित । GD. °श्वस्य । INF. श्वसितुम् । CS. श्वासयति ॥

सञ्ज् sañj, 'adhere,' I, P. सजति ॥ PF. ससञ्ज । AO. असाङ्क्षीत् । PS. सज्यते । PP. सक्त । GD. °सज्य । INF. सक्तुम् । CS. सञ्जयति ॥

सद् sad, 'sink,' I, P. सीदति ॥ PF. ससाद, सेदिथ or ससत्थ; सेदुः । AO. असदत् । FT. सत्स्यति । PS. सद्यते । PP. सन्न । GD. °सद्य । INF. सत्तुम् । CS. सादयति ॥

सह् sah, 'bear,' I, A. सहते ॥ FT. सहिष्यते; सोढा । PS. सह्यते । PP. सोढ । GD. °सह्य । INF. सोढुम् । CS. साहयति ॥

सिच् sic, 'sprinkle,' VI, सिञ्चति, °ते ॥ PF. सिषेच, सिषिचे । AO. असिचत्, °त । FT. सेक्ष्यति, °ते । PS. सिच्यते । PP. सिक्त । GD. सिक्त्वा, °सिच्य । CS. सेचयति, °ते ॥

सिध् sidh, 'repel,' I, P. सेधति ॥ PF. सिषेध । AO. असेधीत् । FT. सेधिष्यति and सेत्स्यति । PS. सिध्यते । सिद्ध । INF. सेद्धुम् । CS. सेधयति ॥

सु su, 'press out,' V, सुनोति, सुनुते (p. 98) ॥ PF. सुषाव, सुषुवे । FT. सोष्यति । PS. सूयते । PP. सुत । GD. °सुत्य । CS. सावयति ॥

सू sū, 'bear,' II, A. सूते । IMP. असूत । IPV. सुवै, सूष्व, सूताम् । OP. सुवीत ॥ PF. सुषुवे । FT. सविष्यते or सोष्यते । PS. सूयते । सूत ॥

सृ sṛ, 'go,' I, P. सरति ॥ PF. ससार, ससर्थ; ससृव; सस्रुः । FT. सरिष्यति । PP. सृत । GD. °सृत्य । INF. सर्तुम् । CS. सारयति ॥

सृज् sṛj, 'emit,' VI, P. सृजति ॥ PF. ससर्ज । AO. अस्राक्षीत् ।

FT. स्रक्ष्यति। PS. सृज्यते। GD. सृष्ट्वा, °सृज्य। INF. स्रष्टुम्। CS. सर्जयति। DS. सिसृक्षति॥

सृप् sṛp, 'creep,' I, P. सर्पति॥ PF. ससर्प; ससृपिव। FT. स्रप्स्यति। PS. सृप्यते। PP. सृप्त। CS. सर्पयति। DS. सिसृप्सति॥

स्तम्भ् stambh, 'prop,' IX, P. स्तभ्नाति। IPV. स्तभ्नानि, स्तभान, स्तभ्नातु॥ PF. तस्तम्भ। PS. स्तभ्यते। AO. अस्तम्भि। PP. स्तब्ध। GD. स्तब्ध्वा, °स्तभ्य। INF. स्तब्धुम्। CS. स्तम्भयति॥

स्तु stu, 'praise,' II, स्तौति or स्तवीति। IMP. अस्तौत् or अस्तवीत्। स्तौतु or स्तवीतु। स्तुयात्, स्तुवीत॥ PF. तुष्टाव। AO. अस्तावीत् or अस्तौषीत्, अस्तोष्ट। FT. स्तोष्यति। PS. स्तूयते। PP. स्तुत। GD. स्तुत्वा, °स्तुत्य। INF. स्तोतुम्। CS. स्तावयति। DS. तुष्टूषति॥

स्तृ stṛ, 'cover,' V or IX, स्तृणोति or स्तृणाति॥ PF. तस्तार, तस्तरे। FT. स्तरिष्यति। PS. स्तीर्यते (as if from स्तॄ stṝ, 58)। PP. स्तृत। GD. स्तृत्वा, °स्तृत्य। CS. स्तारयति॥

स्था sthā, 'stand,' I, तिष्ठति॥ PF. तस्थौ। AO. अस्थात्। FT. स्थास्यति। PS. स्थीयते। AO. अस्थायि। PP. स्थित। GD. स्थित्वा, °स्थाय। INF. स्थातुम्। CS. स्थापयति। DS. तिष्ठासति॥

स्पृश् spṛś, 'touch,' VI, P. स्पृशति॥ PF. पस्पर्श; पस्पृशुः। AO. अस्प्राक्षीत्। FT. स्प्रक्ष्यति। PS. स्पृश्यते। PP. स्पृष्ट। GD. स्पृष्ट्वा, °स्पृश्य। CS. स्प्रष्टुम्। INF. स्पर्शयति। DS. पिस्पृक्षति॥

स्मि smi, 'smile,' I, A. स्मयते॥ PF. सिष्मिये। AO. अस्मयिष्ट। PP. स्मित। GD. स्मित्वा, °स्मित्य। CS. स्मापयति or स्माययति॥

स्मृ smṛ, 'remember,' I, P. स्मरति॥ PF. सस्मार। FT. स्मरिष्यति। PS. स्मर्यते। PP. स्मृत। GD. स्मृत्वा, °स्मृत्य। INF. स्मर्तुम्। CS. स्मारयति॥

स्यन्द् syand, 'drop,' I, A. स्यन्दते॥ PF. सस्यन्दे। PS. स्यन्द्यते। PP. स्यन्न। CS. स्यन्दयति॥

स्रु sru, 'flow,' I, P. स्रवति॥ PF. सुस्राव। FT. स्रविष्यति। स्रुत॥

स्वज् svaj, 'embrace,' I, A. स्वजते ॥ सस्वजे । PP. स्वक्त । स्वक्तुम् ॥

स्वप् svap, 'sleep,' II, P. स्वपिति ॥ PF. सुष्वाप; सुषुपुः । AO. अस्वाप्सीत् । FT. स्वप्स्यति । PS. सुप्यते । AO. अस्वापि । PP. सुप्त । GD. सुप्त्वा ॥ INF. स्वप्तुम् । CS. स्वापयति । DS. सुषुप्सति ॥

हन् han, 'kill,' II, P. हन्ति; हतः; घ्नन्ति । IMP. अहन्; अघ्नन् । IPV. हनानि, जहि, हन्तु; घ्नन्तु । OP. हन्यात् ॥ PF. जघान । AO. अवधीत् । FT. हनिष्यति । PS. हन्यते । PP. हत । GD. हत्वा, °हत्य । INF. हन्तुम् । CS. घातयति । DS. जिघांसति ॥

हा hā, 'leave,' III, P. जहाति; जहति । IPV. जहानि, जहीहि, जहातु; जहतु ॥ PF. जहौ, जहिथ or जहाथ । AO. अहासीत् or अहात् । FT. हास्यति । PS. हीयते । PP. हीन । GD. हित्वा, °हाय । INF. हातुम् । CS. हापयति । DS. जिहासति ॥

हिंस् hiṃs, 'strike,' VII, P. हिनस्ति । IMP. अहिनत्; अहिंसन् । IPV. हिनसानि, हिन्धि, हिनस्तु । OP. हिंस्यात् ॥ PF. जिहिंस । AO. अहिंसीत् । FT. हिंसिष्यति । PS हिंस्यते । हिंसित । CS. हिंसयति ॥

हु hu, 'sacrifice,' III, जुहोति (p. 96) ॥ PF. जुहाव or जुहवांचकार । AO. अहौषीत् । FT. होष्यति । PS. हूयते । हुत । GD. हुत्वा । INF. होतुम् । CS. हावयति । DS. जुहूषति । INT. जोहवीति ॥

हृ hṛ, 'take,' I, हरति, °ते ॥ PF. जहार, जहर्थ; जह्रुः । AO. अहार्षीत्, अहृत । FT. हरिष्यति; हर्ता । PS. ह्रियते । AO. अहारि । हृत । GD. हृत्वा, °हृत्य । CS. हारयति । DS. जिहीर्षति, °ते । INT. जरीहर्ति ॥

ह्री hrī, 'be ashamed,' III, P. जिह्रेति; जिह्रीतः; जिह्रियति । IMP. अजिह्रेत् । IPV. जिह्रेतु । OP. जिह्रीयात् ॥ PF. जिह्राय; जिह्रियुः । PP. ह्रीण or ह्रीत । CS. ह्रेपयति । INT. जेह्रीयते ॥

ह्वे hve, 'call,' I, ह्वयति, °ते ॥ PF. जुहाव; जुहुवुः । FT. ह्वास्यते । PS. हूयते । PP. हूत । GD. हूत्वा, °हूय । INF. ह्वातुम् । CS. ह्वाययति । INT. जोहवीति ॥

APPENDIX II

METRE IN CLASSICAL SANSKRIT

The versification of classical Sanskrit differs considerably from that of the Vedic hymns, being more artificial, more subject to strict rules, and showing a far greater number of varieties of metre.

Classical Sanskrit metres are divided into—

I. Those measured by the number of syllables.

II. those measured by the number of *morae* they contain.

Nearly all Sanskrit poetry is written in stanzas consisting of four metrical lines or quarter-verses (called pāda, 'foot' = quarter). These stanzas are regularly divided into hemistiches of half-verses.

Quantity is measured as in Latin and Greek. Vowels are long by nature or by position. Two consonants make a preceding short vowel long by position. Anusvāra and Visarga counting as full consonants. A short vowel counts as one *mora* (mātrā), a long vowel (by nature or position) as two.

I. Metres measured by Syllables (Akṣara-cchandaḥ).

These consist of—

A. two half-verses identical in structure, while the quarter-verses 1 and 3 differ from 2 and 4.

B. four quarter-verses all identical in structure.

A. The Śloka.

The Śloka ('song,' from śru, 'hear'), developed from the Vedic Anuṣṭubh, is the Epic verse, and may be considered the Indian

verse *par excellence*, occurring, as it does, far more frequently than any other metre in classical Sanskrit poetry. It consists of two half-verses of sixteen syllables or of four pādas of eight syllables.

Dividing the half-verse into four feet of four syllables, we find that only the second and the fourth foot are determined as to quantity. The fourth is necessarily iambic (˘–˘⏓), while the second may assume four different forms. The first and the third foot are undetermined, except that ⏓˘˘⏓ is always excluded from them. By far the commonest form of the second foot is ˘––⏓ (in Nala 1442 out of 1732 half-verses).

The type of the Śloka may therefore be represented thus—

•••• | ˘––⏓ | •••• | ˘–˘⏓ ||

E.g. Āsīd rājā Nălō nāmă | Vīrăsēnăsŭtō bălī |
ŭpăpannō gŭṇair iṣṭai | rūpăvān aśvăkōvĭdăḥ ||

It is only when the second foot has | ˘––⏓ that the first foot may assume all its admissible forms. When the second foot has any of the other three forms, the first foot is limited, as shown in the following table:—

	I.	II.	III.	IV.
1.	••••	˘––• ||		
2.	{ •–˘– / •˘–– }	˘˘˘• ||	••••	˘–˘• ||
3.	•–˘–	–˘˘• ||		
4.	•–˘–	–, ––• ||		

The first (typical) form is called Pathyā; the remaining three, called Vipulā, are in the above table arranged in order of frequency of occurrence. Out of 2579 half-verses taken from Kālidāsa (Raghu-vaṃśa and Kumāra-sambhava), Māgha, Bhāravi, and Bilhaṇa, each of the four admissible forms of the Śloka in the above order claims the following share: 2289, 116, 89, 85.

In the table a dot indicates an undetermined syllable: a comma makes and *caesura.*

The end of a pāda coincides with the end of a word (sometimes only with the end of a word in a compound), and the whole Śloka contains a complete sentence. The construction does not run on into the next line. Occasionally three half-verses are found combined into a triplet.

B. All Four Pādas identical in Form.

1. Of the numerous varieties developed from the Vedic Triṣṭubh (II syllables to the pāda), the commonest are —

a. **Indravajrā:** – – ˘ | – – ˘ |˘ – ˘ | – – ||

b. **Upendravajrā:** ˘ – ˘ | – – ˘ |˘ – ˘ | – – ||

c. **Upajāti** (a mixture of the above two):

⏓ – ˘ | – – ˘ | ˘ – ˘ | – ⏓ ||

d. **Śālinī:** – – – | –, – ˘ | – – ˘ | – – ||

e. **Rathoddhatā:** – ˘ – | ˘ ˘ ˘ | – ˘ – |˘ – ||

2. The commonest forms of Jagatī (12 syllables to the pāda) are—

a. **Vaṃśastha:** ˘ – ˘ | – – ˘ |˘ – ˘ | – ˘ – ||

b. **Drutavilambita:** ˘ ˘ ˘ | – ˘ ˘ | – ˘ ˘ | – ˘ – ||

3. The commonest variety of Śakvarī (14 syllables to the pāda) is—

Vasantatilaka: – – ˘ | – ˘ ˘ |˘ – ˘ |˘ – ˘ | – ⏓ ||

4. The commonest form of Atiśakvarī (15 syllables to the pāda) is—

Mālinī: ˘ ˘ ˘ |˘ ˘ ˘ | – –, – |˘ – – |˘ – ⏓ ||

5. The commonest varieties of Atyaṣṭi (17 syllables to the pāda) are—

a. **Śikhariṇī:** ˘ – – | – – –, |˘ ˘ ˘ |˘ ˘ – | – ˘ ˘ |˘ – ||

b. **Hariṇī:** ˘ ˘ ˘ |˘ ˘ –, | – – – | –, ˘ – | ˘ ˘ – |˘ – ||

c. **Mandākrāntā:**

– – – | –, ˘ ˘ | ˘ ˘ ˘ | –, – ˘ | – – ˘ | – ⏓ |

6. The commonest form of Atidhṛti (19 syllables to the pāda) is—

Śārdūlavikrīḍita:

– – – | ˘ ˘ – | ˘ – ˘ | ˘ ˘ –, | – – ˘ | – – ˘ | ⏓ ||

7. The commonest variety of Prakṛti (21 syllables to the pāda) is—

Sragdharā:

– – – | – ˘ – | –, ˘ ˘ | ˘ ˘ ˘ | ˘ –, – | ˘ – – | ˘ – – ||

II. Metres measured by Morae.

A. Metres in which the sum total only of the *morae* is prescribed (Mātrā-chandaḥ).

The **Vaitālīya** contains 30 *morae* in the half-verse, 14 in the first pāda, 16 in the second. Each pāda may be divided into three feet, the second always consisting of a choriambus, and the third of two iambics; while the first foot in the first pāda consists of a pyrrhic, in the second pāda of an anapaest. The half-verse thus contains 21 syllables. The following is the scheme of the half-verse:—

˘ ˘ | – ˘ ˘ – | ˘ – ˘ ⏓ | ˘ ˘ – | – ˘ ˘ – | ˘ – ˘ ⏓ ||

B. Metres in which the number of *morae* in each foot (gaṇa) is specified (Gaṇa-cchandaḥ).

Āryā or **Gāthā** has 7½ feet to the half-verse, each foot containing 4 *morae* (= 30 *morae* altogether). The 4 *morae* may take the form ˘ ˘ ˘ ˘, – –, – ˘ ˘, or ˘ ˘ –; in the 2nd and 4th they may also become ˘ – ˘; in the 6th they appear as ˘ ˘ ˘ ˘ or ˘ – ˘. The 8th foot is always monosyllabic; the 6th of the second half-verse consists of a single short syllable. Hence the second half-verse contains only 27 *morae*.

APPENDIX III

CHIEF PECULIARITIES OF VEDIC GRAMMAR

1. As several stages can be distinguished in the development of the Vedic language, some of the following statements are strictly applicable only to the Rig-veda, the oldest and most important monument of Vedic literature.

The Alphabet.

2. The sounds are the same as in Sanskrit, which the exception of two additional letters. Cerebral ड् ḍ and ढ् ḍh between vowels regularly become cerebral ळ् ḻ and ळ्ह ḻh; — e.g. ईळे īḻé = ईडे īḍé, 'I praise'; मीळ्हुषे mīḻhúṣe = मीढुषे mīḍhúṣe, 'to the bountiful.'

Sandhi.

3. A. Vowels. Hiatus is not avoided either within a word, or between the members of a compound, or between the words of a sentence; and, in particular, initial a after e and o (21 *a*) is only occasionally elided; — e.g. sū́riasya, 'of the sun'; su-áśviam, wealth in horses'; Váruṇasya Agnéḥ, 'of Varuṇa (and) Agni'; adhí eti, 'he goes towards'; vípro akṣarat, 'the priest poured out.'

a. The e of the pronominal forms (dat., loc.) tvé, 'to or in thee,' asmé, 'to or in us,' yuṣmé, 'to or in you,' remains unchanged before vowels; as does the final o produced by the coalescence of a with the particle u, as in átho (átha‿u), mó (mā́‿u), nó (ná‿u).

B. Consonants. The final syllables ān, īn, ūn, ṝn are treated as if they were āṃḥ, īṃḥ, ūṃḥ, ṝṃḥ (cp. 36 B 1, and 45, 1); i.e.

ān becomes āṁ̐ (except in the 3. pl. subjunctive, where it represents an original ānt), while īn, ūn, ṝn become īṁ̐r, ūṁ̐r, ṝṁ̐r; — e.g. mahā́ṁ̐ asi, 'thou art great' (but ā́ gacchān úttarā yugā́ni, 'later ages will come'); raśmī́ṁ̐r iva, 'like reins.'

a. Sometimes rules which in Sanskrit apply internally only, are extended to the initials of words; — e.g. sahó ṣú ṇaḥ (cp. 67).

Declension.

4. A. Endings. Singular. *a.* Instr. ā is sometimes added to stems in a, less commonly to feminines in ā; — e.g. yajñá, m. 'sacrifice,' instr. yajñéna and yajñā́; manīṣā́, f. 'wisdom,' instr. manīṣáyā and manīṣā́. The a of ena is also often lengthened.

Stems in -man sometimes do not syncopate the vowel of the suffix, while when they do, the m or the n is occasionally dropped; — e.g. bhū-mánā and bhū-n-ā́ for bhū-mn-ā; drāgh-m-ā́ for drāghmán-ā.

***b.* Loc.** Stems in i take ā, though less commonly than au;— e.g. agní, m. 'fire,' loc. agnáu and agnā́.

Stems in -an usually drop the i; — e.g. bráhmaṇi and bráhman. They never syncopate the a of the suffix; — e.g. rā́jani only (cp. 90).

***c.* Voc.** Stems in -mat, -vat, -vas. -yas regularly from their vocative in -as; — e.g. nom. bhānumā́n: voc. bhā́numas; hárivān hárivas; cakṛvā́n: cákṛvas; kánīyān: kánīyas.

Dual. *a.* The nom. acc. voc. take ā more usually than au;— e.g. aśvínā, 'the two Aśvins'; dvā́rā, f. 'the two doors'; nadíā, 'the two rivers.' Feminines in derivative ī remain unchanged;— e.g. devī́, 'the two goddesses.'

b. The personal pronouns of the 1. and 2. pers. distinguish five cases; — e.g. N. yuvám; A. yuvā́m; I. yuvā́bhyām or yuvá-bhyām; Ab. yuvád; L. yuvós.

Plural. Nom. ***a.*** Masculine stems in -a often (feminines in -ā rarely) take āsas beside ās; — e.g. mártyāsaḥ, 'mortals.'

b. Feminine stems in derivative ī take s only; — e.g. devī́ḥ, 'goddesses.'

c. Neuters take ā, ī, ū (sometimes shortened to ă, ĭ, ŭ) as well as āni, īni, ūni; — e.g. yugā́, 'yokes' (cp. Lat. juga, Gk. ζυγά).

Instr. Stems in -a take ebhis nearly as often as ais; — e.g. devébhiḥ and deváiḥ.

B. Inflexional Type. The main difference in type of declension is in the polysyllabic stems (mostly feminines, with a few masculines) in ī and ū, a considerable number of which are inflected like the monosyllabic stems dhī and bhū (100), excepting the gen. pl., where they take nām. (Stems in derivative ī otherwise for the most part follow nadī and vadhū as in Sanskrit: 100.)

E.g. rathī́, m. 'charioteer'; nadī́, f. 'river'; tanū́, f. 'body.'

Sing.	N.	rathī́-s	nadī́-s	tanū́-s
	A.	rathī́-am	nadíam	tanúam
	I.	rathíā	nadíā	tanúā
	D.	rathíe	nadíe	tanúe
	Ab. G.	rathías	nadías	tanúas
	L.	—	—	tanúi
	V.	ráthi	—	tánu
Du.	N.A.V.	rathíā	nadíā	tanúā
	I.	rathī́bhyām	nadī́bhyām	tanū́bhyām
	G.L.	rathíos	nadíos	tanúos
Pl.	N.A.	rathías	nadías	tanúas
	G.	rathī́-n-ām	nadī́-n-ām	tanū́-n-ām
	L.	rathī́ṣu	nadī́ṣu	tanū́ṣu

Conjugation.

5. Augment. ***a.*** This prefix is in some cases permanently long, in others metrically; — e.g. ā́-var, 3. sg. aorist or vṛ, 'he has covered'; ā́-raik, 3. sg. aorist of ric, 'she has given up.'

b. The augment can always be dropped without changing the meaning. Unaugmented forms are, however, often used as injunctives: this use has survived in Sanskrit with the prohibitive particle mā́ (128 *a*).

6. Verbal Prefixes. These generally precede, but sometimes follow the verb. They can be separated from it by particles and other words; — e.g. ā́ tvā viśantu, 'let them enter thee'; gámad vā́jebhir ā́ sá naḥ, 'may he come to us with riches.'

7. Endings. ***a.*** The primary termination of the 1. pers. pl. active, **-masi,** is much commoner than -mas; — e.g. i-mási and i-más, 'we go.'

b. In the 2. pl. **-thana** and **-tana** often occur beside -tha and -ta; — e.g. yā-thá and yā-thána, 'ye go'; yā-tá and yā-tána, 'do ye go.'

c. The 2. sg. impv. has a not uncommon alternative ending in **-tāt** (added to the weak stem), which expresses an injunction to be carried out in the future; rákṣa-tāt, 'protect'; brū-tāt, 'say'; dhat-tā́t, 'place' (cp. Gk. φερέ-τω, Lat. lege-tōd). It is sometimes used for the 2. du. and pl., or 1. and 3. sg.

d. The 3. pers. sg. pres. middle (like the perf. middle, 136) is not uncommonly identical with the 1.; — e.g. śáy-e, 'he lies' (= śéte).

8. Reduplication. Many roots reduplicate with a long vowel in the perfect; — e.g. dhṛ, 'support': dādhā́r-a; vas, 'clothe': vā-vas-e; tu, 'thrive': tū-tāv-a.

9. Tenses. ***a.*** There is a pluperfect, which does not, however, occur often. It is formed from the perfect stem by prefixing

the augment, and adding the secondary terminations; — e.g. from cit, 'appear,' 1. sg. á-ciket-am, 3. á-ciket.

b. The periphrastic future does not exist; the periphrastic perfect is not known to the Rig-veda.

10. Moods. ***a.*** There is a subjunctive, which is much commoner than the optative. Its meaning is imperative or final; it is also often equivalent to a future indicative. Its stem is formed by adding -a to the tense stem. In the a-conjugation it therefore ends in ā; — e.g. bhávā. In the second conjugation -a is added to the strong stem, which remains throughout; — e.g. from kṛ, 'do': kṛṇáv-a. The endings are partly primary, partly secondary. Thus the subjunctive of bhū, 'be,' and su, 'press out,' are formed as follows:—

Par.	1. bhávā-ni	bhávā-va	bhávā-ma
	2. bhávā-si, bhávā-s	bhávā-thas	bhávā-tha
	3. bhávā-ti, bhávā-t	bhávā-tas	bhávā-n
Ātm.	1. bháv-ai	bhávā-vahai	bhávā-mahai
	2. bhávā-se	bháv-aithe	bhávā-dhvai
	3. bhávā-te	bháv-aite	(bháv-anta)
Par.	1. sunáv-ā-ni	sunáv-ā-va	sunáv-ā-ma
	2. sunáv-a-s	sunáv-a-thas	sunáv-a-tha
	3. sunáv-a-t	sunáv-a-tas	sunáv-a-n
Ātm.	1. sunáv-ai	sunáv-ā-vahai	sunáv-ā-mahai
	2. sunáv-a-se	sunáv-aithe	sunáv-a-dhvai
	3. sunáv-a-te	sunáv-aite	sunáv-anta

b. Not only the present, but the **perfect and aorist** as well, have all the **three moods**, subjunctive, optative, and imperative.

E.g. pf. subj. of stu, 'praise': tu-ṣṭáv-a-t; opt. of vṛt, 'turn': va-vṛt-yāt; impv. of muc, 'release': mu-mug-dhí; of bhū, 'be': ba-bhū-tu; Ātm. 2. sg. of vṛt: va-vṛt-sva.

Aor. subj. nī, 'lead': 3. sg. néṣ-a-ti or néṣ-a-t; budh, 'wake': bódhiṣ-a-t; vid, 'find': vid-ā́-t; kṛ, 'do': kár-a-ti or kár-a-t. Opt. of vid: vid-ét; aś, 'reach': aś-yā́t; bhaj, 'share': bhakṣīṣṭá. Impv. of av, 'favour': 2. sg. aviḍ-ḍhí, du. aviṣ-ṭám, pl. aviṣ-ṭána; 3. sg. aviṣ-ṭu; sad, 'sit down': 3. sg. sada-tu, du. sada-tām, pl. sada-ntu; śru, 'hear': 2. śru-dhí, śru-tám, śru-tá; 3. śró-tu, śru-tā́m, śruv-antu.

II. Participles. In addition to those surviving in Sanskrit the Veda has an **aorist** participle, both active and middle; — e.g. Par., from kṛ, 'do': kr-ánt; gam, 'go': gm-ánt; sthā, 'stand': sthā́nt; Ātm., kṛ: kr-āṇá; budh: budh-āná.

a. The part. in -ta-vat is not known to the Rig-veda.

12. Gerunds. In addition to the gerund in -tvā́, there is a commoner one in -tvī́, and a very rare one in -tvā́ya. The vowel of the forms used with prefixes, -ya and -tya, is generally lengthened.

13. Infinitives. About a dozen kinds of infinitives can be distinguished, having the form of an acc., dat., abl., gen., or loc. The last three cases are rare. The vast majority are dat. infinitives, these being about twelve times as common as the acc.

a. The **acc.** inf. is formed either from the root or from a verbal noun in -tu (the latter being very rare in the Rig-veda); — e.g. sam-ídh-am, 'to kindle'; prati-dhā́-m, 'to place upon'; pra-tír-am, 'to lengthen out'; kár-tu-m, 'to make'; dā́-tu-m, 'to give.'

b. The **dat.** inf. is formed from the root or from verbal nouns in -as, -man, -van, -tu, or -dhi; — e.g. dṛś-é, 'to see'; śrad-dhé, 'to believe' (cp. εἴδεσ-θαι); jīv-ás-e, 'to live'; vid-mán-e (ἴδ-μεν-αι), 'to know'; dā-ván-e (δοῦναι from δοϝ εναι), dā́-tav-e, 'to give'; kár-tav-ái (with double accent), 'to do'; gamá-dhyai, 'to go.'

c. Examples of the other cases are: ava-pád-as, 'to fall down'; dā́-tos, 'to give'; neṣ-áṇ-i, 'to lead'; dhartár-i, 'to support.'

Prepositions

14. The genuine prepositions are used only with the acc., loc., and abl. (apart from a few isolated instances of the instr.).

a. With **acc.** áti, 'beyond'; ádhi, 'on to'; ánu, 'after'; antár, 'between'; áccha, abhí, ā́, úpa, práti, 'towards'; pári, 'round'; tirás, 'across'; purás, 'before.'

b. With **loc.** ádhi, 'on'; antár, 'within'; ápi, ā́, and úpa, 'near'; purás, 'before.'

c. With **abl.** ádhi, 'from upon'; antár, 'from within'; ā́, 'away from' or 'up to'; pári, 'from (around)'; purás, 'before.'

Accent.

15. The accent is marked in all the texts of the four Vedas, as well as in two Brāhmaṇas. Of the four different systems of marking it, that of the Rig-veda is the most important. Here the chief accent, the acute (**udātta**, 'raised'), or rising tone, is not marked at all, probably because it comes midway between the grave or low tone (**an-udātta**) which precedes, and the **svarita**, or falling tone, which follows it and marks the transition from an accented to a toneless syllable. The anudātta preceding the acute is marked with a horizontal stroke below, and the svarita following it, with a vertical stroke above; — e.g. अ॒ग्निना॑ ag-ní-nā́. The so-called independent svarita (originally also preceded by an acute, which disappears by removal of hiatus in the written text, but has often to be restored in pronunciation) is marked like the enclitic one; — e.g. क्व॑ kvà (= kúà); the anudātta being also indicated under the preceding syllable; — e.g. वी॒र्य॑म् vīryàm (= vīríam). If an independent svarita precedes an udātta it is marked with the numeral १ (1) when the syllable is short, with ३ (3) when it is long, the figure bearing both the svarita sign and the anudātta which precedes the udātta; अ॒प्स्व१॒॑न्तर् apsvàntár (= apsú antár);

रा॒यो ३॒ वनि॑: rāyò'vániḥ (= rāyó avániḥ). An accented syllable at the beginning of a line remains unmarked; all grave syllables at the beginning of a sentence preceding an acute must be marked; and all graves following a svarita are left unmarked till the one preceding an acute or svarita; — e.g. नमो॑ युजा॒नम् námò yujānám; क॒रि॒ष्यसि॑ karişyásì.

16. Enclitics. ***a.*** The particles u, cid, svid, iva, gha, ha, ca, sma, vā. ***b.*** Certain monosyllabic pers. pronouns, me, te, &c. (109 *a*). ***c.*** The demonstrative pron. ena, and īm, sīm. ***d.*** The indefinite pronouns tva, 'another'; sama, 'some.'

17. Unaccented Forms. ***a.*** The demonstrative pron. a, when unemphatic as replacing a noun; — e.g. asya jánimāni, 'his (Agni's) bírths'; but asyá́ uṣásaḥ, 'of thát Dawn.'

b. The **vocative** loses its accent, unless it begins the sentence, whatever the length of the vocative expression; — e.g. á́ rājānā maha ṛtasya gopā, 'hither, ye two sovereign guardians of great order.'

18. The employment of the **accent** in declension and conjugation may be gathered from the paradigms given in the preceding grammar; but the following peculiarities of its use **in the sentence** should be noted.

a. The **vocative** is invariably emphasized on the first syllable only, all the other syllables of a complex expression losing their accents; — e.g. hótar yaviṣṭha sukrato, 'O most youthful wise sacrificer'; ū́rjo napāt sahasāvan (nom. ūrjó nápāt sáhasāvā).

b. The **finite verb** of a principal clause is unaccented, unless it begins the sentence; — e.g. Agním īḷe, 'I praise Agni.' Since a voc. does not count in a sentence, a verb following it is accented; — e.g. á́śrut-karṇa, śrudhí hávam, 'O thou of listening ears, hear our call.' A sentence being regarded as capable of having only one verb, all verbs syntactically connected with the same

subject as the first are accented as beginning new sentences; — e.g. taráṇir íj jayati, kṣéti, púṣyati, 'successful he conquers, rules, thrives.'

c. In subordinate clauses (introduced by the relative or its derivatives, and the particles hí, 'for,' ca and ced, 'if,' néd, 'lest,' kuvíd, 'whether') the verb is always accented; — e.g. yáṃ yajñáṃ paribhū́r ási, 'what sacrifice thou protectest.' When two principal clauses are in a relation of antithesis, the first is often treated as subordinate, and its verb accented.

d. In principal clauses the verbal prefix is separated from the verb and accented; in subordinate clauses it is compounded with the verb and loses its accent; — e.g. ā́ gacchati, 'he comes,' but yá āgácchati, 'he who comes.'

SANSKRIT INDEX

This index contains all Sanskrit words and affixes occurring in the grammar, except the numerals (104-108), unless declined, and the verbs in Appendix I. The former can be found at once owing to their numerical, the latter owing to their alphabetical order. Indifferent words occurring in examples of Sandhi or of Syntax, as well as in Appendix III, are excluded.

The figures refer to paragraphs unless pages are specified.

ABBREVIATIONS

A. = adjective. adv., adverb, adverbial. ao., aorist. cd., compound. cj., conjunction. cpv., comparative. cs., causative. dem., demonstrative. den., denominative. ds., desiderative. encl., enclitic. f.n., foot-note. fp., future participle passive. ft., future. gd., gerund., ij., interjection, indec., indeclinable. inf., infinitive. int., intensive. inter., interrogative. ipv., imperative. irr., irregularities. N., note. n., neuter. neg., negative. nm., numeral. nom., nominal. ord., ordinal. par., paradigm. pcl., particle. per., periphrastic. pf., perfect. poss., possessive. pp., past passive participle. pr., present. pri., primary. prn., pronoun, pronominal. prp., preposition, prepositional. ps., passive. pt., participle. sf., suffix. spv., superlative. Tp., Tatpuruṣa. v., vocative. vb., verbal. w., with.

A-vowel, pronunciation of, 15, 1.
a, pronominal root, 111.
a-, augment, 128.
-a, sf. of 1st conj., 124; pri. nom. sf., 182, 1 *b*; sec. nom. sf., p. 163; nominal stems in, 97.
aṃś, 'reach,' pf., 139, 6.
akṣi, n. 'eye,' 99, 3.
agni-mat, a. 'having fire,' 86.
agra-tas, adv. 'before,' 177 *d*.
agre, 'in front of,' prp. adv., 177 *d*.
aṅga, pcl. 'pray,' 180.
aṅgiras, m. a proper name, 83 *a*.
-ac, '-ward,' adjectives in, 93.
añj, 'anoint,' 134 D (p. 107).
aṇu, adj. 'minute,' cpv. of, 103, 2.
-at, stems in, 85; 156; 182, 1 *b*.
ati-ric, 'surpass,' w. abl., 201, 2 *a*.
atra-bhavat, m. 'your Honour here,' 195, 1 *c*.
atha, pcl. 'then,' 'now,' 180.
atho, pcl. 'then,' 180.
ad, 'eat,' pr. stem, 127.1; pf., 135.2.
adat, 'eating,' pr. pt., 85.
adas, dem. prn. 'that,' 112.
ádhara, prn. adj. 'inferior,' 120 *e*.
adhas, adv. prp. 'below,' 177 *d*.
adhastāt, adv. prp. 'below,' 177 *d*.
adhi, prp. 'over,' 176, 2 *a*.
adhi͜i, 'read,' 134 A 3 *d* (p. 106); cs., 168, 2; w. two acc., 198, 4.

ud-diśya, prp. gd. = 'towards,' 179, 1.
ud-vij, shrink from,' w. abl., 201 *a*.
-una, pri. suffix, 182, 1 *b*.
und, 'wet,' pr. and impf., 128.
upa-kaṇṭha, m. 'vicinity,' 178.
upa-kṛ, 'benefit,' w. gen., 202, 1 *c*.
upa-jāti, f. a mixed metre, p. 234.
upa-dhmānīya, 6, f. n. 4.
upra-ram, 'desist,' 207 *a*.
upari, prp. adv. 'over,' 177 *d*.
upariṣṭāt, prp. adv. 'above,' 177 *d*.
upā-nah, f. 'shoe,' 81.
upendra-vajrā, f. a metre, p. 234.
ubha, prn. 'both,' p. 81, f. n.
ubhaya, prn. a. 'both,' 120 *b*.
ubhaya-tas, prp. adv. 'on both sides of,' 177 *a*.
-ur, ending of gen. sing., 99, 1. 2; 101; of 3. pl., 131, 6; 136; 142; 14S.
uśanas, m. a proper name, 83 *a*.
uṣas, f. 'down,' 83 *a*.
uṣṇih, f. a metre, 81.
-us, pri. suffix, 83; 182, 1 *b*.

Ū, pri. sf., 182, 1 *b*; stems in, 100.
ūna, pp. 'diminished,' 104 *b*.
ūrj, f. 'strength,' 79 *b*.
ūrdhvam, prp. adv. 'above,' 177 *c*.

Ṛ, 'go,' pr. impf., 128; pr., 133 C 2; cs., 168, 2.
-ṛ, stems in, 101.
ṛte, prp. adv. 'without,' 177 *c*.
ṛtvij, m. 'priest,' 79 *b*.

E, ai, o, roots ending in, 129, 8.
eka, nm. 'one,' 105, 1; 120 *b*; 192.
eka-tama, prn. a. 'one of many,' 120 *a*.
eka-tara, prn. a. 'either,' 120 *b*.
etad, dem. prn. 'this,' 110 *a*.
etā-vat, prn. 'so much,' 118.
edh, 'thrive,' per. pf., 140, 1.
e-dhi, 2. sg. ipv. of as, be,' 134 A 2 *b*.
ena, prn. 'he, she, it,' 112 *a*.
eva, pcl., 180 (p. 149); w. pt., 2055, 1 *d*.
evam, pcl. 'thus,' 180; w. pp., 205, 1 *c*.
eṣa, dem. prn. 'this,' 48; 112 *a*; 195, 2 *a*.

Ai, o, au, nominal stems in, 102.

Au, ending of 1.3. sg. pf., 136, 4.

Ka, inter. prn., 'who?' 113; with api, cana, cid, 119.
kakubh, f. 'region,' 78.
kae cid, inter. pcl. = 'I hope', 180.
ka-tama, prn. a. 'which of many?' 120 *a*.
ka-tara, prn.a. 'which of two?' 120 *a*.
ka-ti, prn. 'how many?' 118 *a*.
kati-paya, prn. a. 'some,' 120 *d*.
kathaya, den. 'tell,' 175 *a*; 198, 2 *a*; 200 A 1 *a*.
kadā, inter. 'when?' 113 *a*; w. cid and cana, 119 *a*.
kaniṣṭha, spv. 'least,' 103, 2 *b*.
kanīyas, cpv. 'lesser,' 103, 2 *b*.
kam, 'love,' 125, 4; pp., 160, 2 *c*.
karma-dhāraya, 'descriptive cd.,' 188.
kalpa, m. 'manner,' 189 *f*.
kaś-cid, indef. prn. 'some,' 119; 192.
kaṣṭam, ij. 'alas!' 181 (p. 158).
kānta, pp. 'beloved,' 97; 160, 2 *c*.
-kāma, compounded w. inf., 211 *b*.
kāmam, adv. pcl. 'indeed,' 180.
kāla, m. 'time,' w. inf., 211 (p. 204).
Kālidāsa, the poet, 185; p. 233.
kim, inter. 'what?' 113; 180; 199, 1 *g*; 210 *d*.
kiyat, prn. 'how much?' 86 *b*; 113 *a*; 118.
kila, pcl. 'indeed,' 180 (p. 150).
kī-dṛś, -dṛśa, prn. 'what like?' 117.
kīrtaya, 'celebrate,' 175 *a*.
ku, prn. as first member of a cd., 113 *a*.
ku-tra, inter. 'where?' 113 *a*.
kup, 'be angry,' w. dat., 200 A 2.
kuśala, n. 'health,' 200 A 3.
kṛ, 'do,' pr., 127, 5 *a*; 134 E (p. 107); pf., 135, 1; 136 *a*; 136, 2; 137, 1; 138, 2; 140; pf. pt., 157; ao., 143 *a*; 144, 2; ft., 151, 1; per. ft., 152 *a*; ps., 154, 3; 154, 7; 155; pp., 160, 3; fp., 162, 1 *b*; 162, 3; gd.,

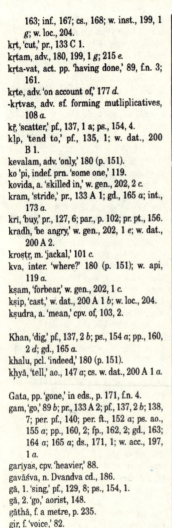

viś, 2. 'enter,' ao. ps., 155; ds., 170, 1.
vi-śeṣa, m. 'difference,' at end of cd., 187 *c*; w. gen., 202, 6.
viśva-jit, a. 'all-conquering,' 187 *b*.
vi-śvas, 'trust,' w. gen., 202, 1 *c*; w. loc., 203 *e*.
vi-śvāsa, m. 'confidence,' w. loc., 204 *d*.
viṣvañc, a. 'all-pervading,' 93 *a*.
vi-sarga, m. 'hard breathing,' 4, f.n. 1; 6, f.n. 1; 15, 8; 27; 29, 6; 31; 32 *a*; 37; 43; 44; 45; 46; 48; 49; 82; p. 49, f.n. 1.
vi-sṛj, 'send away,' w. two acc., 198, 3; w. dat., 200 A 1 *b*.
vi-smṛta, pp., w. act. and ps. sense, 208 *b*.
vṛ, 'choose,' pf., 136 *a*; w. loc., 204 *c*.
vṛt (vartate), w. loc., 203 *c*; w. pt., 207.
vṛddha, 'old,' cpv. of, 103, 2 *b*.
vṛddhi, f. 'strongest vowel gradation,' 17 *a*; 19; 22; 23; 99, 4; 101; 125, 4; 128; 134 A 1 *a*, *b*; 135, 3; 136, 2, 3; 142; 144, 4; 145 *b*; 155; 162, 1 *b*.
vṛdh, 'prosper,' w. diṣṭyā, p. 158.
-vṛdh, 'increasing,' 77 *a*.
veda, pr. pf. 'knows,' 139, 3.
vedaya, cs. 'tell,' w. dat. or gen., 198, 2 *a*, 4 *a*.
vai, expletive pcl., 180, p. 157.
vaitālīya, n. a metre, p. 235.
vyadh, 'pierce,' pr., 133 B 2; pf., 137, 2 *c*; ao., 149 *a* 1.
vyavasita, pp. 'resolved,' w. dat., 200 B 2.
vyāghra-buddhi, f. 'thought of (its being) a tiger,' 187, 5; 199, 1 *a*.
vraśc, 'cut,' pr., 133 C 3.

S, initial, changed to ch, 53.
śaṃs, 'tell,' w. dat., 200 A 1 *a*.
śak, 'be able,' pr., 134 C 2; fp., 162, 1 *c*; ds., 171, 3; w. dat., 200 B 2; w. inf., 211 *c*.
śakya, fp. 'possible,' w. inf., 211 *d*.
śaṅk, 'doubt,' pp. 160, 3.
śaṅkarācāryāḥ, m. pl. of respect, 193, 3 *a*.
śatam, n. 'a hundred,' 106 *c*.
śam, 'cease,' pr., 133 B 1.
-śas, distributive adv. sf., 108 *c*.
śārdūla-vikrīḍita, n. ('tiger-play'), a metre, p. 235.
śālinī, f. a metre, p. 234.
śās, 'rule,' pr., 134 A 4 *a*; ps., 154 *a* 2.
śikhariṇī, f. a metre, p. 234.
śī, 'lie,' pr., 134 A 1 *c*; ds., 169, 2.
śitoṣṇa-kiraṇau, m. du. 'moon and sun,' 189 *c*.
śuci, a. 'pure,' 98.
śunī, f. 'bitch,' 95.
śubh, 'beautify,' ds., 169, 2.
śṝ, 'crush,' ds., 169, 2.
śrad, 'heart,' compounded with dhā, 'put,' 184 *b*.
śram, 'be weary,' pr., 133 B 1.
śrāvaya, cs. 'tell,' w. dat. or gen., 198, 4 *a*.
śri, 'go,' pf., 137, 1 *a*; red. ao., 149.
śru, 'hear,' pr., 134 C 3; pf., 136 *a*; ps., 154; ao., 155: gd., 166; w. part., 207 *c*.
śreyas, cpv. 'better,' 103, 2 *a*.
śliṣ, 'cling to,' w. loc., 203 *e*.
śloka, m. a metre, pp. 232-34.
śvan, m. 'dog,' 91, 3.
śvaśurau, m. du. 'parents-in-law,' 186, 3 *c*.
śvas, 'breathe,' pr., 134 A 3 *a* (p. 106).

Ṣ, internal Sandhi of, 64 *a*.
ṣaṣ, nm. 'six,' 106 *a*.
ṣoḍaśa, nm. 'sixteen,' p. 68, f.n. 3.
ṣṭhiv, spit,' pr., 133 A 1.

S, becomes t, 66 B 1; 89, f.n. 2; 151 *b* 3; 171, 5; becomes ṣ,. 67; disappears, 66 B 2; stems in, 83.
-s, aorist suffix, 143; 144.
sa, prn. 'that,' 48; 110; 192; 195, 2 *b*.
-sa, ao. sf., 141 *a*; ds. sf., 169.
saṃvṛta, pp. 'closed' (pronunciation of vowel a), 15.
sam-śri, 'cling,' w. loc., 203 *e*.
saṃ-skṛta, pp. 'elaborated' (cp. Lat. perfectus), 1.
sakāśa, m. 'vicinity,' 178.

svar, 'heaven,' 46, f.n. 1.
svarita, 'falling accent,' p. 242.
svar-pati, m. 'lord of heaven,' 50 *a*.
svasṛ, f. 'sister,' 101 *a*.
svastri, ij. 'hail.' 181, (p. 158).
sv-āgatam, adv. 'welcome,' w. dat., 200 A 3.
svāmin, m. 'master,' 87 *a*.
svāmī-ya, den. 'treat as master,' 175.

H, 6, f.n. 3; 29, 6; aspiration of initial, 54; internal Sandhi of, 69; noun stems in, 81.
ha, encl. pel., 180 (p. 157).
han, 'kill,' pf. pt., 89 *b*; 92; pr., 134 A 2 *c*; pf., 136, 3; 137, 2 *b*; 139, 4; per. ft., 152 *a*; pr. pt., 156 *a*; pp., 160, 2; gd., 165 *a*; cs., 168, 5; ds., 171, 1.4.
hanta, ij. 'pray,' 181 (p. 159).
hariṇī, f. a metre, p. 234.
havis, n. 'offering,' 83.
hasta, m. 'hand,' at end of poss. cds., 189 *i*.
hasta-gata, pp. 'held in the hand,' p. 171, f. n. 4.
hasty-aśvan, m. du. Dvandva cd. 'elephant and horse,' 186, 1.
hā, 1. 'depart,' pr., 134 B 2.
hā, 2. 'abandon,' pr., 134 B 2 *a*; ps., 201 *b*.
hā, 3. ij. 'alas!' 181 (p. 159).
hi, 1. 'impel,' pf., 139, 4.
hi, 2. cj. 'for,' 180 (p. 157).
-hi, ipv. sf., 131, 4.
hiṃs, 'injure,' pr., 134 D.
hu, 'sacrifice,' pr., 127, 2; pt., 156; 158 *a*; fp., 162, 1 *b*; par., p. 96.
hū, 'call' = hvā, int., 172 *a*.
hrasīyas, cpv. 'shorter,' 103, 2.
hvā (hve), 'cail,' pf., 136, 4; per. pf., 140, 3; ps., 154 *a*; 3; int., 172 *a*.

GENERAL INDEX

The abbreviations occurring in this Index have been explained at the beginning of Appendix I and of the Sanskrit Index.

The figures refer to paragraphs unless pages are specified.

Abbreviation, sign of, 9.
Ablative, syntactical use of, 201; with prepositions, 176, 2; 177 *a*, *b*, *c*; 179, 2.
Absolute cases, 205; participles with eva or -mātra, 205, 1 *d*.
Accent, 15, 10; 104 *d*; 107; 109 *a*; 112; 169; 175; 176, f.n.; App. III, 15-18; shift of, 72 *a*, *b*; 86 *a*; 94, 3 *a*; 126; 131; 189 *a*; Vedic, pp. 242-4; of the vocative, p. 243; of the finite verb, pp. 243-4.
Accordance with, expressed by the instrumental, 199, 1 *b*.
Accusative, syntactical use of, 197; double, 198; with infinitive, not used in Sanskrit, 211; with prepositions, 176, 1; 177 *a*, *b*, *c*, *d*; 179, 1.
Action nouns, 182, 1.
Active, voice (Parasmaipada), 121; sense of past passive participle, 208 *a*, *b*.
Adjectives, 86; 87; 88; 93; 95 *a*; pronominal, 120; expressing identity, equality, likeness construed with inst., 199, 2 *c*; with gen., 202, 2 *d*; construed with the infinitive, 211.
Adverbial compounds, 186, 3; 188, 3; particles, 180.
Adverbs, 180; numeral, 108 *a-c*; indenfinite, 119 *a*; prepositional, 177; constructed with gen., 202, 4.